Israeli and Palestinian Voices

A Dialogue with Both Sides

SECOND EDITION

CATHY SULTAN

To Carole·

*Striving for Peace in
the Middle East!*

Cathy

SCARLETTA PRESS

MINNEAPOLIS

Further information about *Israeli
and Palestinian Voices* and other Cathy
Sultan endeavors, including contact
information, is available on the author's
webpage at the Scarletta Press website.
Go to www.scarlettapress.com/
authors/CathySultan.cfm

Library of Congress PCN
2005938513

ISBN 13: 978-0-9765201-2-2
ISBN 10: 0-9765201-2-5

Book design by
Mighty Media Inc., Minneapolis, MN
Cover: Tracy Kompelien
Interior: Chris Long

First Scarletta edition | First printing

10 9 8 7 6 5 4 3 2 1

Manufactured in the United States
of America

To my grandchildren
that they may live in a peaceful world

CONTENTS

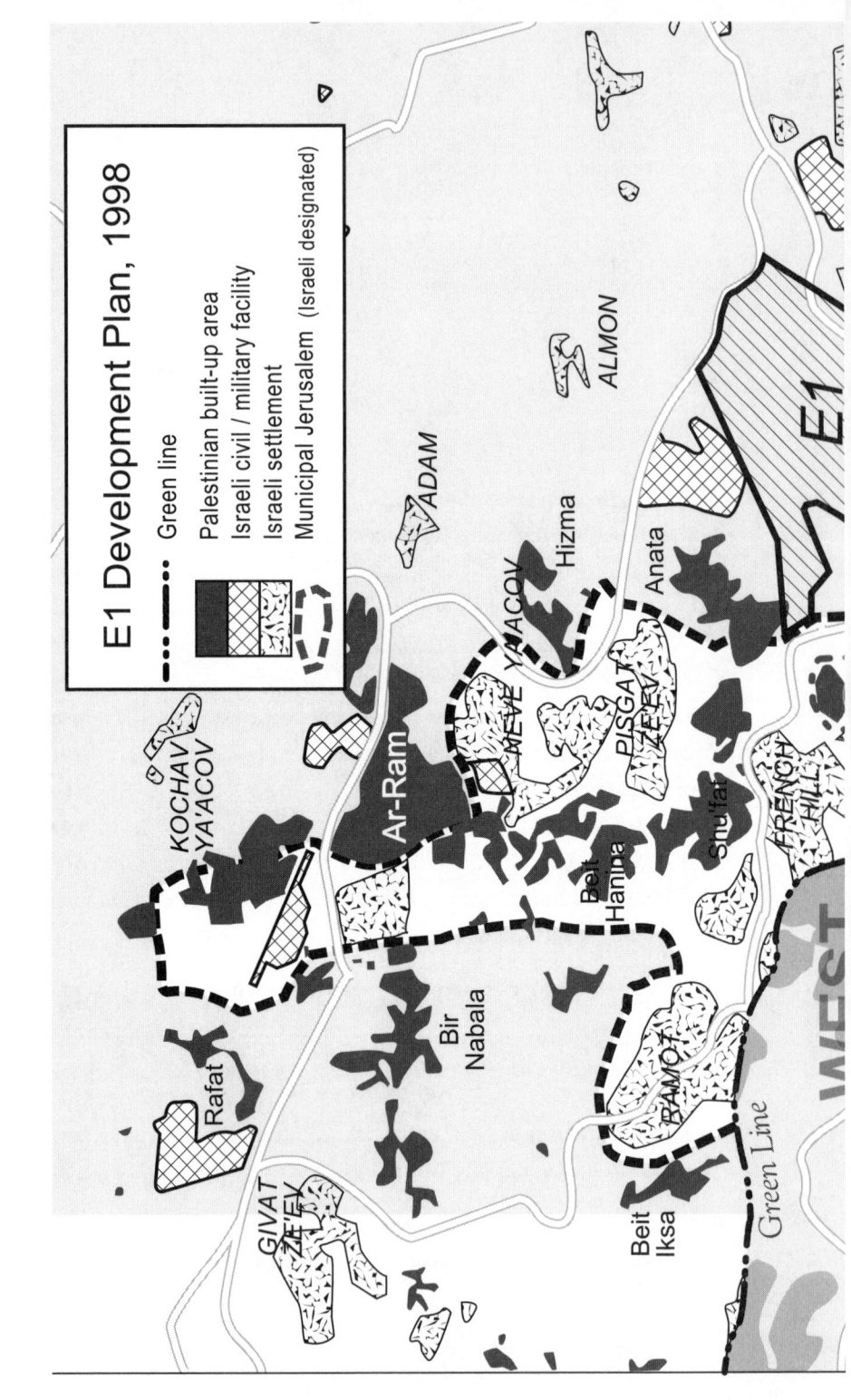

E1 Development Plan, 1998

- ········· Green line
- Palestinian built-up area
- Israeli civil / military facility
- Israeli settlement
- Municipal Jerusalem (Israeli designated)

KOCHAV YA'ACOV

Rafat

GIVAT ZE'EV

Bir Nabala

Beit Iksa

Ar-Ram

ADAM

ALMON

Hizma

Anata

MEVE YA'ACOV

PISGAT ZE'EV

Beit Hanina

Shu'fat

FRENCH HILL

RAMOT

Green Line

WEST

E1

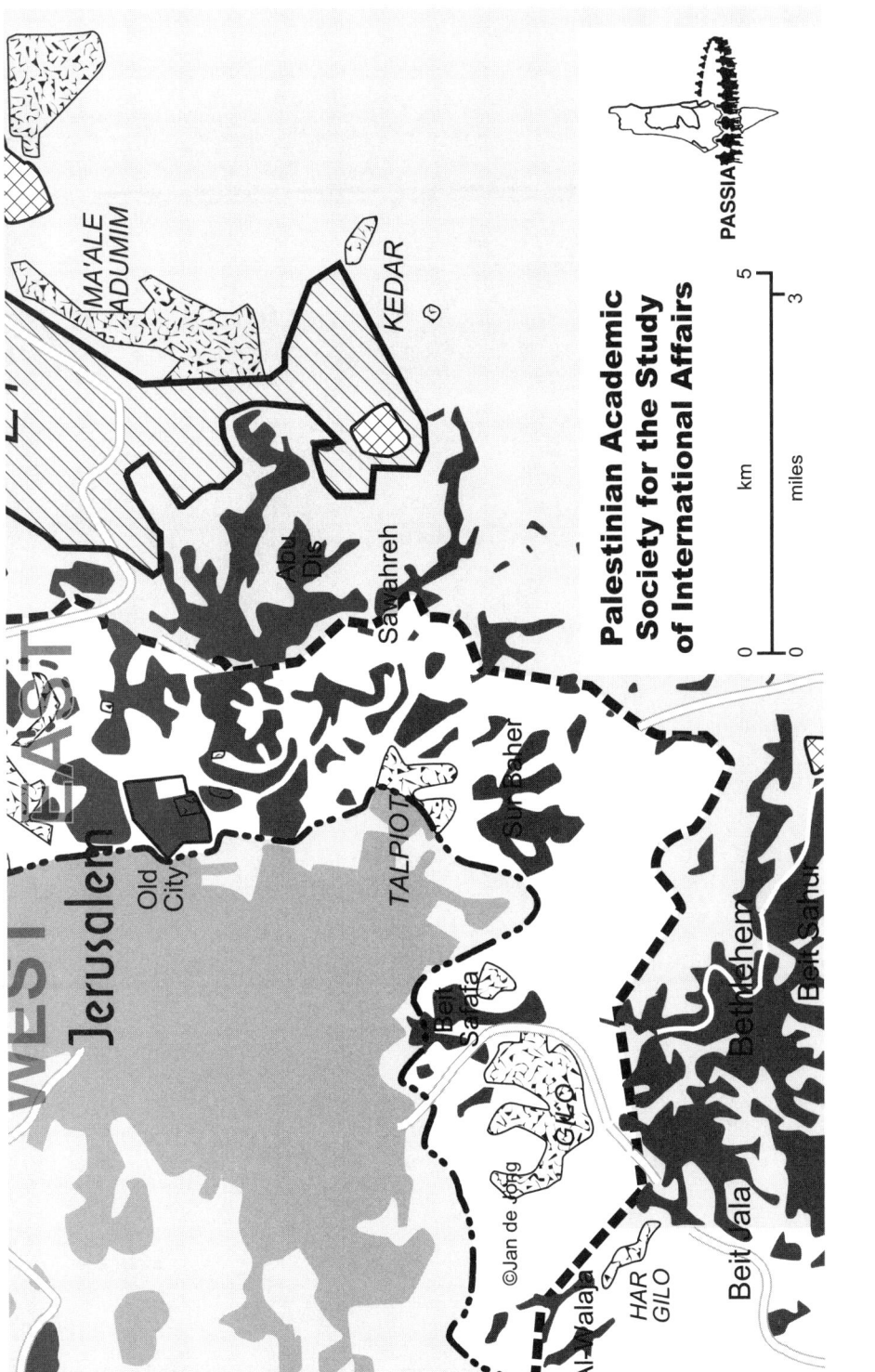

WEST

EAST

Jerusalem

Old City

MA'ALE ADUMIM

KEDAR

Abu Dis

Sawahreh

TALPIOT

Sur Baher

Beit Safafa

GILO

©Jan de Jong

Al-Walaja

HAR GILO

Beit Jala

Bethlehem

Beit Sahur

Palestinian Academic Society for the Study of International Affairs

km

miles

0   5

0   3

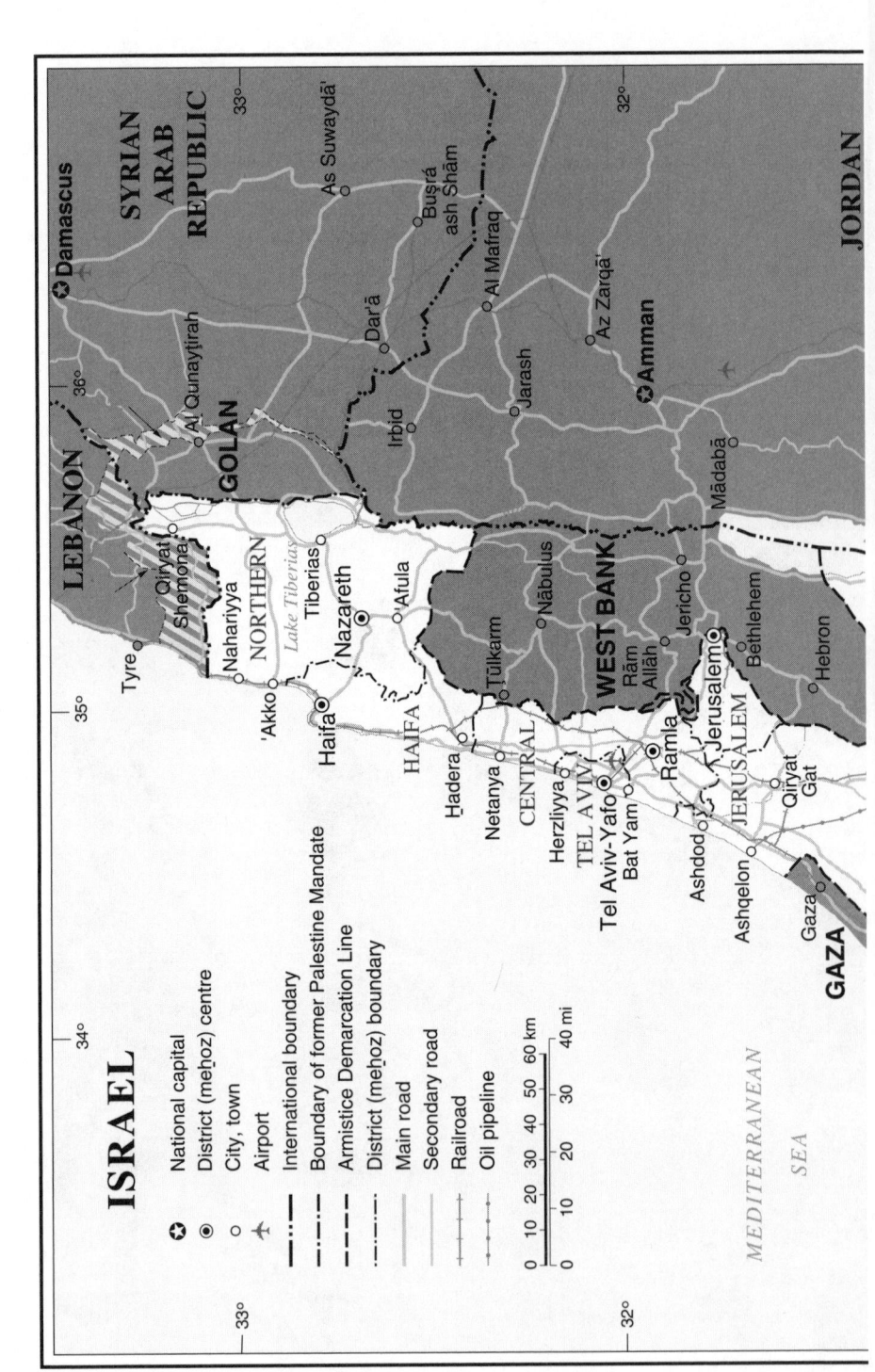

ISRAEL

- ✪ National capital
- ◉ District (meḥoz) centre
- ○ City, town
- ✈ Airport

International boundary
Boundary of former Palestine Mandate
Armistice Demarcation Line
District (meḥoz) boundary
Main road
Secondary road
Railroad
Oil pipeline

| 0 | 10 | 20 | 30 | 40 | 50 | 60 km |
| 0 | 10 | 20 | 30 | 40 mi |

LEBANON

SYRIAN ARAB REPUBLIC

✪ Damascus

Al Qunayṭirah

GOLAN

As Suwaydā'

Buṣrá ash Shām

Al Mafraq

Darā

Irbid

Jarash

Az Zarqā'

✪ Amman

JORDAN

Tyre

Qiryat Shemona

Nahariyya

Lake Tiberias

Tiberias

Nazareth

Afula

NORTHERN

'Akko

Haifa

HAIFA

Hadera

Netanya

Herzliyya

CENTRAL

TEL AVIV

Tel Aviv-Yafo

Bat Yam

Ashdod

Ashqelon

Gaza

GAZA

Ṭūlkarm

Nābulus

WEST BANK

Rām Allāh

Jericho

Ramla

Jerusalem

JERUSALEM

Bethlehem

Hebron

Qiryat Gat

Mādabā

MEDITERRANEAN SEA

33° 34° 35° 36° 33° 32°

32°

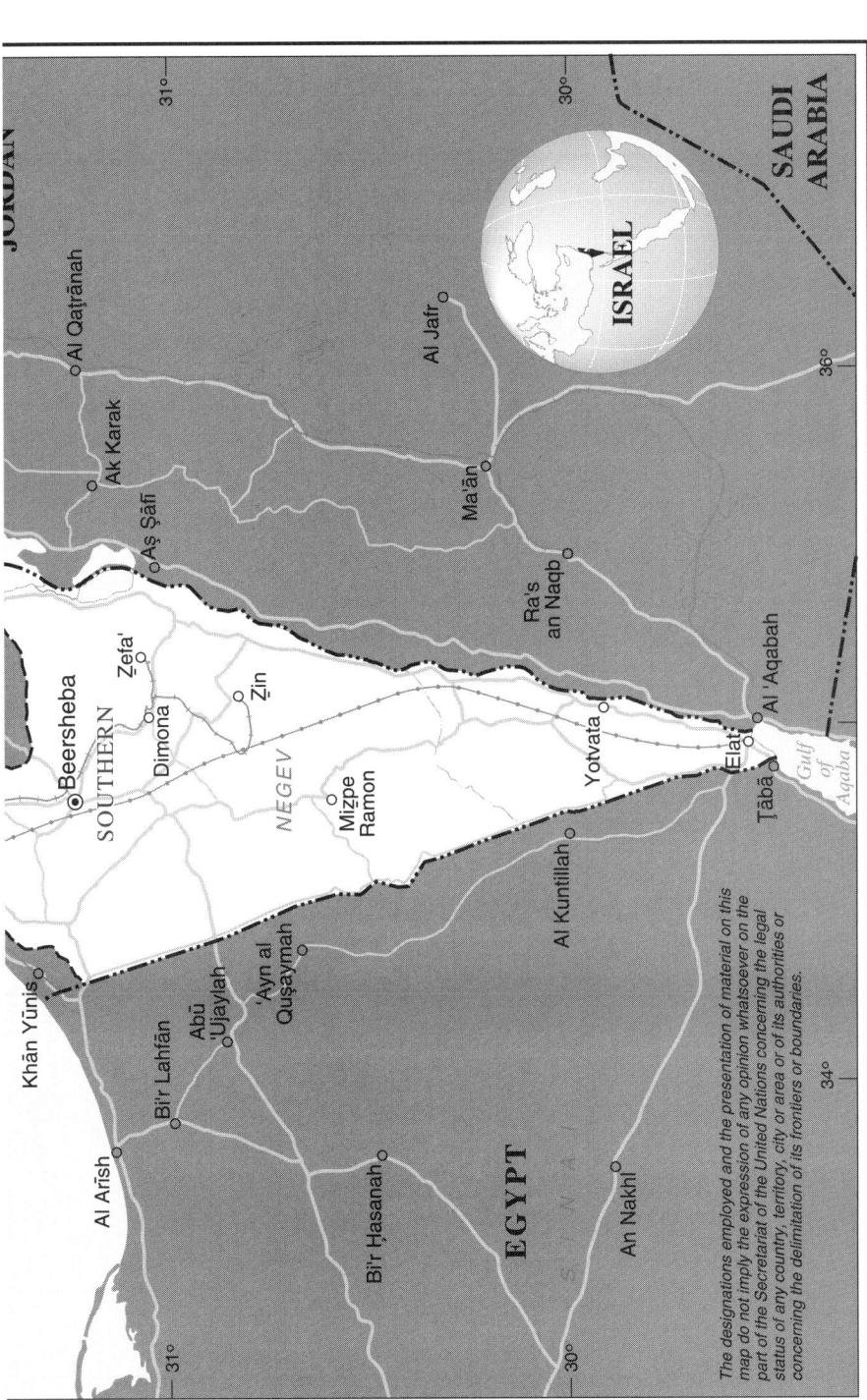

Department of Peacekeeping Operations
Cartographic Section

Map No. 3584 Rev. 2   UNITED NATIONS
January 2004

JORDAN

Al Qaṭrānah

Ak Karak

Aş Şāfī

Al Jafr

Maʿān

Raʾs
an Naqb

SAUDI
ARABIA

ISRAEL

Beersheba

SOUTHERN

Zefaʿ

Dimona

Zin

NEGEV

Mizpe
Ramon

Yotvata

Al ʿAqabah

Elat

Ṭābā

Gulf
of
Aqaba

Khān Yūnis

Biʾr Lahfān

Abū
ʿUjaylah

ʿAyn al
Quṣaymah

Al Kuntillah

Al ʿArīsh

Biʾr Ḥasanah

An Nakhl

EGYPT

S I N A I

31°

30°

36°

31°

30°

34°

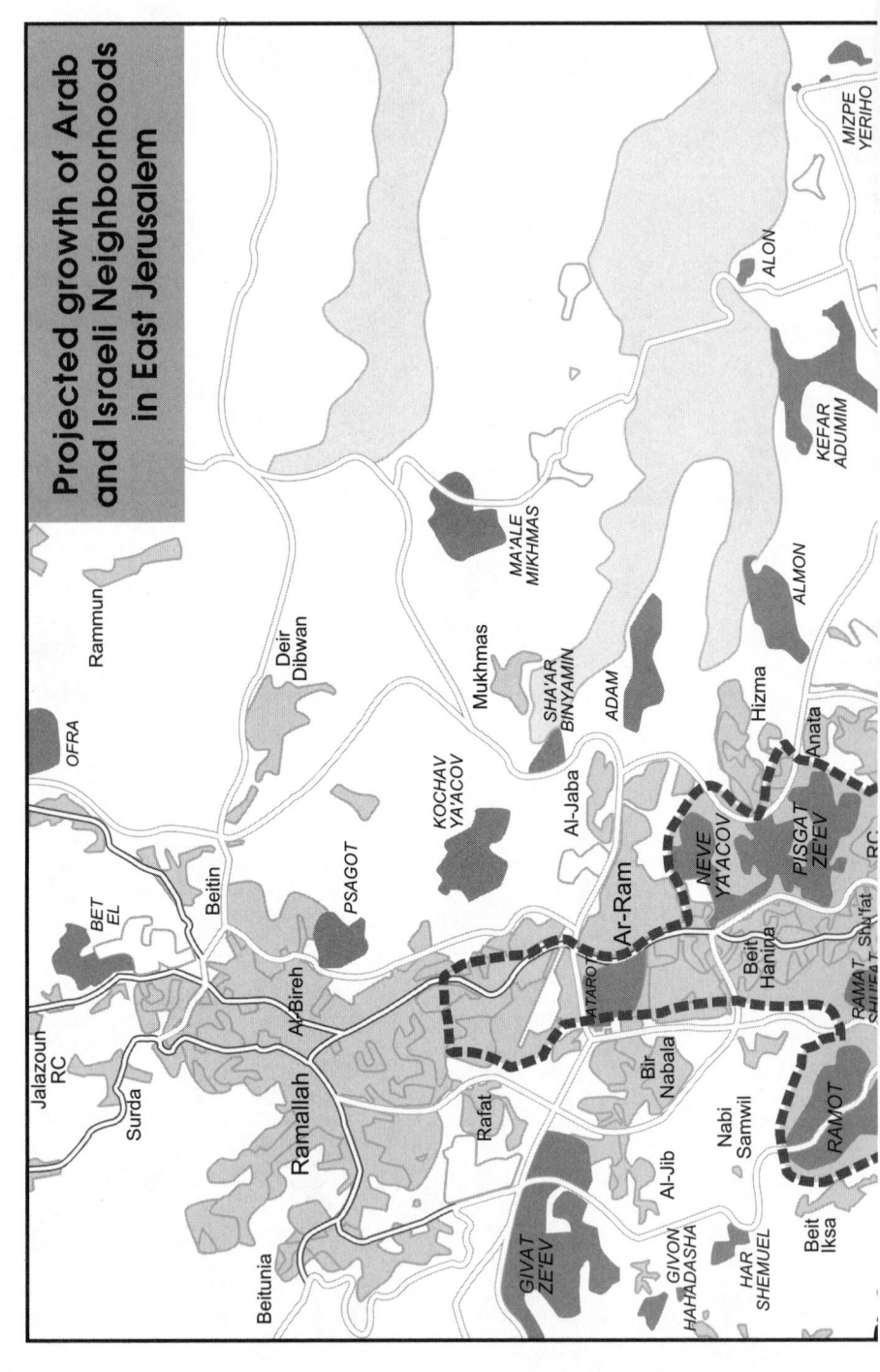

Projected growth of Arab and Israeli Neighborhoods in East Jerusalem

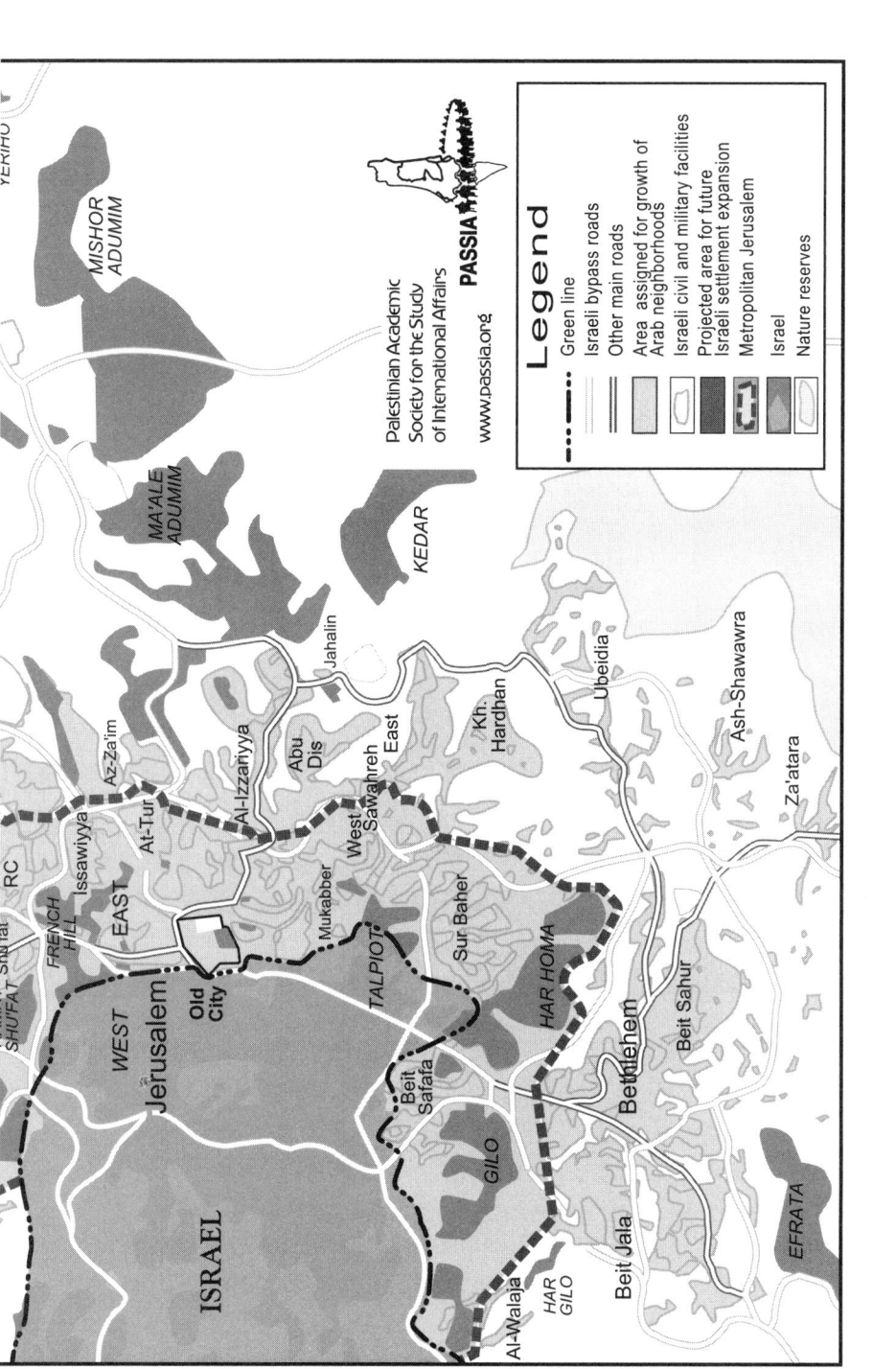

Legend

····· Green line
Israeli bypass roads
Other main roads
Area assigned for growth of Arab neighborhoods
Israeli civil and military facilities
Projected area for future Israeli settlement expansion
Metropolitan Jerusalem
Israel
Nature reserves

Palestinian Academic Society for the Study of International Affairs

www.passia.org

PASSIA

YEKHU'

MISHOR ADUMIM

MA'ALE ADUMIM

KEDAR

Jahalin

Az-Za'im

Al-Izzariyya

Abu Dis

SaWahreh East

West

Kh. Hardhan

Ubeidia

Ash-Shawawra

RC

SHU'FAT Shu'fat

FRENCH HILL

Issawiyya

At-Tur

EAST

Mukabber

Za'atara

Old City

WEST

Jerusalem

TALPIOT

Sur Baher

HAR HOMA

Beit Sahur

Beit Safafa

Bethlehem

ISRAEL

GILO

HAR GILO

Al-Walaja

Beit Jala

EFRATA

Palestinian Sovereign Areas According to the Sharon Proposal, 2001

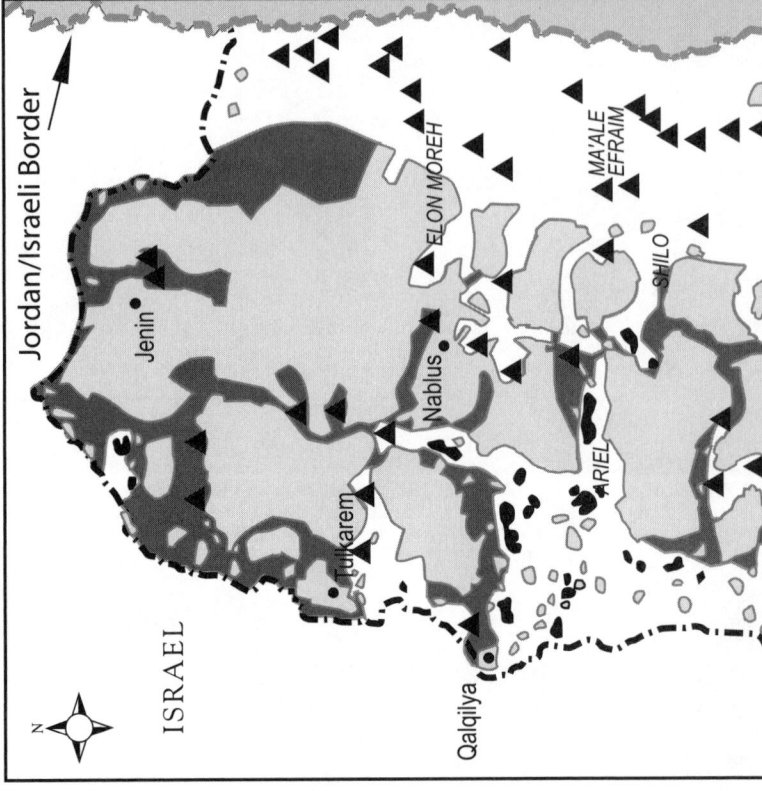

Jordan/Israeli Border

ISRAEL

N

Jenin

Tulkarem

Nablus

ELON MOREH

MA'ALE EFRAIM

SHILO

ARIEL

Qalqilya

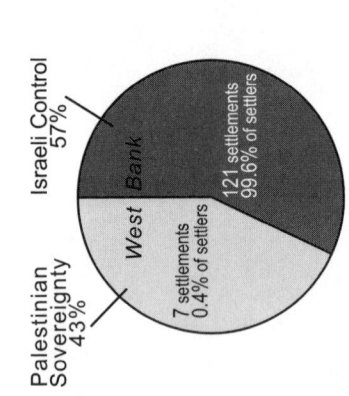

West Bank

Palestinian Sovereignty 43%

Israeli Control 57%

7 settlements 0.4% of settlers

121 settlements 99.6% of settlers

West Bank division
with number of Israeli settlements
and percentage of settlers,
excluding East Jerusalem

PASSIA

Palestinian Academic
Society for the Study
of International Affairs

www.passia.org

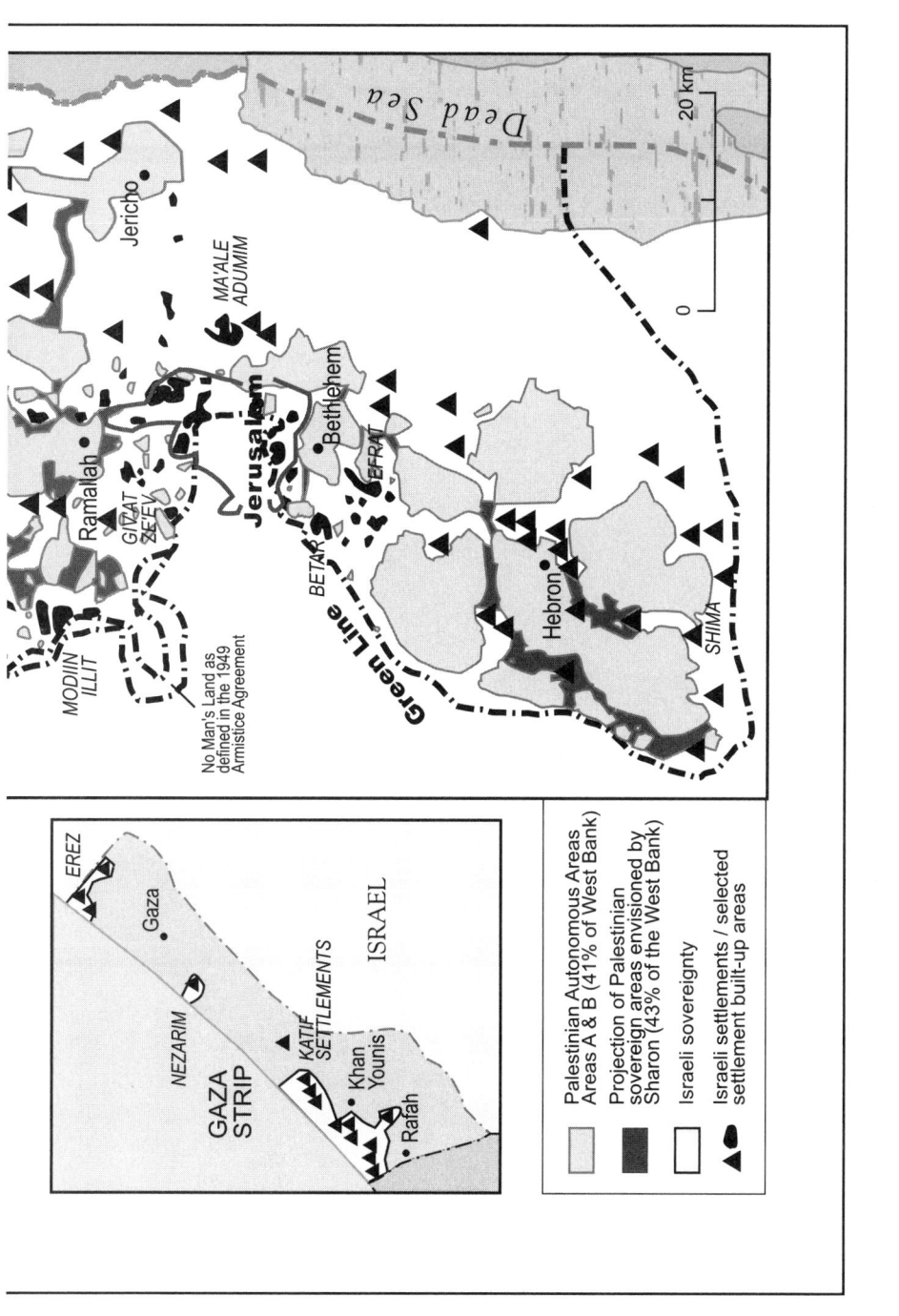

MODIIN
ILLIT

No Man's Land as
defined in the 1949
Armistice Agreement

Ramallah

GIV'AT
ZE'EV

Jericho

MA'ALE
ADUMIM

Jerusalem

Dead Sea

BETAR

Bethlehem

EFRAT

Green Line

Hebron

SHIMA

20 km

0

EREZ

GAZA
STRIP

NEZARIM

Gaza

KATIF
SETTLEMENTS

Khan
Younis

Rafah

ISRAEL

Palestinian Autonomous Areas
Areas A & B (41% of West Bank)

Projection of Palestinian
sovereign areas envisioned by
Sharon (43% of the West Bank)

Israeli sovereignty

Israeli settlements / selected
settlement built-up areas

INTRODUCTION

"Palestinians must come to acknowledge Jewish fears and their need for security, while Israelis must recognize that the only authentic security for them is through justice for the Palestinians." [1]

– Naim Ateek, Canon of St. George's Cathedral, Jerusalem

Peace between Israelis and Palestinians does not require them to agree on the events which comprise their respective histories. Instead, it necessitates a mutual acknowledgement of the injustices each has suffered.

In September, 2005, the world witnessed an extraordinary event when, after thirty-eight years of occupation, the Israeli government pulled 7,800 settlers out of the Gaza Strip without any serious incidents. Many of the soldiers, sympathetic to the settler movement and the violent protests, did not want to be ejecting fellow Jews from their homes. Yet they performed their duties admirably and with great care so as not to harm the civilian population. The world saw the power of moderation transcending the forces of extremism, something which has not been seen before in Israel.

---

[1] Ateek, Naim. *Justice and Only Justice: A Palestinian Theology of Liberation.* Orbis Books, New York 2001.

As I watched the coverage on television, I imagined how wonderful it would be if that same moderation were extended to Palestinian civilians at the military checkpoints. In my mind's eye I saw
an Israeli soldier apologizing to a Palestinian man twice his age for
having to carry out a body search, or to an old woman obliged to
wait hours in a long line in the hot sun. For one fleeting moment
I dared to dream of a day when both peoples would dwell side-by-
side in peace. After all, Jews and Arabs are both indigenous to the
Holy Land, and since ancient times have lived as neighbors, and
often as close relatives through intermarriage. Why then in the
21st century is our thinking not more sophisticated; why can we
not create the same amicable living conditions that existed for long
periods in ancient times?

If events in the last four years are any indication, it appears that
neither the Palestinians nor the Israelis are acting in a reasonable
way to make peace happen.

In March, 2002, while I was in Jerusalem and the West Bank,
Palestinian suicide bombers killed a record one hundred eight
Israelis. These human bombs chose to carry out their deadly mis-
sions in crowded malls, pizza parlors and neighborhood cafes.
That month their favorite target appeared to be buses. The bombers chose mornings when the city buses were crowded with students on their way to school, and evenings when commuters were
returning home to their families. Because March was unusually
hot that year, most bus drivers closed the windows and turned on
the air conditioning, which intensified the blasts and maximized
the number of victims.[2]

Suicide bombers strap home-made explosives to their torsos.
These bombs are packed with nuts, bolts, screws and pieces of broken machinery capable of inflicting maximum bodily damage in
a blast. The explosion – powerful enough to plunge metal shards

---

2   Margalit, Avishai. "The Suicide Bombers." *The New York Review of Books*, Volume 50,
Number 1, January 16, 2003.

through necks and rip open major arteries – transforms the bus into an inferno of twisted metal and burning flesh, leaving intestines, severed limbs and shreds of bloody clothing strewn around the bomb site. Survivors wander about, dazed and deafened.

An Amnesty International report in July, 2002, concluded that the deliberate killing of Israeli civilians by Palestinian terrorist groups constituted crimes against humanity. During approximately the same period in the Gaza Strip, equally senseless deaths of Palestinians occurred.

Until Israel's unilateral withdrawal in August, 2005, Khan Younis was one of eight refugee camps in the Gaza Strip, where 58,891 Palestinians lived in a 147-square-mile area, making it the most densely populated place on earth. Khan Younis is a concrete shanty town; sewage runs in rivulets down the middle of alleyways; there are no gardens; no places for children to play other than the dunes in front of the neighboring Israeli settlements, which, together with Israeli military installations, surround Khan Younis on three sides. The dunes, dotted on their tops with Israeli gun emplacements and sandbagged bunkers, are surrounded by an electric fence. Israeli soldiers routinely taunt young boys – who like to fly their kites along the perimeter of the fence – with racial slurs and invective meant to produce an angry response. The boys run up the sloping dunes to the fence and throw stones, to which the Israeli soldiers reply with their weapon of choice: dart-like needles known as *fléchettes*, which are packed inside shells. On impact the *fléchettes* spray out in a deadly mass, slicing the target to pieces. In one twenty-four hour period Israeli soldiers killed fourteen Palestinian children. Chris Hedges, Middle East reporter for the *New York Times*, witnessed such an incident. "Children have been shot in other conflicts I covered but I have never before watched soldiers entice children like mice into a trap and then murder them on the spot."[3]

---

3   Hedges, Chris. "A Gaza Diary: Scenes from a Palestinian Uprising." *Harper's Magazine*, October 2001, pp. 35–46.

Amnesty International considers the Israeli government's violations of human rights so grave that many of them meet the definition of crimes against humanity under international law.[4]

If – as frequently stated in the media – strict religious doctrine on both sides is stalling the peace process, and fundamentalist values have taken control of the decision-making of both the Palestinian Authority and the Israeli government, we urgently need to use every resource to marginalize fanaticism and narrow-mindedness. Failure to counter the threat of rising fundamentalist influence could ultimately overwhelm the larger, moderate brands of the three Abrahamic religions. According to Rabbi Michael Lerner, this will not be an easy task. "The Palestinian fundamentalists have entered into a de facto alliance with Ariel Sharon. They engage in acts of terror against Israeli civilians whenever acts of occupation become so outrageous that recruiting suicide bombers becomes possible. The Israeli government then responds by engaging in acts of retaliation and obliterating the infrastructure of the Palestinian Authority. Israel then demands that the obliterated infrastructure take powerful steps against the Palestinian terrorists."[5]

Palestinian extremists seek the destruction of Israel and the replacement of the Palestinian Authority with an Islamic state in the West Bank and Gaza. The Likud Party government of former Prime Minister Ariel Sharon is committed to the idea of a Greater Israel, and hold the view that the Palestinians are not entitled to self-determination. The Israeli Settler movement believes Palestinians should be 'transferred' out of Israel because only the Jewish people have the biblical right to Judea and Samaria.

---

4   Amnesty International Report, November 4, 2002. "Sharon's Rival Netanyahu signs on as foreign minister." *St. Paul Pioneer Press*, November 4, 2002. Algazy, Joseph. "Israel Defense Forces Operating in Jenin and Nablus During Operation Defensive Shield." *Ha'aretz*, November 4, 2002. McGreal, Chris. "Amnesty calls for Arrest of Israelis for War Crimes." *The Guardian*, November 4, 2002.

5   Lerner, Rabbi Michael. "Can Colin Powell Rescue Us?" *Tikkun*, Vol. 17, No. 1, March, 2002, pp. 7–9.

Long before I visited Jerusalem and the West Bank in March, 2002, my opinion about the Israeli-Palestinian conflict shifted several times. I attribute this metamorphosis in large part to the fourteen years I lived in Beirut, Lebanon. Between 1969 – when I moved there as a self-absorbed young woman – to 1983, when I was forced to leave because of civil war – I went from being a knee-jerk supporter of Israel to having sympathy for the Palestinians. I became embarrassed at the extent of my own ignorance and set out on a life-long journey – which remains very much in progress – to understand one thing properly. The Middle East was my obvious choice, and I quickly found all the areas of inquiry spreading out from it, as one expects from a deep study of almost anything. It became clear to me that the most stable times in this region have occurred when the inhabitants adhered most closely to the Golden Rule: 'Do unto others what you would have them do unto you'; or, simply, 'live and let live.' Whenever extremism, fanaticism or fundamentalism raises its obdurate head, the Golden Rule is quickly set aside and the bloodshed begins. Therefore, as an agitator for peace and cohesion among all people, I advocate the marginalization of extremism on both sides of the Israeli-Palestinian conflict. I am convinced it is the middle ground which promotes sustainable safety, comfort and prosperity in any civilization. In various ways this book attempts to demonstrate that most people gravitate to this middle ground.

Currently there are approximately five million Israelis and 4.8 million Palestinians – only two percent of the original thirty percent Christians remain; the rest are Sunni Muslim – living in Israel proper and the occupied territories. Whether it is the Iranian President's outrageous call for the destruction of Israel, or Benjamin Netanyahu's equally offensive threat – stated in a speech at Bar-Illan University in 1989 – to carry out mass expulsion of Palestinians, these two peoples are not going to disappear. Rather, they must find a way to make compromises in exchange for peace.

. . .

There has been a Jewish presence in the area of Palestine for thousands of years. The Holocaust made the formal creation of a Jewish homeland in Palestine in 1948 morally justifiable, and its continued secure existence must be guaranteed in final peace negotiations with the Palestinians.

The Palestinians are ethnic cousins of the indigenous Jews of ancient Canaan, and have shared a presence in this land for thousands of years. From prehistoric times this tiny area of the Middle East has witnessed a twisting continuum of factions, with one city or state rising and then falling. Empires have come and gone. More significantly, the fleeting power of people and ideologies has emerged and disappeared, sometimes almost without a trace. Egyptians, Assyrians, Babylonians, Macedonians, Romans, Israelites, Philistines, Crusaders, Arabs, Ottoman Turks, and finally the British, can all claim strong historical connections to this land either through bloody warfare or benign conquest. The multitude of ruins in the Golan Heights – contested since the Amorites first dominated it in the 3rd Millennium BCE – and Tel Megiddo[6] – a town in northern Galilee where historians believe more battles have been fought than anywhere else in the world – bear witness to the vulnerability of the most powerful armies. Time after time the inhabitants have been slaughtered, driven into exile or subjugated under a new political power which held sway for a few centuries. Who are the rightful claimants to this ancient land? Does the Jewish claim that they were driven out by the Romans two thousand years ago[7] override the Palestinian Arabs' claim that as descendants of the inhabitants of ancient Canaan, they too have a right to this land?

The State of Israel has existed for almost sixty years, an infini-

---

6   The Armageddon of biblical prophecy.

7   Slater, Jerome. "Can Zionism be Reconciled with Justice for the Palestinians?" *Tikkun*, July/Aug 2000.

tesimal speck of time compared to the litany of events which have taken place in this area since human habitation began. Israel's current leadership and its extremist supporters believe their policies will forever protect the Jewish people and the Jewish state; in the same way, Palestinian fundamentalists believe their ideology will endure as dogma; but history has shown otherwise. The many warriors who fought for their beliefs at Tel Megiddo and are now forgotten and faded into oblivion are ironic proof.

According to Rabbi Lerner, "There will be no peace for Israel, no safety, no matter how many walls they build or how repressive they get, until the occupation of Palestinian land ends. Anyone who wants to save Israeli lives has to focus on that. There will be no safety for Palestinians, either, if they cannot find a way to stop the fundamentalists who want to disrupt any chance of peace. But the Palestinian leadership is powerless to stop them as long as their conditions are so intolerable."[8]

While a resolution between Israelis and Palestinians may appear impossible, doing nothing could lead to the dissolution of the State of Israel, which would be a tragedy. According to Tanya Reinhart, Israeli journalist and professor, "The current Israeli government is not reflective of its people, the majority of whom want some form of negotiated settlement even if it means dismantlement of some or all settlements in a framework of peace."[9]

However, Uri Avnery, former member of the *Knesset* and founder of *Gush Shalom* – one of Israel's most influential peace organizations – believes that the majority of Israelis – who want peace – have allowed a minority to take over Israeli politics. "When a majority doesn't have a clear and dominant ideology, and is faced

---

8   Lerner, Rabbi Michael. "Stop the Murders of Israelis and Palestinians: How Many More will have to die," *Tikkun*, July/September, 2003. www.networkingtheinternet. com/zxm198.htm

9   Reinhart, Tanya. "Interview With Tanya Reinhart: Israel/Palestine: How to End the War of 1948." ZNet, Nov. 8, 2002, www.zmag.org/content/showarticle.cfm?SectionID =22&ItemID=2595

with a strongly motivated, ideologically fanatical minority, the majority is at a great disadvantage."[10]

Recent polls in Palestine show that a majority of Palestinians, while dreaming of peace, are convinced that a genuine peace with Israel – one based on UN resolutions 242 and 338 and the land-for-peace formula – is no longer attainable because of the expansion of Jewish settlements in the West Bank. Palestinians feel betrayed by terrorist groups like *Hamas* and *Fatah*, who appear to wantonly thwart every effort toward stability, and by an ineffectual, corrupt leadership unable or unwilling to negotiate some concessions from the current Israeli government.

I decided I needed to go there and see for myself.

. . .

I interviewed both Israelis and Palestinians in order to find the middle ground, since I am fully aware that each side has been terribly wronged by historical events, that each side has a story which needs to be heard and understood.

Accusations of anti-Semitism are frequently used to silence any discussion of Israel and its policies toward the Palestinians. My criticism of Israel is directed at the political agenda of the current Israeli government, not against Judaism or an ethnic group.

On the other hand Islamic fundamentalists do not represent Islam. So any criticism of groups like *Hamas*, Islamic Jihad and al-Aqsa Martyrs Brigade is not an attack on Islam but on the goals of these groups: the complete destruction of the State of Israel and the establishment of an Islamic state in Palestine.

This book is in three parts. The first is a travelogue which tells how I arranged for the interviews with a variety of people, and what I underwent to get them.

The second section is a verbatim account of the interviews I held in Israel/Palestine. Four additional interviews, conducted by

---

10   Interview with Uri Avnery. "Leaving Gaza." *Tikkun*, Vol. 20, No. 5., pp. 33–39.

telephone in October and November, 2005, may further enhance the reader's understanding of the complex issues at hand.

The third section consists of a brief history of the Israeli-Palestinian conflict, compiled for myself because I knew very little about its origins despite all the years I lived in the Middle East. For thirty-eight years I was a housewife; only recently have I become a peace activist; and I am not an historian. In preparation for my trip I read Noam Chomsky, Simha Flapan, Israel Shahak, David Fromkin, Robert I. Friedman, Avi Shlaim, David Hirst, Benny Morris and Mark Tessler.[11]

For a basic primer on the complex relationship between these two peoples, read the history section first. This may help to better understand the interviews in the middle section of the book.

Finally, it is my hope that you come away better informed and more willing to help publicize this tragedy. Western governments, and the American government in particular, must change the way they conduct foreign policy in the Middle East. We have everything to gain. Peace between Israelis and Palestinians is one of the missing cornerstones of world peace.

---

11   See the Bibliography.

JOURNEY

When I announced my intention to go to Israel in March, 2002, my Lebanese husband, Michel, still overly protective after 38 years of marriage, insisted I could not possibly do any such thing.

"It's much too dangerous. Besides, you've got plastic and metal for knees. If you have to run from danger, what will you do?"

"I'm doing my exercises and I'm getting stronger by the day. By the time I leave, I'll be able to leap over tall buildings."

Michel, used to being manipulated with humor, rolled his eyes.

"What good is it having new knees if I'm not going to use them?" I asked, sounding very serious.

At this, he threw up his hands, saying, *"Allah E Najjina"* (God save us from such stupidity).

My original plan was to accompany Rabbi Andrea Cohen and a delegation from Mid-East Citizen Diplomacy. Their itinerary included a stay with Father Elias Chacour in the Galilee in northern Israel, and with Israeli settlers in the Gaza Strip. Mid-East Diplomacy, seeking to play a role in reconciliation between Israelis and Palestinians, launched The Compassionate Listening Project in 1990. It is modeled on the work of Gene Hoffman, a Quaker and international peace activist. I e-mailed Andrea, told her I was encountering stiff opposition from my husband and asked if there was something she could say to convince him I would be safe.

By e-mail she replied, "Dear Cathy, I am running into the same problem. I will tell you what I have told my husband and children: I would not take people to Israel, particularly under current conditions, if I did not feel I could provide for their safety. I have every confidence in the Israeli-Palestinian team I work with over there. They understand the political climate, and are prepared to change our itinerary and arrange alternative plans at the slightest sign of trouble."

I showed her response to Michel. His reaction was, "We'll see."

I left the room smiling. Whenever I get to the 'We'll see' stage with Michel, I know I have won.

"Don't worry," I said, popping my head back though the door, "the violence always escalates before it slows down again. By the time I get to Israel, things will be calm."

He responded with a grunt.

Two weeks prior to the departure date, Mid-East Diplomacy canceled the trip. Rabbi Cohen and I were the only two participants. I decided not to share this information with Michel, who was still very reluctant to let me go.

In fact, every time he saw me, he came right up to my face and said, "You're going to cancel your trip, aren't you? You know it isn't safe. Please don't go."

While taking his shower, he would serenade me, imitating The Platters: 'You're just the great pretender, telling me you're going when you aren't.'

"And what happens if you die?" Michel finally asked.

"I'll leave you the name of our lawyer, accountant, broker and insurance agent. Did I forget anyone?"

"That's not funny."

"And remember. The key to the safety deposit box is in the bottom drawer of the ..."

"I remember," he mumbled, taking me in his arms. "You just come back, okay?"

"I will."

. . .

Rabbi Cohen shocked me by deciding not to go after all. I knew of one other person who was planning to travel to Israel at the same time. Her name was Mary. I had made her acquaintance the year before at a conference in Washington, D.C., on Israel/Palestine. She worked with several non-governmental organizations (NGO) and traveled to Israel frequently. I telephoned her and swore her to secrecy about Rabbi Cohen's pullout. Because of the lack of security in Israel she was having the same problem with her husband, and assured me I need not worry.

"But I have to tell you one thing, and it may cause you to change your mind," she said.

"What?"

Mary, a very straightforward person, replied, "If you're going to come with me, this is what you have to know. I have a lot to do there and I can't baby you. I will fix you up with a cell phone and a taxi driver I know. The rest is up to you. When you're done with your work, and me with mine, we'll meet back at the hotel for a stiff drink before heading back to the airport. Can you do this?"

I assured her I could.

"Okay then, we're out of here on the first of March. I'll meet you at the Toronto Airport in the Air Canada departure lounge."

"Mary, one more thing," I said before hanging up, "thank you for your help."

"You're welcome."

. . .

I needed to get a new passport for this trip. My old one had multiple visas for Lebanon since Michel and I travel there every year to visit relatives and friends. Israel could have denied me entry because of these visas. Except for Egypt and Jordan, Israel is technically at war with its other Arab neighbors, Lebanon and Syria. An Israeli who has contact with these countries is committing treason. Non-Israelis – particularly those with Arab sounding names and whose travel documents show contact with an enemy nation – are often denied entry visas.

I spent months reading dozens of books and articles in order to better understand the history of the Israeli-Palestinian conflict. With a solid foundation I was confident I could ask my interviewees the questions that would best inform my readers. On the Internet, I read *Ha'aretz* and the *Jerusalem Post*, two Israeli newspapers. In addition to the mainstream media, I routinely perused alternative news sites like ZNet, The Nation, CounterPunch, the BBC, *Al-Ahram* from Egypt, *Le Monde* from France, *L'Orient-Le Jour* from Beirut. I subscribed to *Tikkun*, a magazine published by Rabbi Michael Lerner, and to a number of Israeli news services both right and left of center. I telephoned Jewish and Palestinian organizations asking for contacts in Israel. I e-mailed people whose articles I had read, told them when I would be in Israel, and asked if I could see them. The response was so overwhelmingly positive that by the time I left I had a dozen names and phone numbers.

Michel must ultimately have trusted my decision to go because he did not block the door when I opened it to leave.

Kissing him good-bye, I said, "I'll call you every day."

"Promise me you won't go to Ramallah, or anywhere else in the West Bank. It is much too dangerous."

"I promise."

. . .

I flew from Minneapolis to Toronto and met Mary near the Air Canada gate. I barely recognized her. I had forgotten how petite she was and that her hair was so dark it was almost black. As we had at least an hour before boarding our flight, Mary and I decided to get something to eat. We found two seats at a bar near the gate; over hamburgers, French fries and draft beer, we got better acquainted.

Because of the situation in Israel I was convinced that the plane for the flight to Tel Aviv would be empty. Instead, every seat was taken. Mary was seated in the last seat of the last section of the plane and my aisle seat was in the third row of the middle section. Thanks to the midnight departure and a very effective pill, I was able to sleep for about nine of the eleven hours of the flight. My stomach gave a quick turn when I heard we were about to land in Israel, but I reminded myself I had survived Beirut and I could handle an Israeli adventure.

As I was stuffing my inflatable pillow and earplugs back into my carry-on, a flight attendant approached a young Palestinian couple seated directly in front of me, traveling with their four young children.

Leaning toward the man's right ear, the Air Canada attendant said, "Please remain seated. Someone will come to escort you off the plane."

My Arab friends in Eau Claire had told me the Israeli government often makes it difficult for Palestinians to enter Israel. I did not know these people but I felt sorry for them, particularly since they were traveling with small children. They appeared to take their predicament in stride. They exchanged looks but did not utter a word. Instead they gathered up the children's things and began stuffing them into their hand luggage.

Our plane landed on the tarmac some distance from the terminal. Although it was already night – a little after seven PM with the eight-hour time change – it was quite warm for the first of March. When I descended the steps there were a number of empty buses waiting. I boarded the one closest to me but as the doors were about to close, I abruptly jumped off.

"What do you think you're doing?" asked the Israeli security guard.

"I decided I wanted to wait here for my friend," I replied, a bit surprised at my boldness. After all I did have an Arab name, and I was at Ben-Gurion Airport. Mary was among the last to leave the plane.

What I really wanted was to find out what would happen to the Palestinian family. Before Mary and I boarded the last bus, I watched the couple and their children being escorted from the plane, helped into a van and driven off.

On the short drive to the terminal, someone standing behind me whispered, "Those poor bastards. They're going to be kept in detention for twenty-four hours, then expelled on the next available plane."

I have no way of knowing whether or not they were interrogated and eventually given entry visas, or expelled, as the stranger on the bus suggested.

When I finally walked through the glass doors at Ben-Gurion terminal, most of the passengers had already passed through immigration. Mary had somehow gotten off the bus ahead of me and proceeded inside. With a choice of agents I chose a woman.

I was so fearful of having my new passport stamped that before she had a chance to open her mouth I blurted, "If at all possible, please don't stamp my passport."

Because I spoke so emphatically, she must have felt curious enough to ask why.

I explained I had plans to travel to Lebanon the following month, so she issued my visa on a piece of paper and slipped it inside my passport. I thought this was a generous gesture on her part; had she stamped my passport I could not have entered Lebanon, since Israel is considered an enemy nation. Apparently it was standard procedure to give visitors the choice whether to have their passport stamped.

Keeping one eye on Mary, who was answering questions a few booths away, I heard the lady say, "This is not a good time to be visiting Israel."

"Thanks, I appreciate the warning. You're very kind."

I caught up with Mary at baggage claim where she was talking to two women who had been on our flight. When I collected my suitcase I followed Mary toward the exit. Perhaps other parts of Ben-Gurion Airport were more modern, but the section we walked through to find a taxi into Arab East Jerusalem was shabby, something I did not expect in an Israeli airport. Outside the terminal we turned right, walked a short distance along a narrow sidewalk and turned right again. We took our place in a long line and waited our turn for a taxi.

"Where are you going?" asked the dispatcher when we finally reached his stand.

"The Golden Walls Hotel on Saleh el Din Street in East Jerusalem," replied Mary.

Israeli currency is called shekels. I do not remember the exchange rate at that time but we agreed on the equivalent of a fifty-dollar fare and the driver threw our luggage into his trunk.

"It never seems to matter how often I come here," Mary said. "I still get excited at the thought of seeing Jerusalem again."

I was not thinking about Jerusalem because I could not get that poor family out of my mind. It is one thing to be traveling alone but to have to involve the children … I had inadvertently done that in Beirut during the war when I got caught up in a mob scene one day and had to drive over burning tires to escape. For days following that episode my children were alarmingly distraught.

"Cathy, didn't you hear me?" Mary asked.

"No, sorry, what did you say?"

"What you saw back there is nothing," Mary said. "If you visit a refugee camp in the West Bank you'll see much worse."

. . .

Although it was night, I expected to see some signs of life along the way during the forty-five minutes it took to drive from Tel Aviv to Jerusalem. What appeared to be long stretches of total darkness were partly the sheer cliff-faces of a mountain through which the road had been carved. However this did not explain the open spaces seemingly devoid of human existence. I asked Mary about this.

"There are a few clusters of Palestinian houses along this route. Since they're not hooked up to electricity they're difficult to see, particularly if a veil of fog is hanging over the valley," she told me.

"What about that?" I asked a few minutes later, pointing off to my right. "See all those lights up on the hill? It looks like an amusement park at Christmas time."

"That's an Israeli settlement."

It was an amazing display of light but I wondered if it was not a bit excessive given the cost of electricity.

When we got to West Jerusalem our driver pulled over and got out his map. It was almost 9:00 PM, and the neighborhood in which we stopped bustled with traffic and pedestrians. To my great surprise one of the actors who starred in a PBS Point of View Special entitled *Promises* – which aired some months earlier – was standing on a corner waiting to cross the street just outside my taxi window. He was taller than I remembered, but even though I could not recall his name he was definitely the same Israeli who befriended a Palestinian in the Dheisheh refugee camp near Bethlehem in the story.

"Don't you know where you're going?" I idly asked our driver, still staring at the young Israeli.

"No," he replied. "I live in Tel Aviv. I never go into East Jerusalem."

Then, without any explanation, he jumped out of his car and ran to a taxi parked ahead of us. Mary and I watched, mesmerized. Even with the windows closed, we could hear the shouts. Flinging his arms in the air, our driver looked like he was trying to fly. Eventually, the second driver opened his door, got out, slammed it shut and walked toward us.

"My friend does not want to enter East Jerusalem, so I have accepted to take you. It will cost you twenty dollars."

I immediately agreed, quite certain we did not want to be dumped on a busy street corner, luggage in hand, in the center of Jerusalem. We paid the first driver his fare while the second transferred our bags to his car.

As soon as we were settled in the back seat he said, "There's going to be trouble in Jerusalem tonight."

"What do you mean?" I asked.

"My brother called me an hour ago. He was told to close his shop. They are expecting a suicide bomber."

"I don't understand," I said. "How do people know ahead of time that a person is going to blow himself up?"

The minute I opened my mouth I realized I sounded a bit naïve, but his certainty that a bomber would strike made no sense to me.

I had no sooner said this than we were forced to the side of the road by the sound of sirens coming from all directions. Fire trucks, ambulances, police vans, and scores of press cars – cameras already dangling out of windows – sped past. Our new driver pulled in behind them and headed in the same direction.

"You see!" he shouted. "It has already happened." Pointing directly ahead of us he said, "Look down there. See the crowd? That is where the bomb just exploded. Now, how am I going to get you to your hotel?"

Sure enough, we were within a block of the explosion. Had we arrived minutes earlier, we would have been at the wrong place at the wrong time. Sabbath had just ended in this Hasidic – Ultra-Orthodox Jewish – neighborhood, and the bomb had exploded in one of the schools. Jewish schools are closed during Sabbath from sunset Friday to sunset Saturday.

Men and young boys in black hats and suits, white shirts and *payos* (side curls), congregated on the sidewalks on either side of my taxi. I knew no Hebrew but from the commotion and shouting it was obvious they were worried about who might have died or been injured in the blast.

The driver suddenly turned right at the next corner and stopped.

"I cannot take you any farther," he said. "I do not like to drive into East Jerusalem at night, and I certainly will not do it tonight. You will have to walk the rest of the way."

For a brief second, I thought of telling him that I had artificial knees, and that I was unable to lift heavy bags. Mary had already jumped out, as if there was nothing we could do, but being me, I was ready to argue. Finally, something clicked in my mind, something I had already decided back in Wisconsin: I was not going to complain. I had put myself in this situation, and I had to deal with it. I got out, collected my bag and backpack and started walking.

I did not know where we were, and I was too nervous to ask, but our taxi driver left us off near the Jerusalem Hotel on Nablus Road. Mary knew that we still had three long blocks to walk before reaching our hotel on Saleh el Din Street, just outside the Damascus Gate of the Old City. Aside from the rhythmic smack of our suitcases rolling along the cobblestone street and echoing off high stone walls along the perimeter, this area of East Jerusalem was eerily silent. All businesses had closed for the day; every storefront's metal shutter was padlocked shut. The only indication of life, or death, was the sad wail of sirens, still transporting the wounded or dead to hospitals. When we turned left onto Saleh el Din Street, we almost bumped into two Israeli policemen patrolling the deserted streets. I do not know who was more surprised, us or them, at seeing two foreign women loaded down with luggage, walking past them. In normal times, this would not have been an aberration but in March, 2002, when suicide bombings were averaging two a day, very few tourists were crazy enough to venture into this tense situation.

"Look," said Mary, pointing off to her right. On the otherwise dimly lit, deserted street, I saw the ancient wall of the Old City illuminated in splendor against the night sky. I was really in Jerusalem. Under other circumstances I would have taken the time to look around, to study the skyline and discover that, from the point where our taxi driver dropped us off, we were quite near the Dome of the Rock, the familiar Jerusalem landmark. However, my arrival that evening was anything but normal.

. . .

"Welcome," said Nabil, the hotel owner, greeting us as he helped us with our bags.

'Indeed,' I thought, as he showed me to my room which was small but clean with view on an inner alleyway strewn with garbage cans. 'I cannot imagine what the next two weeks are going to be like if this is how they have begun!'

After unpacking my suitcase, I returned to the reception area to find the hotel staff watching the news on television. On the screen flashed our taxi and our two heads in the back seat. At the time I was concentrating on the car full of journalists and cameramen ahead of us. Our taxi had obviously been sandwiched between two cars. It was painfully clear from the footage just how close we had been to the blast.

When the news finished, I approached the hotel owner.

"Nabil, I'd like to get something to eat if that's possible. Do you have a restaurant in the hotel?"

"I used to," he said, "but I was obliged to close it last year. I couldn't afford to keep it open."

"What a shame. He had the best food in town," Mary said, joining us at the front desk.

"Last year, I was down to a five percent occupancy rate," explained Nabil. "I am already worried, with the worsening *Intifada* and lack of tourists, that this year will be even worse."

Turning to me, Mary explained that Nabil used to keep a staff of sixty-five. "What are you down to now, five?" He nodded sadly.

"Aside from the excellent cuisine," Mary said, "just imagine sitting at a table on a terrace overlooking the Old City. It was truly spectacular. Nabil," she asked, "could you at least fix us some hummus or *lebneh* (dried yogurt) with olives? If a plain cheese sandwich and tea is all you can throw together, well take it. We're famished."

That was an understatement. It had been a long time since my hamburger and fries at the Toronto airport. I passed up dinner on the plane so I could sleep. Now I was ready for a five-course meal but I politely agreed to whatever food Nabil could scrounge up.

While we waited, I asked Mary if Nabil was Christian or Muslim. "That name could be either, so I can't tell."

"What do you mean?"

"If his name were Michel or Joseph, I would automatically know he was Christian. If his name was Mohammad or Ali, he would be Muslim."

"Nabil is Greek Orthodox."

"Lebanon has a large Greek Orthodox community along with a number of other Christian sects. What about the Palestinian Christians?"

"The majority are Greek Orthodox," Mary said. "There are also Roman and Greek Catholics, and some Egyptian Copts. There are quite a few Anglicans and Lutherans. And there are some Armenian Christians in the Armenian Quarter in the Old City."

"What is the percentage of Christian Palestinians?" I asked.

"Approximately a fourth, but most live in the Diaspora."

"I had no idea it was that many."

In fact, when I looked into the different Palestinian Christian sects, I learned that the remaining Christians in East Jerusalem, the West Bank and the Gaza Strip belong to fifteen different denominations, the largest of which are Greek Orthodox (fifty-one percent) and Roman Catholic (twenty-one percent).[12] Among the Palestinian Christians there are also Protestants – Lutherans and Anglicans – Quakers, Copts, Greek Catholics (officially called Melkites), Syrian Catholic, and Syrian Orthodox.

The Armenian presence dates back to 254 AD when pilgrims flocked to the Holy Land. Large numbers remained and took up residence in the proximity of the sanctuaries owned by the Patriarchate, the Armenian Convent.[13] While Palestinian Christians are Arabs, Armenians are not. Eventually the area around the Armenian Convent, located in the southwest corner of the Old City in

---

12 Sabella, Bernard, Bethlehem University, Palestine. "Palestinian Christians: Challenges and Hopes." www.al-bushra.org/holyland/sabella.htm

13 Hagopian, Arthur. "Armenians in Israel." Jerusalem Center for Public Affairs, VP:51 25 Sivan 5746/2 July 1986. www.jcpa.org/jl/hito4.html

Jerusalem, became the Armenian Quarter. The three other components of the Old City are the Muslim, Christian and Jewish Quarters.

Of the 750,000 Palestinians forced to flee their homes in 1948, thirty-five percent were Christian. In West Jerusalem alone – now part of Israel – fifty percent of the Christians living there lost their homes to the advancing Israeli army. Numerous convents, hospices, seminaries, and churches were either destroyed or cleared of their Christian owners and custodians. On May 17, 1948, in one of the most spectacular attacks on a Christian target, the Armenian Orthodox Patriarchate in Jerusalem was shelled with about one hundred mortar rounds by Zionist forces from the already-occupied monastery of the Benedictine Fathers on Mount Zion. The bombardment also damaged St. Jacob's convent, the Archangels' Convent, their appended churches, their two elementary and seminary schools, and their libraries, killing eight people and wounding one hundred twenty.[14]

From the middle of the 4th Century CE until the Arab Conquest in the middle of the 7th Century, Palestine was a Christian country with Jerusalem as its capital. In fact, since the time of Christ, Palestine has had a continuous Christian presence.[15] Today, of the 4.8 million Palestinians living in Israel/Palestine, just two percent are Christian. The vast majority have migrated to countries in Central and South America, the United States, Australia and Canada. No reliable figures are available but is it estimated that between 100,000 and 300,000 Palestinian Christians currently live in the United States.[16]

. . .

14   Strindberg, Anders. "Forgotten Christians: Not all Displaced Palestinians are Muslims." *The American Conservative*, May 24, 2004. www.amconmag.com/2004/2004_05_24/article.html#

15   Palestine Facts. "What about Christians in Palestine?" www.palestinefacts.org/pf_early_palestine_christians.php

16   Strindberg, *loc. cit.*

When I returned to my room after devouring two cheese and tomato sandwiches on pita bread, I undressed and climbed wearily into bed. With my throbbing knees propped up on two pillows, I fell asleep listening to explosions in the distance. As I drifted off, I wondered how people in this city knew ahead of time that a bomb was going to explode. I gave thanks that Michel knew none of this.

The next morning, Mary and I walked four city blocks into West Jerusalem to rent cell phones.

"They're an absolute necessity here. Before you go anywhere, you call first to make sure it's safe."

I assured her I would.

"And another thing," she added as we walked back to our hotel, "always have bottled water with you. Jerusalem is 2,500 feet above sea level. It's high desert and extremely dry. You can get dehydrated very quickly if you aren't careful."

"I can believe that, especially in this heat. This is unusual for March, isn't it?"

"Nabil said they were having an early *khamsine*. Do you know what that is?"

"Yes, it's a hot sand storm that blows in from North Africa. How unfortunate that it arrived now. I only packed wool clothes."

As Mary and I walked, I took in the sights and sounds. East Jerusalem is an exotic blend of ancient East meeting a more modern West. It is older women in *chador* or head scarves, the younger generation in mini skirts, tight jeans and form-fitting sweaters; it is men in dress suits and ties; old timers in baggy pants and *tarbouche* (red cap, or fez); it is donkey-driven push carts alongside automobiles on congested, narrow streets; it is the biblical Old City; the Al Aqsa Mosque with its golden dome; the Church of the Holy Sepulcher; the Western (Wailing) Wall; streets lined with graceful umbrella pines, the sound of their fine needles trembling in the light breeze; it is gardens lush with rosemary, jasmine, fuchsia, and pink laurel.

It is a place where knowing how to haggle in Arabic – whether over a kilo of tomatoes, a carton of cigarettes or a spool of thread – is a must; it is neighborhoods full of colorful scenery; the merry chatter of street vendors – their carts overflowing with eggplant, zucchini, baby green okra, lemons and *haricots verts* – gathered as if for some joyous occasion on the corner opposite the Post Office on Sultan Suleiman Street. Just around the corner, not a hundred feet away on a quiet residential street, is the upscale greengrocer. The owner painstakingly arranges his soft and ready-to-eat burnt-orange persimmons, red pomegranates, yellow quinces, prickly pears, and wrinkly-skinned pomelos – the size of grapefruits – in wooden crates lined in golf-course-green shredded paper.

It was said the half dozen women, seated along the narrow cobblestone alleyway of the Muslim Quarter just inside the Damascus Gate, walked here all the way from Jericho to sell their herbs and brown eggs. East Jerusalemites, happy for the rare opportunity to buy Palestinian-grown goods, scooped them up as quickly as the old ladies could unpack them. One woman, having no other place to carry her eggs, cradled them inside her purse, closing the clasp gently.

"I will have these for dinner tonight," she said.

The mouth-watering smell of flat bread dusted with thyme and olive oil drifts onto the street from a nearby oven, joining the scent of spit-roasted chickens, of coffee beans toasting, and the rich aroma of Lattakia tobacco burning slowly in *nargillas* (bubble pipes). It was not yet noon, but on the corner of Nablus and Saleh el Din Streets, vendors were already busy grilling cinnamon-scented meat kabobs and carving marinated lamb which they layered into warm flat bread, dousing the sandwich with a sauce of tahini, garlic and lemon.

"I have some time before my first meeting," Mary said. "Why don't I call the driver I know. This way you can meet him and, if he is free, we can take a quick tour of the city."

"I'd love that."

. . .

Naim, our Palestinian taxi driver, was a resident of Jerusalem. He carried a blue ID card which identified him as an Israeli Arab and gave him the right to circulate in both Israeli West and Arab East Jerusalem. Palestinians living in the West Bank carry orange IDs and are not allowed to leave their towns and villages without Israeli-issued travel permits.

Naim drove us through some Arab East Jerusalem neighborhoods and, as we headed south toward Bethlehem, he pointed off to his left.

"My family used to live there," he said, and began to tell us his story. One of the things which upset me was the part about the ancient olive grove.

No one knew how old the hundreds of trees really were. Some of the old-timers swore the olive grove was 300 years old or perhaps even older. The trees probably did not need irrigation because they had been there so long. Their roots intermingled with the rich, dark dirt and delved deeply into the earth. A small village nearby had an olive press, and every day during the season the villagers brought their freshly-picked crop to be pressed for oil.

Naim still remembered the exact location of his house, what time the sun shone through the kitchen window, and where each tree was planted. He remembered because he was the one who scurried up the trees and shook the branches at harvest time, carefully aiming for the sheet spread around the base of each tree to catch the olives as they fell. Now there is no sign of a Palestinian presence. The villagers, if not already dead, had been dispersed to one of the many refugee camps. As for the ancient olive grove, it was uprooted to make way for Har Homa, a massive Israeli settlement.

Har Homa sits atop Abu Ghnaim Mountain, once a forest of 60,000 pine trees and a refuge for wild animals and plants. On the southwest edge of Bethlehem, this entire area was stripped bare to build 7,000 identical red roofed, multi-storied square housing units, arranged in layers some two kilometers in circumference.

When completed, the project looked from afar like asymmetrical Lego blocks. Gilo, another Israeli settlement, dominates the eastern perimeter of Bethlehem, sandwiching the Christian village between two Israeli colossi.

. . .

Tony, a friend in Eau Claire, had asked me if I could possibly deliver some important papers to his parents. He assured me that either his brother or his parents would come to East Jerusalem to meet me. They lived in Ramallah in the West Bank. Before leaving Eau Claire I had promised Michel that I would not venture into the West Bank. When I returned to the hotel after my tour with Naim and Mary, I decided to call Tony's parents to arrange a meeting place.

"Hello, this is Cathy ..."

"Oh, yes, Tony said you would call," replied his brother Charlie. "Why don't you come and have lunch with us today?"

"I don't think so, not today. The people at the hotel say its too dangerous to cross, that the Israeli army is bombing Ramallah."

"Not to worry. It will be over by the time you get here."

"I don't know, Charlie ...," I said, remembering my promise to Michel not to enter the West Bank.

"Look, I have a friend. She will pick you up at your hotel, and drive you to the Israeli checkpoint at Qalandya. The worst thing that can happen is that the Israelis will not let you through. In which case, she will bring you back to your hotel. Okay?"

Before I could stop myself, I had agreed.

"Great! She lives nearby. Her name is Vega. She'll be there in fifteen minutes."

Two minutes later, the phone rang.

"Cathy, this is Charlie. Come prepared to stay as long as you want with us in Ramallah. My mother would like you to accompany her to school and we'll do our best to assist in any way we can with any other interviews you might want. And don't worry. After you walk through the checkpoint, I'll be waiting for you at the other end. I look like my brother."

I stuffed my toiletries, a few changes of clothes and my trusty recorder with extra tapes and batteries into my backpack. I had no sooner closed my bag than I heard a knock on my door.

"Hi, I'm Vega, Charlie's friend."

We drove through the congested, poorly-paved streets of East Jerusalem.

"You see how bad these roads are?" Vega said. "We pay the same taxes as the Israelis, but their neighborhoods don't look like this."

I nodded, glancing at the hodge-podge of apartment buildings and low-end stores, at a car repair shop with rusted equipment and piles of tires strewn along the side wall, the many abandoned gas stations, corner stores so dilapidated you wondered what they could possibly have inside, alongside small cafes selling falafel balls wrapped in warm bread and doused with tahini, garlic and lemon.

"That's Hebrew University up there," she said, pointing to my right. "The area is called French Hill."

"What beautiful houses," I remarked.

"Those are Israeli settlements," Vega explained.

"That's a huge complex. Aren't we still in Arab East Jerusalem?"

"Yes. And look to your left. There are even more. About a month ago, the Israeli government began constructing a wall around the settlements."

These Israelis were probably told that the land they were living on was 'disputed territory,' a frequent Israeli government claim, not confiscated Palestinian land. I supposed, too, that since decent housing in Israel proper was out of reach for most Israelis, a lovely house with garden sounded like an offer few people could refuse. The increase in suicide bombings made a high wall around their complex sound like a perfectly logical thing.

This particular area of Jewish settlement was obviously pricier than the one I had seen earlier near Bethlehem. Resplendent perennial beds full of pink laurel, red bougainvillea and yellow jasmine surrounded the settlements, and Vega assured me that they had well-paved roads, playgrounds for their children and parks to sit and play in.

A few minutes later Vega said, "There it is up ahead."

"What?"

"Qalandya, the Israeli checkpoint."

It took less than fifteen minutes to arrive at the checkpoint, and I was not at all mentally prepared. I could not seem to get enough air to my lungs and my throat felt dry from hyperventilating. At first glance the checkpoint looked like the huge sand dunes that line the Atlantic coast of France near Arcachon; except here they were divided into four distinct parts. The checkpoint sat in a large open space in the center.

"Are you ready?" Vega asked.

I could not speak. My heart was beating furiously. Finally I was able to ask, "What am I supposed to do?"

"Get out your passport."

I adjusted my backpack and retrieved my passport while trying to practice deep breathing.

"You see all those people standing over there?" Vega said. "We'll join them and see what happens."

From the top of the sand dune to my right, I heard someone shout. I looked up to see an Israeli soldier pointing his gun, shouting furiously at a man behind me.

I turned to Vega. "Why is he shouting so hysterically?"

"It's not our business. Don't look up again."

I glanced at the faces of the dozens of Palestinians standing alongside me. They were waiting for a sign, a nod, a grunt from the Israeli soldier – wearing dark glasses, standing behind a chest-high sandbag barricade, the barrel of his gun clearly visible, his finger on the trigger – to advance and show their ID.

I studied the soldier, following the way he stared long and hard at each person in line, nodding at one of them from time to time. This was their cue to advance, to stand before him, to hand over ID. If they were lucky, he motioned them to squeeze around the cement barricade, and walk through the large hole – intentionally dug to fill with water when it rained – then across a metal bump – purposely built so if you were careless or nervous you stumbled and fell in front of the soldiers.

The soldier nodded in my direction. I hesitated; I had only just arrived. When I glanced over at the others waiting, they smiled. "*Maalishe*" (it's all right), one woman said.

"I'm sorry," I said. "I'm truly sorry."

As I maneuvered my way through the checkpoint, I turned and waved good-bye to Vega.

I have since learned that some foreign nationals place themselves at the end of the line at an Israeli checkpoint, refusing any invitation to move ahead of the others. In the presence of foreigners, Israeli soldiers generally tend to speed up the line because they are embarrassed to have outsiders see how they treat the Palestinians.

Three years later, I better understand the behavior of many of the Israeli soldiers at the checkpoints. While any inhumane behavior is unacceptable, the young soldiers must always fear for their lives. With the increase in Palestinian extremist activity this is completely understandable.

US servicemen and women in Iraq face the same daily challenges. They too react defensively out of fear. Human beings do irrational things, often cruel things, when they feel their lives are threatened.

RAMALLAH

As I cautiously walked across the no-man's land – a dusty, garbage-strewn terrain full of potholes and craters separating the Qalandya checkpoint from the outskirts of Ramallah – I looked up to see a cluster of about fifteen people waiting ahead. I saw only one car, a white one, with a tall young man standing alongside it next to a shorter, older man. I knew instantly the tall one was Charlie. Except for having much less hair, he did resemble his brother Tony. As I walked toward them I attempted the impossible task of dusting off my black shoes and pants. Finally I gave up and rushed toward my hosts, grateful to have made it safely across the checkpoint. Charlie advanced toward me, hand extended.

"Hi, Cathy, welcome to Ramallah." Gesturing toward the other man, he said, "I would like you to meet my father." In his mid-sixties and bald except for a halo of white hair, Issa was a handsome man, dressed in a dark grey suit and white dress shirt. He smiled warmly.

"How do you do," I said, shaking his hand.

"Did you have any problems?" Issa asked in perfect English.

"No, I was very surprised."

"The soldier saw your American passport," he said, laughing. "An Israeli wouldn't dare say anything to you."

"Let's get out of here," Charlie said, opening the passenger door. "My mother has prepared us a lovely lunch."

Charlie made a U turn out of the checkpoint zone, and we zig-zagged – to avoid the potholes – up a deserted boulevard lined with vacant buildings, their façades sprayed with bullet holes, their windows shattered. The sidewalks on either side of the street were in major disrepair and the trees along the median were either dead or dying.

"You'll have to excuse our roads," said Charlie. "The Palestinian Authority does not have the money to repair them every time the Israeli Army sends a rocket into Ramallah, or an Apache hits a so-called target."

"What happened here?" I asked, pointing off to my right.

"That was a police station before the Israelis destroyed it," explained Issa. "There is still one standing in the center of Ramallah. For how long, I do not know."

"In the States, Bush insists that Arafat should do more to control terrorism. How can he do that if the police stations are routinely demolished?"

Issa shrugged. "Ask the Israelis when you interview them."

Charlie let his father and me out at the front entrance and headed to the garage to park his car. Issa preceded me into the building to call the elevator. He must have also beeped his apartment because as soon as the elevator arrived on the fourth floor, his wife, Regina, was there to open the door.

"*Ahlan, Ahlan*," she said, kissing me on both cheeks. "Welcome to our home."

Charlie and his family are Greek Orthodox Christians. They are one of five Christian families living in a modern apartment building on the north side of Ramallah, overlooking a quiet, largely arid valley dotted with off-white stone houses and modern-style villas; traditional Mediterranean red tile roofs glistened in the afternoon sun. Beyond what I assumed were the city limits the landscape changed dramatically. The earth took on a lush, deep red color and the narrow road wound across a vista of steep terraced hills dotted with silvery-green leafed olive trees.

After washing up, and before joining them on the living room couch, I unpacked a manila envelope which I had carried from Eau Claire, and handed it to Charlie's parents. Their faces beamed when they opened it and saw the first photos of their new grandson, born just weeks before my departure. There were also snapshots of Tony's three other children. Regina, at least for now, was much more interested in newborn Zade. Teary-eyed, she gently kissed his photo before placing it on a nearby table already crowded with family photos. Tony's four children resembled Regina with her finely chiseled nose, high cheekbones and green eyes more characteristically Caucasian than Semitic. Then I handed Issa and Regina another envelope. This one contained their immigration papers which Tony's wife, Mary, had carefully assembled. In normal times, Issa and Regina lived in Amman, Jordan. He was a retired banker; she taught high school French. They had moved to Ramallah three years earlier to take care of Charlie. After the Oslo Accords were signed, Charlie assumed there would be many opportunities for a young architect in Ramallah.

Regina excused herself and retreated to the kitchen, where she put the final touches to our meal. She refused to even let me enter her space, insisting I was guest not helper. I was famished by the time we sat down to her golden roasted chicken stuffed with lamb, rice, pine nuts, pistachios, and walnuts, and seasoned with a pinch of cinnamon and grated lemon zest.

I found it perfectly normal, given the turmoil in which they lived, that Issa would be a news junkie, but I did not expect Regina to be a devoted soap opera fan. Lunch was eaten and the dishes were done in time to watch *Days of Our Lives*, and another soap opera, whose name I cannot remember. I almost burst into laughter. Here I was – someone who never turned on her own television – watching American soap operas in Ramallah in the West Bank.

Later that afternoon, Charlie suggested we take a drive.

"Come on, I will give you a tour of Ramallah, and then we will stop by my office so I can show you my building projects."

Issa and Regina came along.

Ramallah, which means "Heights of the Lord," sits some 2,900 feet above sea level, about 400 feet higher than Jerusalem. At first glance it reminded me of Aley in the Metn Mountains in Lebanon which overlooks Beirut. Like Aley, Ramallah was the region's most affluent area, with large and luxurious villas. Before the 1967 Six Day War and subsequent Israeli occupation, Ramallah was a popular resort for wealthy Arabs from Jordan and the Gulf states. French Crusaders invaded the area in the 12th Century, building a stronghold on the highest hill. Ramallah, which is mostly Christian, was settled in 1550 and today has a population of about 200,000.

The first thing one sees when driving into al-Manara Square, the city's downtown area, is the enormous poster of Yasser Arafat strung across the middle of the intersection. Tightly knit rows of stores line the maze of streets that wind in and out of the main thoroughfare, selling everything from ladies' intimate apparel to blaring Arabic music to kitchen appliances and fast food. But mostly, Ramallah's center is full of people, jockeying for a place on the crowded streets, talking, hands gesturing every which way, as though they had not seen their friends for years or talked to another human being for months.

After the tour of the town center we drove to the highest point in Ramallah from which you could look down at Jerusalem. Charlie parked the car, got out, invited me to do the same, and pointed skyward.

"You see it?"

"What?" I asked.

"The Apache helicopter!"

"From here, it looks like a regular helicopter."

"Regular helicopters don't fire missiles, Cathy."

"What is it doing here?"

"It's on a surveillance mission. The Israeli Army sends them over Ramallah every day. They photograph their intended targets. At night, they return to take them out."

"How do they know where to shoot?"

"Palestinians who operate as Israeli collaborators mark the targeted cars with a special kind of infra-red ink." I could not independently verify this but with Israeli technology the best in the world I don't think they need anyone's help detecting a specific target.

"Why would a Palestinian work for the Israelis?" I asked.

"Some do it because they need the money, others are blackmailed. Say a man is in prison. The Israelis approach his son. They threaten him, 'If you don't work with us, we will torture your father to death.' If you were the son, what would you do?"

The number of Palestinians collaborating with Israel in the West Bank is unknown. When Prime Minister Ariel Sharon evacuated Gaza in August, 2005, seventy-four Palestinian collaborators and their families were evacuated along with the settlers. These Palestinians petitioned the Israeli High Court requesting evacuation from the Gaza Strip, citing fear of revenge should they remain.

. . .

As we sat in Charlie's office our conversation turned to politics. Among other things Charlie wanted to know why the media in America was so anti-Palestinian.

"Don't they know how many of us die here every day? At least the European media gives an unbiased version of events. They talk of killings on both sides. If necessary, they put the blame on both parties. American papers only talk of Israeli dead. Aren't we human beings in your country's eyes?"

"America has always been sympathetic to Israel," I replied. "And the Bush administration is no different."

"But things have changed in the world," said Charlie. "Here in the Middle East, hatred of America has never been so high. People want a solution to the crisis. They're sick of the billions of dollars America gives free of charge to Israel each year, without asking anything in return. They want to see the sanctions ended in Iraq. People in the Arab world, particularly in Egypt and Saudi Arabia,

know that Washington is responsible for propping up their governments. And they know it's done to protect American oil interests."

"Most Americans are not aware of any of that, Charlie. And to
be fair, Bush has asked Sharon recently to show some restraint."

"Oh, come on, Cathy," he replied. "Admit it. The Israelis have
beaten your government at the game of chess. America is nothing
more than a checker player."

"Not to change the subject," Regina said, turning to me, "but
when you come to school with me tomorrow, you could talk to the
girls in my class as well as to some of the teachers."

"What a wonderful idea. I am very grateful for your hospital-
ity but …"

"You can stay with us as long as you need to," Issa said. "You
have come here to try to help the Palestinian people. We are honored to be able to play some small part in your project."

"Thank you, you are all very kind."

Turning to Charlie, I asked if he knew a particular businessman
by the name of Sam B.

"Yes, of course, I worked with him on a number of projects," he
replied, a bit puzzled. "But how do you know him?"

"He writes articles that are published in some of the online sites
I read. I wrote him, told him that I was hoping to get to Ramallah
and asked if he could see me. He replied immediately, giving me his
phone number. He even gave me some other names to contact."

"I'll call him right now. When would you like to meet with
him?"

"Since tomorrow I will be joining your mother at school, why
not try for Tuesday."

"And Charlie, I have another favor to ask. My cell phone does
not work from Ramallah, even though the Israeli merchant said it
would. I promised Michel that I'd call him every day so he wouldn't
worry. May I please give him a quick call?"

Moments later – pretending all the while that I was calling from
Jerusalem – I had Michel on the line.

"Hi, Mich," I said. "Yes, everything's fine. I took a lovely walk with Mary this morning past the Old City and the Damascus Gate. I can't believe I'm actually here. It's such an amazing place."

To his comment about the situation in the West Bank, I responded, "No, I didn't know the Israelis bombed Ramallah today. I'll have to give Tony's parents a call again to see if they're okay.

"Yes, I spoke with them this morning, but they didn't mention any bombing.

"Please don't worry. I'm safe. I'll call you tomorrow. Love you, too. Bye."

After I hung up the phone, I said, "I didn't tell him I was calling from Ramallah."

"Why not?" a shocked Regina asked.

"I promised him I wouldn't go to the West Bank. If he knew, he'd just worry himself to death."

Apparently my lie displeased Regina. Her rolled eyes expressed what she was too polite to say. Charlie, on the other hand, thought it was funny.

"I'm afraid you've gotten yourself caught anyway, Cathy," he said, laughing.

"How?"

"The evidence is already in my brother's hands. I just e-mailed him the photo I took of you and my parents."

"Damn it, Charlie! E-mail him again and tell him to destroy it."

. . .

The next morning Regina and I walked through a quiet residential neighborhood to get to her school. The white stone houses along our route were built on terraced hills awash with fruit and olive trees. Since the weather was warm the buds on the apple and lemon trees were already in bloom. I knew Ramallah was dry like Jerusalem but I did not expect it to be so hilly. Our fifteen minute uphill walk felt more like an hour by the time we reached our destination.

Regina taught French at St. Joseph's High School, run by the Sisters of the Sacred Heart. I sat in on Regina's first hour class. She introduced me first as a friend of her son, then as an American who had come to Ramallah to interview Palestinians.

"She speaks fluent French," Regina said, "because she lived in Lebanon, and will answer any questions you have."

Hands darted into the air. 'Was my husband an Arab?' 'How many children did I have?' 'Did they speak Arabic?'

When I told them I had lived in Beirut during the civil war, and my children had also suffered through nightly bombing raids and indiscriminate machine gun fire, I saw in their eyes an acknowledgement that I was someone who could appreciate their fears and understand why they reminisced about lost childhoods. Three of the girls were Israeli Arabs who lived in Jerusalem. They crossed the Qalandya checkpoint every morning and afternoon to get to and from school, and were often kept waiting in long lines.

"One morning," one said, "the Israeli soldiers made a man strip down to his underwear and parade around, while the soldiers laughed their heads off. I felt so sorry for the man. I hoped his children were not there to see the way their father was being humiliated."

"What would you do," I asked, "if an Israeli girl your age walked into this classroom right now?" Several hands shot up.

"I would ask her to be my friend, and invite her to my house."

"I would ask her to please tell Sharon to end the occupation. I want to be able to go visit my grandmother in the next village."

"I would ask her what she and her friends do together. Do they go to movies, amusement parks or beach outings? Did they do sleepovers with their friends? We can't do any of those things, so I am very curious."

Regina explained later that her students' fantasies would not become reality anytime soon. Israelis were not allowed to enter the West Bank or Gaza. Those Israelis who used Israeli-only roads to reach their Israeli settlements were the only ones allowed to cross into the occupied territories. If Israelis were to show up at the Qalandya checkpoint wanting to cross into the West Bank, they would be denied entry for their own safety. That same evening, Daniel Barenboim, who had performed with the Tel Aviv Orchestra the evening before, was scheduled to give a recital in Ramallah. He was denied entry.

"Why?" I asked. "Is he an Israeli?"

"He holds Israeli citizenship even though he is an Argentinean-born Jew who lives in Germany," explained Regina. "But the Israeli government does not want anyone, certainly not a world famous musician, to see how they treat the Palestinians."

Six months after my visit to the West Bank, I read in an Israeli newspaper that Daniel Barenboim made another visit to Israel. This time, amid much fanfare, he was not stopped at the Qalandya checkpoint, and was able to play Beethoven's "Moonlight Sonata" to a hundred young admirers in a Ramallah school, "… to stretch out a hand and share music, to silence the hatred," he said. "People asked me all over the world why I wanted to be in Ramallah today. The answer is very simple: I am not a politician. I do not have a solution to solve the conflict, but believe each of us has to think about his responsibility as a human being, and stop depending on governments."[17]

. . .

My first interviewee was Elias, a social studies teacher and father of two. He had some free time and suggested we take advantage of the warm, sunny day to sit outside. He had spent eighteen months in an Israeli prison during the first *Intifada* (uprising) (1987–93) for throwing stones at Israeli soldiers.

When I asked him if he saw an end to the Israeli occupation, he laughed. "Bush's war on terrorism has been a disaster for the Palestinians. It has literally given Ariel Sharon a green light to lock up

---

17 AFP News Service, Sept. 10, 2002, www.islamic-world.net/warnews/quote/week053.htm

three million people behind barbed wire, and impose strict curfews and closures. Did you know that if I wanted to go to Beit Shahour, a village near Bethlehem, that I couldn't? The Israeli government says I must apply for a travel permit if I want to leave Ramallah. They say that, but even if I tried, I would be denied. That is their policy now."[18]

Regina and two of her colleagues had organized a French competition that afternoon in the auditorium, open to all high schools in Ramallah. Because of the day-long sound of explosions and F16 sonic booms overhead, I was surprised at how many people came. Even the judge, the French Consul, crossed over from East Jerusalem. As I watched the children, singing and dancing as if first prize meant a performance at Carnegie Hall, I thought back to my own children's activities in Beirut: a track and field event, a karate tournament, a school play. Then, as now, it was not about winning. It was the thrill of being allowed to act like normal children, albeit for a very short time.

. . .

One of the news channels Regina and Issa watched was *al-Jazeera*, the Arabic News Service, which is based in Qatar, a tiny nation located between Bahrain and Abu Dhabi, off the east coast of Saudi Arabia. Much of the world considers *al-Jazeera* uncensored news at its best. Secretary of State Condoleezza Rice asked the Qatar government to close the network down during the initial days of the Afghan campaign because it broadcast the horrors of the US bombing raids to the Arab world, something American audiences were spared.

News from either the West Bank or Gaza is horrible any day of the week. What follows is a sampling of the nightly news, either in English or Arabic, I watched during my week in Ramallah:

---

18   The rest of my interview with Elias and the others mentioned in this section can be found in the Interviews section at the end of the book.

Footage of the Israeli Army in Gaza shows massive amounts of damage already inflicted on the worst hellhole on earth. The camera follows an Israeli tank as it rolls down a narrow street. There are two ambulances in its path, one parked along the left wall, the other, along the right. The Israeli tank turns abruptly, smashing the first ambulance against the wall. It then does the same to the one on the right. The television screen switches from Gaza to Tel Aviv where Prime Minister Ariel Sharon is giving a news conference: "The Palestinians have to be hit hard. We are at war with a bloodthirsty enemy. It is us or them."

Today, Messianic Jewish settlers cut down 300 olive trees belonging to Palestinians in Hebron in full view of Israeli soldiers, who provide protection for the settlers. Our reporter saw Israeli troops open fire on the farmers, as they rushed to stop the settlers. Over the last seventeen months, the Israeli army and Jewish settlers have destroyed more than 100,000 olive trees throughout the West Bank. Palestinians call the acts a deliberate environmental holocaust.

The last remaining police station in Ramallah was hit today. An Apache helicopter gunship fired a missile through a window, destroying the interior of the building.

In Gaza, gunmen opened-fire on Israeli troops as they entered the Khan Younis refugee camp. Two soldiers sustained injuries. They were transported to Israel for treatment.

American Vice President Dick Cheney arrived in Tel Aviv today to meet with Prime Minister Ariel Sharon. When asked by a reporter to describe his mission, he replied: "I have come to Israel to lend my support to Mr. Sharon and his government."

To the question: "Will you be traveling to Ramallah to meet with Mr. Arafat?"

"Not at this time. Mr. Arafat has yet to exhibit the leadership qualities we expect of him. He has done nothing to curb terrorism and refuses to safeguard the stability and security of Israel."

A Palestinian suicide bomber killed ten and wounded fourteen inside a popular pizza parlor on Emek Refaim Street in West Jerusalem this evening. The dead and injured were all Israeli teenagers.

A Jewish group, in retaliation for the explosion at a Hasidic school the night I arrived, placed a bomb in an Arab school in East Jerusalem today. It was detected in time.

On an English-speaking Israeli news channel we heard a different version of the same story: Today gunmen placed a bomb in an Arab school in East Jerusalem. Our sources tell us that Palestinians probably planted the bomb so they could blame Israel.

. . .

Night after night, it was the same horrible stuff that had been going on since September, 2000, when the current *Intifada* began. Even though I knew intellectually what I was getting into, I was nonetheless constantly astounded at the level of violence on both the Israeli and Palestinian sides, at the wanton destruction, at the targeted assassinations, the escalation of suicide bombings, the indiscriminate arrests, and the collective punishments.

On one side were the Palestinians, the vast majority of whom disavowed the suicide bombers. They had no army, no Apache gunships, no tanks, no armored personnel carriers, no FI6s. They were defenseless against one of the most powerful military forces in the world.

On the other side innocent Israelis died in suicide bombings. To take a bus to work, to meet friends at a sidewalk cafe for lunch or to walk the dog along the neighborhood street was to risk a deadly encounter with a suicide bomber ready to take as many people to their deaths as he could.

. . .

On my second morning in Ramallah, I accompanied Regina to school again. While she taught her first class, I chatted with some of the other teachers, one of whom I had met the day before. She showed me a letter her husband had sent to George W. Bush in November, 2001.

"Dear Mr. President, I am a Palestinian who was forced, by Jewish gunmen, to flee my land and home in Haifa in 1948. In light of the Palestinian history, I am shocked by the blind bias of American policies in support of Israel, despite its forceful occupation of our land. You are the leader of the largest and strongest country in the world. This gives you the moral authority to stand with the oppressed. We are not asking for the moon. We are asking for the liberation of our land from occupiers and the right to live in freedom. These are just and human demands that should be supported by those who claim to represent justice, freedom and democracy."

. . .

Shortly before 11:00 AM I walked toward the city center to Charlie's office. Stores, their metal doors bolted shut, were crammed in along the narrow side streets all the way to the busy intersection. On a normal day I should have been on a street corner with cars careening past as in any crowded Arab city – taxi drivers shouting out their destinations like auctioneers, Arabic music blaring from car radios, coffee shops filled with men smoking *nargillas* and sipping strong Turkish coffee. But that day all the stores were closed.

Charlie and I were scheduled to meet Sam B. at one of the outdoor cafes before we discovered everything was closed.

"Charlie, please call Sam and ask him what he wants to do."

As it turned out, all shops in Ramallah were closed in support of the Gazans under Israeli military siege.

Sam agreed to come to Charlie's office. When he walked through the door I was surprised to see such a tall, powerfully built man.

"I was born and raised in Ohio," he said, laughing. "It must have been the milk."

If I had seen Sam on any street corner in America, given his complexion and dark wavy hair, I would have said that he was Mediterranean without being able to identify which particular country he was from. Convinced that peace was about to be declared, Sam left the States in 1995 and moved to al-Bireh, a city adjacent to Ramallah in the West Bank, where he lives with his wife and their two young daughters.

"Charlie, I will take Cathy to my place for coffee. I will drop her back here in about an hour and a half. Okay?"

On the way to his house, Sam gave me a tour of the main attractions in al-Bireh: the Ministry of Culture, the municipal building, and the shopping complex he and his business associates were building. He lived in a seemingly quiet neighborhood.

As he pulled into his driveway, he said, "As you walk toward the house, look behind you. You will see the Israeli settlement of Psagot."

It looked like a fortified bunker, surrounded by lookout towers and high walls. Every few meters along the wall were holes large enough to fit what I assumed was the turret of a tank.

"That is exactly what it is. And this one is particularly dangerous. My wife and I had to abandon our bedroom. For whatever reason, the soldiers would fire randomly at our windows and bullets would fly through the room. We finally barricaded the room off completely. Take my advice. Whatever you do while in Ramallah, do not get too close to Psagot. They just might open fire."

"Do you know any Israelis?" I asked. "Do you work with any?"

"I studied at Tel Aviv University in an exchange program while I was a student at Northwestern in Chicago. It was an eye-opening experience for me. I found the majority of Israeli students very out of touch with what was going on around them."

"Surely that is not still the case," I said.

"Unfortunately, for the most part it is. If they have not served in the army in the occupied territories, Israelis have little knowledge of the occupation."

While this was Sam's personal opinion, one of my Israeli interviewees, Tali, said similar things. According to her, Palestinian suicide bombers were having a tremendous impact on Israeli society and Israelis were in awe that the Palestinians would commit such atrocious acts.

"This is their reaction," she said, "because most Israelis do not know what is happening in the territories. Israel is humiliating a whole people and they hate us for what we do to them."

Over the course of the current *Intifada*, more and more Israelis have learned of the Israeli occupation of the West Bank and Gaza. A number of factors have contributed to this awakening. Israeli soldiers who did their military service in the territories have come forward to expose the human rights abuses in which they participated. Soldiers who served in Hebron organized a much publicized – and criticized – exhibition of photos and essays about their time in Hebron, calling the event "Breaking the Silence." Israeli pilots as well as some 1,665 military personnel now refuse to serve in the territories. Israeli women who are part of Machsom Watch monitor Israeli checkpoints for abuses. Their reports are read by military and civilians alike.

In June, 2005, Haim Yavin, the respected nightly-news anchorman of Israel's state-run TV channel – who is called Israel's Walter Cronkite – produced a documentary entitled *Yoman Masa* (Diary of a Journey). Over a two and a half year period, Yavin traveled throughout the West Bank and Gaza with a hand-held video camera. He spoke with settlers, soldiers and Palestinians. In his documentary he concluded, "Since 1967, we have been brutal conquerors, occupiers, suppressing other people. I cannot really do anything to relieve this misery other than to document it, so that neither I, nor those like me, will be able to say that we saw nothing, heard nothing and knew nothing."[19]

---

19 Schoffman, Stuart. "Smelling the Coffee." Excerpt from *The Jerusalem Post*, reproduced in the Foundation for Middle East Peace, July 11, 2005.

Israelis are not the only ones speaking out against atrocities.

Prominent Palestinians have strongly condemned suicide bombers. In fact Sam, my interviewee, published an article on suicide bombers in which he said that "Suicide bombers are never ever justified in their actions. The innocent Israeli lives, especially those of the children, which such attacks so abruptly end, are mourned by Israelis and Palestinians alike. The memory of those lost lives serves as an eternal burden to both sides. Without an end to the occupation there are no winners or losers, only more mourners on both sides."[20]

Naim Ateek, Director of the Sabeel Ecumenical Liberation Theology Center in Jerusalem, condemns all forms of violence and terrorism whether coming from the Israeli government or from militant Palestinian terrorist groups. Father Ateek writes, "The Israelis seek peace with security and the Palestinians seek peace with justice ... By three things does the world endure: justice, truth and peace. Wherever justice is done peace will be found."[21]

Sam talked about the Palestinian Authority (PA) and its lack of power. According to him, the Palestinian Authority is blocked from exercising its right to collect money the Israeli government owes it for taxes collected on goods imported into the territories. As of December, 2001, it was estimated Israel owed the Palestinian Authority half a billion dollars.

"Our men are out of work, unemployment is at an all-time high. Many families can hardly afford to put food on the table, and the Israelis are sitting on money that even the World Bank says belongs to the Palestinian Authority."

Over juice and cookies, we talked for another hour.

Two weeks after I visited Sam, Israeli tanks broke down the

---

20 Bahour, Sam. "The Making of a Suicide Attacker: Are Palestinians Human?" Dec. 5, 2001, www.counterpunch.org/sbahour8.html

21 Ateek, Naim Stifan. *Justice and only Justice: A Palestinian Theology of Liberation.* Orbis Books, Maryknoll, New York, 2001, p. 181.

outside walls of the al-Bireh municipal building, crushing the jeeps parked outside. They shattered windows, vandalized every room, and destroyed every computer. According to Israeli journalist Amira Hass, "Culture Ministry employees discovered what appeared to be urine and feces strewn across floors, in emptied flowerpots, on the photocopier, in drawers that had been pulled out of desks and even inside plastic bags, which were then thrown in every direction."[22]

Sam was lucky. His project was only at the concrete and mortar stage; there was nothing to destroy.

After he dropped me back at Charlie's office, I decided to walk back to the apartment. Issa was watching the afternoon news; I joined him. A few minutes later, we heard an explosion.

"It's another Apache," Issa said, "and probably nothing to worry about."

In fact it was a strike; and it was major news. The Israeli Army fired missiles from inside the Psagot settlement – the one in front of Sam's house – hitting a car thought to be driven by a wanted Palestinian. His wife and four children were killed instead. Two other children, standing on a nearby sidewalk, were also killed.

Suddenly, I heard an Apache helicopter gunship hovering overhead. As much as I tried to ignore the distinct noise of metal clacking and engine churning, I could not resist dashing to the balcony and looking out. I was so startled to see hordes of people, standing, unafraid in the middle of the street, pointing at the gunship like it was a strange bird, I burst out laughing. 'People here are just as crazy as we were in Beirut,' I thought.

While my eyes were still glued to the sky, I saw the gunship fire a missile. Seconds later, I heard the explosion.

"Another targeted assassination," Issa said, shaking his head.

By the time Charlie arrived an hour later the city had quieted

---

22   Hass, Amira. *Ha'aretz*, May 6, 2002.

down. He brought with him W., a second cousin who lived with his mother two floors below. He was a producer at the Educational Television at al-Quds University.

As we were being introduced, W. said, "When Charlie told me where you lived in Beirut during the war, I was not sure I wanted to meet you. You didn't like the Palestinians, did you?"

"No, not at all," I replied. "When I moved to Beirut in 1969, I knew nothing about the Middle East, and I did not speak the languages. I was busy with two small babies and had no time to study the region's history. And then, when the war started and we were being bombed by the Palestinian-Muslim coalition, I didn't know enough to distinguish between a leader and his people."

We spent the rest of the evening discussing politics while Issa and Regina slept in their chairs. W. was a very quiet man in his mid-fifties. He was well-educated, and spoke perfect French. Because of his work at the al-Quds television station – where he produced documentaries on Palestinian issues – foreign journalists interviewed him frequently as a reliable source of information. In spite of his vast knowledge, however, he was unaware of the American Christian Fundamentalist support for Israel. He knew nothing about Christian Zionism as it pertained to the birth of Israel. I took him back to 1837 and Lord Shaftesbury; then into the next century, to Lloyd George, who was instrumental in acquiring Palestine for Britain so as to create a Jewish homeland.

"I have never heard any of this," he said. "I think you have your facts wrong."

"When I get home, I will send you a copy of David Fromkin's book, *A Peace to End All Peace*. It is all there."

When we had talked a while longer I finally said, "Now that you are convinced I am more open-minded, will you introduce me to some of your friends?"

He agreed, took out his telephone book, and gave me several names.

"Just tell them that I told you to call them. And if you would like,

I will ask my mother to let you interview her on Friday night when she returns from my brother's home. Recently, the BBC spoke with her. She is a '48 Arab' and has an excellent memory."

Regina and Issa were also '48 Arabs' – a term that refers to those who refused to leave Palestine in 1948. Over breakfast the next morning, I asked Issa about his childhood.

"In 1944, I was eleven years old and living in Jaffa," he said. "There was already a Jewish settlement there. The men trained as a military force. I remember seeing them parade through the streets of Jaffa carrying their weapons. If an Arab was caught with a small gun, or even a bullet in his possession, he was hanged."

"Was Palestine still under British Mandate at the time?"

"Yes, of course," Issa said. "And even though all this activity was going on in broad daylight, the British soldiers never said a word."

"Were you frightened?"

"Never! In my mind, these were small weapons. They did not pose a threat. However, when the killing started, people became very scared. We were told to leave Jaffa for a few days, until the fighting stopped. We were also told we would be able to return. Of course, this never happened."

"Where were you when the killing started? Do you remember?"

"Oh, yes, I remember very well. I was at school. When I heard the news, I ran home as fast as I could. My parents were not in the house. I did not know where they were, and I began to cry ..." Issa suddenly stopped talking. His eyes swelled. "Please turn off your tape recorder, Cathy. I cannot continue. This is something I still find very difficult to discuss."

After talking to Issa, I walked to Charlie's office. I had four interviews lined up and he was going to play chauffeur. Before we left, I called Michel. I had missed a day and was feeling very guilty.

"Hi, Mich," I said.

"Where are you?" Michel asked, before I could say another

word. "You're in Ramallah, aren't you? I thought you promised me you wouldn't go there?"

"Well, it ended up being such an easy thing to do," and I went on to explain how it had happened. "How did you find out?"

"Yesterday, when you didn't call, I called your hotel. Do you know what they told me?"

"I can't imagine." Of course I could imagine and I didn't want to hear it.

"Mrs. Sultan? She is crazy. She went to Ramallah."

"Well, my secret's out but the good news is you need worry no longer. I am being well taken care of and doing lots of interviews. I'll be returning to East Jerusalem in a few days. Oh, before I forget, here is Issa's number. Now, you can call me every day to make sure I'm safe. Love you, Mich, take care. Bye."

. . .

Fouad M. is Director of the Qattan Center for Educational Research and Development. After the Oslo Accords were signed, he quit his teaching post at the University of Tennessee and returned to Ramallah. Oslo, for the very first time, allowed Palestinians to write their own history. Prior to Oslo, Jordan wrote the history of the West Bank, while Egypt wrote the one for Gaza. The Palestinian Authority asked Fouad to help. The Oslo Accords, however, forbade Palestinians to speak of historical Palestine. They could only talk of the area under the Palestinian Authority, and the twenty-two percent of the West Bank and Gaza that constitutes a future Palestinian state.

"Restrictions were placed on us," Fouad said, "while maps in Israeli textbooks show Israel extending from the Mediterranean to the Jordan River. Their map of the West Bank and Gaza Strip shows only Israeli Jewish settlements, no Palestinian villages or towns. Additionally, we have been attacked by the Israeli Settler Movement for promoting hatred toward Jews, which, at least in the new textbooks, is not the case. I should know; I helped write them.

"Israeli textbooks, on the other hand, teach that Jews are involved in a justified, even humanitarian war against an Arab enemy that refuses to recognize the rights of Jews in Israel."

"Would it be possible to purchase some of the new Palestinian textbooks?"

"I will make it possible," replied Fouad. "I will even have one of my staff drive you to the warehouse. You would never find it on your own," he said, laughing.

When I returned to Fouad's office, Charlie was waiting to take me to my next interview. We got lost trying to find the right apartment near Ramallah Hospital. When we finally arrived, Huwaida was standing on her fourth floor balcony, waiting. I waved and began walking up the stairs. Huwaida Arraf is a Greek Orthodox Palestinian in her early thirties. After college, she worked as a Program Coordinator for Seeds of Peace, an Israeli organization that fosters understanding between Israeli and Palestinian children. There she met her husband, Adam Shapiro, a Brooklyn-born Jew. She left Seeds of Peace to co-found The International Solidarity Movement (ISM) with Neta Golan, a Canadian-Israeli peace activist. It is an organization which promotes nonviolent resistance to the Israeli occupation.

When I visited Huwaida she had just returned from the Balata refugee camp in Nablus, where 22,000 refugees live in squalid conditions.

Huwaida and her group usually enter a refugee camp when they suspect the Israeli Army is preparing to attack. The ISM volunteers position themselves between the Palestinians and the Israeli soldiers. Generally, Israeli troops enter refugee camps to demolish houses, launch attacks and round up suspects. When Israeli soldiers know they are being watched, that their actions are being recorded, they are much more reluctant to inflict bodily harm, cause property damage, and otherwise commit human rights violations.

Through Huwaida I met Brian, a member of the Christian Peacemaker Team, an NGO (non-governmental organization) based in Chicago. He worked out of the West Bank town of Hebron, home to 120,000 Palestinians. I asked Brian what he did as a member of the CPT.

"I engage Israeli soldiers in dialogue. When they become aggressive against a Palestinian, I try to help them resolve their conflict. Sometimes it works and both parties back off."

Brian explained that the Tomb of the Patriarchs was located in Hebron. It is where Abraham and his first wife, Sarah, are thought to be buried. A site holy to both Israelis and Palestinians, it is the site of frequent and violent clashes.

Palestinians are allowed out of their homes three days a week, from 8:00 AM to 1:00 PM; otherwise they are confined to their homes. In spite of these hardships – as anyone from the CPT can tell you – the Palestinians are amazingly calm and gentle. I do not for the life of me know how they do it. There are 450 Israeli settlers who literally rule the city of Hebron. They terrorize the Palestinians: they stone their houses, shoot holes in their water tanks, dump sewage in their water system, uproot fruit and olive groves, and fire on any Palestinian who tries to get into his field to pick his crop. These settlers are protected by 1,200 Israeli soldiers.

"I was there one day when the Palestinian market was open," Huwaida said. "Above us, on the roof of one of the houses, there were half a dozen Israeli settlers. Out of the blue I heard one of them yell, 'Go to hell!' Pretty soon, another settler shouted, 'You are all Nazis, all of you,' then another yelled, 'You are going to die.'"

"Where are these settlers from?" I asked

"Many are from Brooklyn, New York," replied Brian.

When I was ready to leave, Adam walked me down the hill through Ramallah back to Charlie's office.

"What is a nice Jewish boy from New York doing in Ramallah?" I asked, laughing.

"When I was at Georgetown I studied international affairs and mediation," he replied. "After college, I went to Africa, where I worked with different groups, helping them settle their disputes. I also grew up reading a lot about the Holocaust. It taught me how important it is to heal wounds, to reconcile differences, to learn to be tolerant of one another in the interest of bettering mankind. I know I can make a difference. That's why I'm here. That's why Huwaida is here."

We said good-bye when we arrived near the city center, not far from Charlie's office.

"Good luck, Adam," I said, shaking his hand. "I'm awfully glad our world has people like you and Huwaida."

That evening I had an interview with a quietly spoken woman named Maise, who made documentary films for the Palestinian Authority. We met in the lobby of The Park, an elegantly furnished hotel with an impressive view of Psagot, the dangerous Israeli settlement.

One week after my interview with Maise, Italian journalist Rafaele Ciriello would be shot six times in the chest on the roof of this hotel while covering the Israeli take-over of Ramallah. A journalist from the Boston Globe would also be injured on the same roof.

Maise insisted on taking me to lunch the following day. She also promised me a walking tour of the al-Amari refugee camp, a few minutes from downtown Ramallah. Over lunch in a lovely outdoor restaurant I asked Maise what she thought of Arafat signing the Oslo Accords.

"Arafat always said to take something is better than having nothing. Take a small thing and then ask for another small thing. Step by step, we will have a Palestinian land. It is very important that there are people called Palestinians. And if, in the end, he gets a small Palestinian state and a passport for every Palestinian inside and outside Palestine, it will be enough for him. He will feel that he has protected the needs of the Palestinian people. That is what he did, or thought he did, when he signed Oslo.

"Would you like to interview Arafat?" Maise asked. "I could arrange it very easily. I meet often with Arafat and it wouldn't be hard to do."

"No thank you. In America people don't want to hear what Arafat has to say. Besides, I want my audience to know that there are Palestinian people like you, that all Palestinians are not suicide bombers, or like Yasser Arafat."[23]

When I commented that most Palestinians appeared to have enormous hearts in spite of their struggles, she replied, "I think this is because we have experienced huge dramas in our lives which have enabled us to grow in many ways."

When I commented that Israelis would say the same about themselves, she agreed. "Of course, they suffered through the Holocaust."

On the issue of suicide bombers, she said, "We Palestinians should never act like the Nazis acted toward the Jews. We should act like human beings and treat everyone with dignity. I am happy to say that most of us act that way. Did you know that before Sharon came to power, there had only been a dozen suicide bombings? In light of this, one must wonder if it is not his brutal treatment of Palestinians that drives a small number of us to do desperate things. If there were some small recognition of our humanity, there would not be such terrible acts perpetuated against the Israeli people."

On nonviolent resistance to the Israeli occupation, "I agree in

---

23 Yasser Arafat signed the Oslo Accords so he would not lose his place as head of the Palestinian Authority, and in doing so he duped his people into believing they would realize their dream of an independent Palestinian state. By signing Oslo, Arafat conceded not only the fifty-three percent of the land partitioned to the Jewish State by the UN in 1947, but also the additional twenty-two percent conquered in June, 1967, from the proposed Palestinian State, a concession of seventy-eight percent of the original Palestine. Conceding the twenty-two percent violated the rights of the Palestinians under the Fourth Geneva Convention, Article B: "Protected persons may in no circumstances renounce any part of the rights secured to them by the present convention." If the basis for the Oslo peace accords had been international humanitarian law rather than power negotiations on the part of the US and the Israeli government, the occupation would have ended and the conditions for a just peace between Israelis and Palestinians would have been established.

principle that Palestinians should practice nonviolent resistance. However, explain that to those in the camps who suffer Israeli aggression every day, who see their children die, their homes demolished, and their gardens and trees bulldozed."

I wondered why Maise and her family had not ended up in a refugee camp.

"My mother was from a wealthy family who lost everything in 1948. She is the one who refused to take us to a refugee camp. 'I would rather die than take my family there,' she said. Instead, she sent my oldest brother, eleven at the time, to work for the British troops. He was not paid, but he received one meal a day, which he brought home and shared with my mother, my sister and another brother. My father went to Jordan to work, returning every two months. My mother worked as a seamstress. She was an incredible woman, and we grew up never knowing we were poor."

When I asked if she had a message for Americans, she said, "Perhaps if Americans had to endure what we have had to suffer, they would show more compassion toward others. In America, you have rules, but you do not necessarily have feelings attached to those rules. Here, we have support with feelings. We are never alone. Someone is always beside us, helping us through the worst of times. These are not written rules. They are norms of human decency. In America, you are always in a hurry. You work hard to make money. Do you also take the time to be compassionate human beings?"

After lunch, we headed for the al-Amari refugee camp on the south side of Ramallah to visit her friend, Seham, a forty-three-year-old widow. In 1989, the Israeli Defense Forces (IDF) shot and killed her husband, leaving her to raise six children. A midwife by profession, Seham is currently unemployed, like nearly seventy percent of the Palestinians in the West Bank and Gaza.

"The Israelis have been striking the camp all day," Maise said. "I don't know how long we will be able to stay."

Apache helicopters continued to hover overhead as we entered the camp. One of the men told Maise they had been there for the last five hours.

"They will probably attack us at nightfall."

As I walked alongside Maise, I felt like one of Huwaida's international volunteers. While I stayed in the camp, would the Israelis hold off attacking?

"Most of the refugees in this camp come from Ramle, a Palestinian village destroyed by the Israelis in 1948," Maise explained.

"That was fifty-four years ago," I said, staring at the row of dilapidated hovels as we walked, most of which looked like they had been glued together – a cardboard slab or plasterboard for a wall, a piece of rippled tin as a roof, someone's discarded window as a door. Even though these were improvements over their original makeshift tents, a strong wind could have blown any one of them down. Imagine the terror of someone living in a dwelling like that, anticipating an Apache missile or worse at any time of the day or night; or the deadly consequences of an F16 fighter plane dropping a one-ton bomb.

"We are here," Maise said, stopping in front of a door.

Seham answered the knock, and after receiving a kiss on each cheek, Maise introduced me.

"I would like you to meet my friend. She has come from America to talk to people in Ramallah."

Then I got the same wonderful, warm greeting as Seham took our hands and led us inside.

"Seham, please tell Cathy about yourself, because she wants to convey your story to her fellow Americans."

I was embarrassed by the assumption that Seham might think I was there to help her specifically, as if unbiased fact-finding could state her case. Yes, I was there to gather the Palestinian point of view, but I was also there to listen to the Israeli side and make both opinions known.

Seham insisted I sit in her best chair, while she sat on the floor and recounted her husband's death at the hands of Israeli soldiers.

Maise and I left the camp about an hour later, the Apaches still hovering overhead.

. . .

What is the perfect antidote to a refugee camp? The theater!

Maha directs *Ashta*, an acting troupe that works with Palestinian children, teaching them to let loose of their fears and emotions and re-interpret them through self-expression and acting.

"We are the only institution in Palestine that works in drama with children. We do not have enough staff or actors to go into the schools, but at least we have this studio which was donated to us. It is here that our children come after school and on weekends. We are an NGO and receive our funding from international organizations, primarily European. Drama is another way, another technique whereby you can affect attitudes, and let out all sorts of feelings. This is greatly needed in these difficult times. Let me give you an example: my husband and I are Israeli Arabs which means we have freedom of movement. Recently, when we tried to return to Jerusalem from Ramallah, and the checkpoint was closed, we had to pass through very rough roads, all the while fearful of an Israeli soldier spotting us and shooting. My son suddenly said, 'Look at the green fields ... Look how we are happy among the flowers.' Given a chance, my son wanted to see something beautiful, and God bless him, he tried to do this on a dirt road in full view of Israeli soldiers."

After the tour of Maha's theater, I took a taxi back to Charlie's office. He wanted to attend a conference on development in the West Bank, and I decided to accompany him. One of the participants was a French architect named Sylvaine. After her presentation, Charlie stayed to talk to her. She had spent the last three years going back and forth between France and Ramallah, working in the West Bank on her second PhD in Urban Development. She was very interested in Charlie's work. Eager to share his projects with a fellow architect, he proposed a tour of his sites the next day.

The rumors began on Thursday. The Israeli Army was preparing to enter Ramallah. On Friday, the Israeli government issued an advisory to all foreigners living in Ramallah to leave. Charlie insisted I should not leave on my own. He had a friend who worked for a German company. They were taking their nationals out the next afternoon. He thought perhaps I could leave with them.

He called an hour later. "Sorry, Cathy, they only want Germans on their van. That will make it easier for them at the checkpoint. Don't worry, I'll ask Sylvaine. I think she intends to cross Saturday afternoon. I'll get back to you."

I still had a number of interviews scheduled. I worked non-stop Friday and again until noon on Saturday to complete them.

I interviewed Walid's mother, and she was as interesting as her son had promised. She and her family had lived in Beirut in the early 1980s. During the Israeli bombardment of 1982, her husband died of a heart attack. Walid is her only unmarried son; like Charlie's mother, she was intent on finding her son a wife.

Um Walid (*Um* means "mother of") travels to the US frequently to visit relatives. While she is fond of America, she is not shy about telling me how ignorant she finds Americans on the subject of the Middle East, particularly about the Palestinians.

"Let me tell you a story," she said. "Then you will understand what I am trying to say. When I was in New York one time, my nephew's neighbor came to pay me a visit. During the course of the conversation, he asked why Palestinians were so fond of Communists. I asked him to explain what he meant. 'Well, you invited Russians to your cities and towns. You allowed them to build you schools and hospitals. Why would you do that if you did not like the Russians and their communism?' "

"How did you respond?" I asked.

"I began by asking him whether he thought I was Muslim or Christian. He answered, 'I thought all Palestinians were Muslims.' As calmly as I could, I replied that, in fact, a quarter of all Palestinians were Christian, and that I was a Greek Orthodox Christian. He had never heard of a Greek Orthodox. I explained that in the Middle East we call ourselves Greek Orthodox. In Russia those Christians practicing the same religion call themselves Russian or Eastern Orthodox. We both follow the Byzantine tradition of the Orthodox Catholic Church. When his eyes opened wide enough, I told him that the Russians who came to our towns and villages were Russian Orthodox priests, and that they came, not to spread Communism, but to open schools, to build and staff hospitals."

Um Walid began laughing. "I wonder if Americans even know that Yasser Arafat's wife, Suha, is a Christian Palestinian?"

"I recently read in *The Economist* that seventy percent of all Arab-Americans are Christian," I said. "At a time when Arabs are being demonized in America, this important statistic is left out of the American media. What about the rest of the Palestinians? Are they Sunni Muslim?"

"Yes," *Um* Walid said, "but we also have a small number of Druze who serve in the Israeli military."

"I didn't know any Arabs served in the Israeli military."

"Druze are the exception. They are a feisty lot and very good fighters."

In the 16th Century, the Druze migrated south from what is present-day Lebanon into Palestine, settling in the Galilee, in northern Israel and in the Negev.

Um Walid explained that those who are in the Negev live in absolute squalor. In exchange for certain economic improvements – better jobs, schools and medical facilities – they agreed to serve in the army. Unfortunately, the Israeli government has not kept its side of the bargain, and the Druze in the Negev are no better-off today.

The Druze religion, which is monotheistic, was born in 11th Century Egypt as an offshoot of Shiite Islam. Their first prophet was al-Darazi, whence comes the name Druze.

. . .

I was late for my next interview. My taxi driver, following written instructions, left the center of Ramallah and climbed to another of the hills sounding the city. He searched in vain for the offices of the General Union of Palestinian Women. Instead, we kept finding ourselves in front of Psagot, the Israeli settlement.

"We have been driving around these same streets for quite a while. Won't the soldiers at Psagot find this suspicious?" I asked nervously.

"Not to worry." The driver laughed. "They will see a blonde woman in my car."

When we finally found the building, and I climbed the four flights of stairs to the office, I was chided for having waited so long to contact these women.

"Why didn't you come to see us the first day?" Khadija, Maise's sister-in-law, asked. "We could have gotten you hundreds of interviews. And you missed the International Women's Day celebration. It was yesterday."

"Did Hanan Ashwrawi speak?" I asked, disappointed at myself for having forgotten all about it.

"No, she could not cross from East Jerusalem. The Israelis held her up at Qalandya."

Khadija led me into a sunny room with windows, where she offered me a seat.

"Is that the Israeli settlement?" I shrieked, pointing straight ahead.

She nodded.

"But the army can look right into this room. How can you sit here so calmly?"

"We are used to it," she said, laughing. "But you aren't. Come, we will move to another room and talk there."

Khadija showed me the memorandum her organization had sent to Israeli women on March 8, 2002, commemorating International Women's Day.

It read: "We call on the Israeli community in general, and

women in particular, to stand against Israeli occupation, oppression, war, apartheid, humiliation and poverty. It is time to raise our voices loud and clear. There has been enough bloodshed ... Today we need one another more than ever before. We have to fight for our children's rights and freedom. We must stand for morality, while working for genuine peace and co-existence. Let us start now, with a new vision that is based on respect for human rights and mutual trust. There has been enormous suffering, hatred and dehumanization on both sides. Women have been the most affected, yet the least involved in finding solutions. Together, we can break this vicious cycle."

· · ·

I returned to St. Joseph's School for my last interview in Ramallah. Three of the girls from Regina's class had agreed to talk to me after school ended at noon. This was only a day after fifty Palestinians had been killed by Israeli soldiers in the West Bank. Despite the heavy death toll I was struck by their heartfelt belief that they could change the world.

I asked them, "If you were in charge of the PA, what would you do to implement peace with the Israelis?"

Their response: "I would forget about Jerusalem, and the boundaries, and the right of return, and just be one nation. We are all brothers and sisters, all from the same family. Why can't we just have one country for all, no boundaries?"

"Because that is an ideal world, not the real one," I replied.

"No, we just need to talk to the ordinary people. They will understand. Forget the leaders, the generals. All they want is war."

· · ·

Issa, Regina and I had just finished a very late lunch when Charlie called. "I'll be there in an hour. Sylvaine is with me now, and you'll be crossing with her. Don't worry. As long as you leave before nightfall, you'll be safe."

I could barely get my bag closed, and I still had not packed my two dozen Palestinian schoolbooks. In the end, I double-lined a thick plastic bag. I only hoped I would not have to walk any great distance with my load.

Issa hung his head out the window looking for Charlie. As soon as he spotted his white car he yelled, "Cathy, are you ready? Charlie has arrived."

Regina called the elevator and the three of us rode down in silence. They must have been wondering if I would pass safely. I was worried about the very same thing.

Charlie was encouraged by the lack of traffic as he made his way through the city center. I, on the other hand, found it very worrisome. When we got to Qalandya, I understood why no one was driving about. Instead of a checkpoint, a dozen Israeli Merkava army tanks were standing guard. Charlie swerved to the left and slammed on his brakes.

"You'll have to get out here. Hurry," he said, jumping out to open the trunk so we could retrieve our bags.

"But what do we do?" I asked, petrified by the noise of the tank engines, churning away like a bunch of mammoth race cars revving up their motors, showing everyone who was boss.

"Follow me," said Sylvaine. "And put your passport away. You won't need that now."

I fiddled with the clasp on my backpack, but my hands were shaking so badly they could hardly function. I gave Charlie a hug before he jumped back into his car and sped away.

"Let's move it," yelled Sylvaine over the noise. "We'll take this dirt road," she said, pointing to her left. "It winds around an old refugee camp. Only walk where I walk, okay? If we hug these abandoned buildings to the right of the path, the tanks will not be able to see us."

"I'm right behind you, Sylvaine," I said, momentarily feeling relieved to be out of the view of Israeli tanks. My heavy bag of books even felt lighter and my knees hurt less. This was only a brief respite however, because Sylvaine was constantly on my case.

"Keep up with me, Cathy," she insisted, "we can't afford to slow down for a second. We must cross before nightfall. Otherwise, we won't be able to see where we're walking."

We turned right at the end of the row of buildings, marched up a small incline, took a left and hit an open field back in full view of the tanks. I glanced up to my right. A turret was following my every step. I stumbled. The sun was setting. I could barely see to walk. Suddenly, I heard gunshots.

"Sylvaine, what's that noise? Are they shooting at us?"

"I don't know. If they are, we don't have a place to hide, so just keep walking. We have to reach the other side of the valley."

Sylvaine and I joined a silent parade of frightened people heading out of Ramallah, each of us looking at the ground, fearful of falling, slipping on the loose gravel and the rocky terrain. Since we were doing everything humanly possible to get ourselves out of this predicament, I was quite surprised to meet scores of people on the same path trying to get back into Ramallah. I supposed they wanted more than anything to get back to their families in case the Israelis sealed off Ramallah.

When I began to lag behind, Sylvaine said, "Hand me your bag. I'll carry it for a while."

"No, thank you. I'm fine." 'Fine,' I thought, 'who am I kidding? I can barely breathe.' My mouth was dry. I was hyperventilating again and I was covered in dust. And then that million-dollar question kept popping into my head: what was a middle-aged American housewife doing here, carrying twenty-five pounds of textbooks in her arms with a heavy pack on her back?

Forty-five minutes later we were forced to climb down a steep hill at the end of the dirt road. My knees throbbed. I was sure I would fall.

"I can't get down here, Sylvaine, I said. I have bad knees."

"You what …? Here, lean on my arm."

When we had reached the bottom safely, she whispered, "Military patrols pass through here all the time. Be prepared to hit the ground if they start shooting."

We hugged the embankment and walked toward a waiting row of mini-van taxis, similar to the multi-passenger VW Vans of the 1960s. By now night had fallen and it was difficult to see. That worked to our advantage vis-à-vis the Israeli patrols. The taxi-van would take us to al-Ram, near the next Israeli checkpoint, where a second van would take us into East Jerusalem. The driver waited for a full load of passengers before leaving. Minutes seemed like hours as I thought of an Israeli patrol appearing suddenly and forcing us out of the taxi.

We piled out of the van when we reached al-Ram.

"Now what do we do?" I asked.

"Just follow me," said Sylvaine.

At that point, I would have followed her anywhere. I was immensely grateful to have her at my side. With the other passengers from our van we walked along a barricade separating us from the Israeli checkpoint a half-block away. I could clearly see Israeli soldiers stopping cars and I was sure they could see us. But they failed to stop us and question us, even though there could have been a terrorist intent on infiltrating Jerusalem among our small group. Given the way these checkpoints were so selectively manned, how could they ensure security?

Our next challenge was to climb a four-foot fence around the barricade. I momentarily panicked, wondering how I would manage.

"Sylvaine, I didn't tell you the whole truth back there. I don't really have knees. They are artificial. I can't climb fences."

"Of course you can. Let me help. Hand me your bag."

When she took it, she cried, "Jesus, Cathy! This is heavy. Okay, watch what the others are doing. Put your right foot here. Now, with the left one … *voilà*, you're over."

"Thanks, Sylvaine."

We crossed the main boulevard again in full view of Israeli troops, and waited for a taxi to take us into East Jerusalem, a fifteen minute trip. As we stood alongside the road, the neighborhood suddenly went dark. We heard the sound of steel blades churning. Apaches hovered overhead.

"They're going to attack," said Sylvaine, "and probably tonight. We got out just in time."

The taxi van made a U turn in the middle of the road to stop and pick us up. It actually sat with its motor idling, waiting for more fares, in full view of an Apache helicopter gunship. Mercifully, minutes later we were on our way. As we drove toward East Jerusalem, I could not help but think that this was how it must have been to be the last non-Jew walking out of the Warsaw Ghetto. I felt terrible guilt making this comparison, but I could not help it. At that moment I could not distinguish between SS troops about to enter the Warsaw Ghetto and Israeli soldiers and tanks about to invade Ramallah. Even the overall passivity of the Palestinians was very much like that of the Jews, with the exception of the small band of Jewish resistance fighters who, coincidently, only did then what *Hamas* and the Al-Aqsa Brigade are doing now.

JERUSALEM

I LEFT SYLVAINE AT HER HOTEL ON NABLUS ROAD SO SHE COULD freshen up before rejoining me later. As I was one of the only guests at the hotel, my return was quite an event. I might even say I was given a heroine's welcome. When I came up the last of three short flights of stairs to the hotel lobby, the two men at the desk rushed to take my bag.

"*Ahlan, Ahlan,* Mrs. Sultan," one said, while the other, shaking my hand, added, "After all the bad news coming out of Ramallah, we thought we would never see you again."

"Thank you," I replied, reaching the desk and unloading my backpack onto the counter. "That is very kind of you. Did anyone call me while I was gone?"

"Oh yes, your husband called one day. He was ..."

"I know ... very upset. I finally spoke to him from Ramallah. Everything is fine now, thank you."

From behind me I heard, "What about me? I was worried, too."

I turned to find Mary standing there, tears in her eyes. I wrapped my arms around her and gave her a big hug.

"I'm so sorry. My cell phone wouldn't connect to Jerusalem. I asked several people I met there to call the hotel and leave you messages. I'm sorry you didn't get any of them. How was your week?" I asked. "Were you busy with meetings?"

"Unfortunately, many of them were canceled at the last minute. And the Israelis closed Bethlehem, so I couldn't get to my favorite orphanage. I brought a suitcase full of clothes for the children so I'm terribly disappointed. And the news tonight is awful, so I doubt this coming week will be any better."

"I doubt that, too, considering how bad things are right now around Ramallah. Listen, if you're not going out, please join me. Sylvaine, the woman who helped me get back to Jerusalem, will be here in a few minutes. I'd like her to meet you. We could sit in the lobby and tell you about our adventure. Will you join us?"

"Yes, with pleasure."

. . .

Thanks to a few beers, a Darvon for pain and two extra-strength Tylenols for good measure – which helped soothe the burning in both my knees – I slept from 10:30 until my telephone rang the next morning at 9:15. I answered, but I must have still been half asleep because I remember asking Sylvaine to repeat what she was saying.

"What about Ramallah?" I bolted up in bed. "The Israelis invaded? When did they go in last night? Oh, Sylvaine," I started crying. "We were so lucky. Yes, I'll call Charlie right away, then I'll call you back."

I connected with Ramallah easily from my hotel phone.

"Hello, Charlie."

"You are one lucky lady," he said. "I can't believe it. You got out just in time."

"How are your parents holding up?" I asked.

"Pretty well, considering …" Charlie went on to tell me that 160 Israeli tanks and armored personnel carriers had entered Ramallah. Residents were under total curfew until further notice.

"We can't even open our windows to look out," he explained. "The Israelis drive around with loud speakers warning us they'll shoot anyone on sight."

"Charlie, I'm so sorry …"

"It's all right. We're used to this. The Israelis invaded and occupied Ramallah about six months ago. At that time, we had an Israeli tank outside our front door. At least this time, they're parked on a different street."

"Please give my best regards to your parents. I'll check on you this evening. Take care."

I called Sylvaine back.

"Charlie is safe, at least for now. He sends you his regards, and thanks you for helping me get out."

"Listen, Cathy, I am going to spend the day with my friend, Christa. She's a German archeologist who has lived here for thirty-five years. Would you like to join us for a drive around the city, then lunch?"

"I'd be honored."

"Meet us in front of *L'École Archéologique* at noon. That's where Christa has her office. It's on Nablus Road, just past the Jerusalem Hotel. Just ask for directions. See you then."

Since it was only 9:30, there was plenty of time to shower and have breakfast. I wanted to call Michel, to tell him that I had returned safely to East Jerusalem, but it was 1:30 AM in Wisconsin.

I had just finished eating two slices of toast and a hard boiled egg when Nabil, the hotel's owner, arrived. He came over to my table and welcomed me back. I invited him to join me.

"You had us all very worried," he said.

"I know, and I'm terribly sorry."

I told him about my week, whom I met, whom I interviewed.

"Did you interview Arafat?" asked Nabil.

"No, but I could have. One of the women I met, who actually lived across the street from his compound, offered to arrange it. I was more interested in talking to the people, hearing what they had to say. It's a voice Americans never hear. No one in America believes Arafat anyway."

"I surely don't," Nabil said. "He's corrupt, and so are the men around him."

"Why do so many Palestinians still like him?" I asked. "In Ramallah, no one said a bad word against him."

"In people's eyes, he symbolizes Palestine. He's their only hope for ever attaining statehood. The Palestinian people cannot live without the hope that one day they will have an independent state."

"How do you see things evolving, Nabil?" I asked.

"Frankly, I'm not very optimistic. Economically, things are a disaster. I can barely afford to keep my hotel running. If I close it, I worry the Israelis will confiscate the building. They're doing that all over East Jerusalem. Wherever they see a vacated building, they move in."

"Who?"

"Israeli settlers."

"But this is Arab East Jerusalem."

"Tell that to the Israelis," he retorted.

. . .

Two months after my conversation with Nabil, I read in a *Christian Science Monitor* article that Jewish settlers were moving into vacant buildings in Arab East Jerusalem at an alarming rate. In one area forty-three Palestinian families had already been evicted. The settlers' apparent aim is ultimately to cut off the Palestinian core of the Old City from the more populous northern Palestinian neighborhoods. Severing this link – and thereby breaking the continuity of Palestinian East Jerusalem – would make it very difficult to establish a peace plan which included Palestinian control over Arab East Jerusalem.

. . .

I was surprised to find the streets of East Jerusalem bustling until I remembered Sunday was not a holiday here. I bought my first copy of the English version of *Ha'aretz* from a newspaper stand along my route; for some reason it is only sold tucked inside the *International Herald Tribune*. As I walked up Nablus Road to meet Sylvaine and Christa, I came upon a fortress-like building with security cameras, floodlights, iron bars on all the windows and a seven-foot-high revolving cage for a door. As Christa explained later, this was the Israeli Population Administration office, a place where Palestinians from East Jerusalem had to go to get birth certificates, renew their identity cards, and all the other bureaucratic necessities. According to Christa, the office was officially open from nine to noon, but the line was already very long in the earliest hours of the morning, some days winding around the corner into the next street. Since I did not reach *L'École Archéologique* until close to noon, I did not get a sense of the chaos. Christa explained that those Palestinians who wanted to avoid the wait, and could afford the privilege, hired youngsters to stand in line, often all night, to secure them a place at the front of the line.

On the following day when I returned to *L'École Archéologique* to see Christa, I witnessed the bizarre scene for myself. Three men, each carrying a clunky old typewriter, set up small tables on the opposite side of the narrow street against the wall of *L'École Archéologique*. They came supplied with stacks of application forms, a prerequisite for any request from the Population Ministry. For a modest fee, these men filled in the forms for those unable to read or write. During the busiest hours of the day other Palestinians added to the surreal scene by setting up stalls to sell snacks, drinks and cigarettes.

According to Christa, the Israeli guard inside the cage could decide to close the doors for the day at any time between 9 AM and noon, and turn everyone away. I did not witness this personally but was assured by Christa that it was common.

In Israeli West Jerusalem – considered Israel proper – the Population Office is called the Interior Ministry. It is reserved for the exclusive use of Israeli Jews, who can obtain ID cards and other legal documents in spacious, air conditioned offices in less than half an hour.

. . .

Sylvaine was waiting for me opposite the Population Ministry.

"You made it," she said, smiling. "Christa is already in the car. Let's go."

As we walked through the high, black iron gates of *L'École Archéologique*, for an instant I forgot I was in congested, dirty East Jerusalem. Even the horn-honking, motor-idling noises stayed outside for some reason. Inside the walls I was reminded of the well-kept grounds of the French-owned schools and universities in Beirut. Here, too, beneath the shade of tall eucalyptus and umbrella pines, I strolled among overgrown beds of blue and white jasmine, of roses that thrive lavishly in the Mediterranean climate, and bushes of rosemary, so full and green I felt obliged to touch them to make sure they were real.

Except for Sylvaine, I could not have met a kinder, more helpful person than Christa, who was delighted to be able to give me a tour of her city. We drove past Makkased Hospital on the Mount of Olives to a point overlooking Jerusalem. As we got out of the car to take photos, young boys approached us trying to sell trinkets. When we refused, they began yelling at us, something I did not expect. Christa and I returned immediately to the car, while she harshly rebuked them in Arabic to mind their manners.

They shot back, "Jew-lovers," and ran away.

Christa apologized for the boys' bad behavior and what they had said, since the young Arab boys are generally better-behaved.

"Usually this city is full of tourists. Now, no one comes. Who would dare? These boys are hungry and scared. We are women, easy targets, and they have simply taken their frustrations out on us. Please do not be offended."

As we drove around the different neighborhoods and along the main highways, I was struck by the vast amounts of vacant land.

"I expected East Jerusalem to be more crowded. Instead, there's so much open space."

"This was all Arab land at one time before the State of Israel confiscated it," Christa explained. "Look over there to the left. See the roadwork underway? The government is constructing a ring around the city of Jerusalem, which will connect all Israeli settlements, north and south of Jerusalem, with Israel's coastal area. Unfortunately, this project will ultimately extend well beyond the 1967 borders."

"How will the Palestinians get from East Jerusalem to Ramallah?"

"They won't. That's the whole point. And, when the ring is completed, there will be no territorial contiguity for a Palestinian state."

"Was this Ariel Sharon's idea?" I asked.

"No, this project was actually approved back in 1996."

In one quiet Arab East Jerusalem neighborhood the road was cut off by concrete blocks. We parked the car, got out and began walking toward the enormous pile. A group of young men was standing alongside the road.

"What is this?" Christa asked.

"Last week, the Israeli Army dumped these blocks here for no apparent reason, other than to force us to go four blocks out of our way to get back into our own neighborhood."

"Come tomorrow and watch what happens," said another man.

"What do you mean?" Sylvaine asked.

"Our children have to cross this pile of blocks to get to that school down the street. Israeli soldiers show up fifteen or twenty minutes before school starts. They throw tear gas at our children."

"Where are you from?" one man asked. Sylvaine and Christa told him, but when it came my turn I replied, "Canada."

Lunch with Christa and Sylvaine was the first time I had relaxed since my arrival. I felt some degree of guilt sitting on the terrace of a grand old hotel in East Jerusalem sipping chilled white wine, a luxury many of my fellow Americans enjoy every day. Back in the States our biggest worry is getting stuck in traffic and being late for an appointment, or getting caught in the rain without an umbrella.

. . .

Early the next morning, Christa called before leaving for work.

"I have only a few hours at the office. I can drive you around Jerusalem after that. Then if you like, I could give you a tour of the Old City."

"That would be wonderful."

Christa showed me the Israeli settlements in East Jerusalem, built on land captured by Israel after the 1967 war. Although the United Nations has deemed these settlements illegal, the American government continues to give Israel billions of dollars every year, knowing full well much of that money goes toward the construction of these settlements.

"You know," Christa said, "this would stop if your government turned off the flow of money."

"George Bush Senior and Secretary of State James Baker tried that with then-Prime Minister Shamir. Bush ended up losing the election to Bill Clinton."

"So what does that mean?" Christa asked sarcastically, "that these settlements will continue to grow, and that more and more Palestinians will be thrown off their land, because American politicians are afraid of risking their political necks and offending the Israeli government?"

All I could do was shrug.

After the tour we returned to Nablus Road and parked the car inside the iron gates and walked down Nablus Road toward Saleh el Din Street. Old Mercedes-Benz city buses – their idling diesel engines spewing grey fumes – lined the narrow street, almost touching the walls and forcing us to walk in the cobblestone street. Chauffeurs shouted out their destinations like auctioneers – Qalandya, al-Ram, Nablus, Jenin, Bethlehem, Hebron – creating a cacophony that bounced off the high walls.

It was market day on Saleh el Din Street. Peddlers Market – the area outside the Damascus Gate of the Old City – was full of vendors selling everything from nightgowns and underwear to tennis shoes, scarves and plastic slippers. The steps leading down from the street were so congested I dared not look around unless I stopped dead in my tracks, and then I risked being pushed from behind by the throngs of people descending toward the Gate.

From the moment I walked into the Muslim Quarter through the Damascus Gate – one of eight gates leading into the Old City – I felt as though I were stepping back into antiquity. The walls surrounding the Old City date back more than 2,000 years. In a place which in ancient times must have smelled of cedar, musk, incense, and myrrh, it was easy to conjure up the image of women draped in brightly colored reds and blues sitting along the cobblestone walkway hawking their pottery and precious purple dye while their men traded livestock and grain to Hebrews and Canaanites. The original water-delivery system to the Old City is still in use – an open gutter along either side of the narrow walkway. The walkway – called *Al Wad Road* – gives way to a step or two about every ten feet. If you do not pay attention to where you place your feet you can find yourself on the ground in very quick fashion. The Crusaders – whose capital Jerusalem was for most of the 12th Century – built the massive stone walls lining both sides of the walkway.

Crammed into every conceivable space along either side of *Al Wad Road*, the shops are full of colorful local ware: exquisitely embroidered cloth in Palestinian motifs; unique Armenian artisan dinner dishes painted in browns, turquoise and blues; or shelves of hand-painted pottery and glass jars, replicas of ancient Phoenician vases used to store precious oils and perfumes. For the leisurely stroller who wants to treat himself to the mouth-watering taste of hot flat bread dusted with thyme and olive oil, or spicy grilled meat kebabs and spit-roasted chickens, he has to spend only a few shekels. He only needs to sit back at any of the numerous cafes along *Al Wad Road*, order a Turkish coffee, smoke a *nargilla*, and marvel at the 15th Century Mamuluk architecture surrounding him.

Merchants must haul in massive amounts of goods, so they hire men with small tractors who are incredibly adept at navigating the narrow streets and steps, the throngs of people, and the ever-present Israeli guards patrolling the streets of the Old City, M16s slung across their chests.

Continuing our walk through the Muslim Quarter, across the *Via del Rosa*, we came to a junction approximately twelve feet wide in the Old City; if we turned left, we would find ourselves not far from a door leading to the Dome of the Rock; if we continued straight, we would enter the Jewish Quarter; to our right were the Christian and Armenian Quarters. We turned left and walked into the *Suq al-Qattanin* (cotton market), a bustling, covered bazaar with an arched tile roof at least a thousand years old. I strolled to the end of the bazaar, where I caught a close-up glimpse through an open door of the glittering, gold eight-sided *Haram-al-Sharif* (Dome of the Rock) on the Temple Mount. The Dome is centered over a sacred rock believed to be the place where Abraham was about to sacrifice his son Isaac,[24] and from which Muhammad ascended into heaven. This magnificent piece of Islamic architecture – laced with intricate mosaics and bordered with tiles that bear quotations from the Quran – was built by Abd el-Malek in 691 CE. Abraham, David, Solomon and Jesus are said to have prayed at the Well of Souls in the downstairs level.

The Al-Aqsa Mosque, next to the Dome of the Rock, is Islam's third holiest site after Mecca and Medina. It was built between 710

---

24 According to the *Quran*, 37:99–111, Ishmael was the intended sacrifice. Abraham's willingness to sacrifice his son, Ishmael, for God is celebrated by Muslims every year at *Eid al Adha*.

and 715 CE. Intricate stained glass windows – installed by Suleiman in the 16th Century – brighten what would otherwise be a musty and dimly-lit mosque.

. . .

Religion and politics aside, Jerusalemites – Israeli and Palestinian alike – agree on one thing: a love affair with hummus. The Israelis like to eat it for breakfast with hot green peppers; the Palestinians eat it for lunch with crushed garlic. No matter. They also agree that the *Al Baraq* Restaurant, a stone's throw from the *Suq al-Qattanin* bazaar, serves up the best hummus in all Jerusalem. That masterpiece of the Middle Eastern table, kibbeh – which the Israelis call *kibbe*, the Palestinians, *kubba* – is also a specialty at *Al Baraq*.

That particular morning our mission was to find someone to interview, so Christa and I retraced our steps to the Al-Quds University at the entrance to the *Suq al Qattanin*. We entered the small campus looking for a friend of Christa's, only to discover she was away on holiday. Instead we met Carmen, who, with her delicately sculptured face and long, black wavy hair, reminded me of Bizet's tragic heroine. In addition to being beautiful, she was articulate, with a perfect command of English. She spoke with us for several hours about the limits placed on Palestinian travel, the daily hassles she and her fellow classmates had to endure at Israeli checkpoints to get to Bir Zeit University in the West Bank, and the vision for peace she shares with her Israeli friends.

"Separating everyone will not be the solution," she said. "We need to heal together. If we live together, we will all be required to make peace work. It is the only way."

. . .

Before I left Eau Claire my husband's aunt, Mère Michèle, a Carmelite nun who used to work in Israel, gave me the name of her Israeli-born friend, Shira W. I called her after Christa dropped me back at my hotel, and she invited me to her house the following afternoon. Mark, a retired professor from Hebrew University and another friend of Mère Michèle's, would also be there and we would all have dinner together.

Shira is a Professor at Hebrew University on Mount Scopus in the French Hill area, on the northern edge of East Jerusalem. Had I seen this petite woman with long, voluminous black hair on a street corner in Rome, I would have taken her for an Italian. But an Italian – like anyone else from the Mediterranean basin – would have greeted me more warmly. While I may have been indirectly related to her friend Mère Michèle, I had yet to establish the reason for my visit and my credentials to interview her. Since her 'prove-yourself-to-me' attitude was quite obvious, I knew I had only a few moments to state my purpose or lose my credibility. Momentarily I panicked. Here I was, a housewife from Eau Claire, Wisconsin. What qualified me to ask questions of this professor from a major university? What could I possibly say which would convince her of my sincerity? It felt as if this were a David-and-Goliath moment, and I was not at all sure I was up to the challenge of playing David.

It made matters worse that Shira seemed perfectly content to let me struggle. She sat back, her shoulders squared, her arms folded across her chest, and as much as said, 'You are no one, and know nothing.'

I had done my homework before coming to Israel. Shira's combative attitude made me realize my study of Israeli/Palestinian history was about to pay off, because I knew exactly what to say when she accused Arafat of blowing his chance at peace with the Israelis.

"He did not accept Barak's generous offer," she said. "Everyone knows that."

"There was no generous offer," I retorted.

"Of course there was. It was all over the Israeli newspapers."

"Look, Barak's offer meant no territorial contiguity for a Palestinian state, it meant no control of its external borders, limited control of its own water resources, and no full Israeli withdrawal from the occupied territories, as required by international law. At best, the Palestinians would have had some kind of autonomy within a greater Israel. Does that sound like a generous offer?"

"No, but that is not what we were told and nothing of what you just said has appeared in our Israeli newspapers."

"To my knowledge, *The New York Times* is the only newspaper that ran a front-page story recounting what really happened at Camp David, and that was four months after the fact. And instead of trying to set the record straight, certain journalists still insist on telling the world that Arafat refused Barak's generous offer."

"Could you please send me the article when you get back to the States?" asked Shira. "I would like to show it to some of my friends."

I assured her I would.

"There is something else you should know," I said. "Robert Malley, who was Clinton's special assistant for Arab-Israeli Affairs, said no other Arab leader had ever come as close to considering such compromises as Arafat. Barak, on the other hand, was a fraud. He was intent on convincing the Israeli public that Arafat wanted to drive the Israelis into the sea. His plan succeeded and the whole world turned against the Palestinians."

"We don't know any of these things here in Israel," said Shira.

"I've come to the realization that there is really little difference between the Israeli and American public," I said. "They are both willfully ignorant of the truth. The Israelis think Ariel Sharon is protecting them by doing something to fight terrorism. The Americans think President Bush is doing the very same thing."

As we continued our conversation Shira commented several times that I appeared to know what I was talking about, a compliment which pleased me immensely.

Mark walked in as we were discussing Barak and Arafat. I stood, greeted him, gave him a message from Mère Michèle, and invited him to join our discussion.

In a barely audible voice, Mark said, "Years ago, when I moved to Israel from Europe, I was one hundred percent for the Jews having their own homeland, particularly after what I saw happen to them in Europe. Now, I am profoundly hurt to see a people that I truly love behave like those who persecuted them in Europe. What is wrong with them? How can they inflict such punishment on people, when they themselves have had such awful things done to them?"

Shira, who acted as Mark's care-giver, saw how agitated he had become and urged him to calm down.

"It's not good for your health. Shall I make you a tea?"

"No, I am fine," he said. "I just wanted our guest to understand how sad I am about what I see happening around me."

Before I returned to my hotel, Shira made arrangements for me to interview several people she knew.

"And I will send my driver to take you anywhere you want to go."

. . .

Over the next few days, I interviewed Amira, an Israeli Arab, who had been hired by Hebrew University to coordinate early childhood programs in the Arab sector because of her Arabic language skills. During my conversation with her I learned that Israel's 1948 Declaration of Independence refers specifically to Israel as a Jewish State committed to the ingathering of Jewish exiles. Palestinians who are classified as Israeli Arabs, and non-Jews who by religious or ethnic affiliation – as in the case of Armenians – have citizenship rights. They can vote in elections for members of the *Knesset* (parliament) and for prime minister.

All other rights are nationality rights defined on the basis of religion, and are reserved for only Jews. If you are a Jew you have exclusive use of the land, since Israeli law states that ninety-four percent of the land in Israel belongs to the Jewish people. If you are a Jew you have privileged access to private and public employment, special educational loans, home mortgages, and priority admission to all universities. Special privileges are reserved for those who serve in the military. Military service is compulsory for all Jews, male and female, except the ultra-Orthodox, who receive the special privileges anyway. Palestinians, both Muslim or Christian, are not allowed to serve in the Israeli Army. The Druze, who are originally from Lebanon and who practice an offshoot of Shiite Islam, are allowed to serve in the Israeli Army.

Intrigued by this distinction between citizenship and nationality, I learned later that Israel does not define itself as a state of its citizens but as a state of all the Jews in the world. Jews from anywhere can make *aliya* (emigration) to Israel, declare citizenship and be granted the nationality privileges of being Jewish while these rights are denied Palestinians who have lived in Palestine for centuries.[25]

Shira introduced me to her professor of Arabic, Omar, who also teaches at Hebrew University. In his interview he offered a very insightful glimpse of academic life in Israel, particularly for Israeli Arabs.

Tali, another of Shira's friends, works for an Israeli agency which promotes tolerance. By her own admission, she now lives in a society incapable of showing tolerance.

"I do not think there will be peace with Sharon. The optimistic viewpoint is that some day Israel will have a good leader. The pessimist in me says that until Palestinians kill more Israelis, we will never begin to talk about peace."

B.D., Professor of Philosophy and Theology at Notre Dame University, and another of Shira's friends, is Director of Tantur Ecumenical Institute, a center which promotes world peace and social justice through theological studies. The campus – which sits in a fifteen acre park of umbrella pines, fruit trees and olive groves

---

25 Elbaum, Max. "For Jews Only: Racism Inside Israel." Interview with Phyllis Bennis. *Color Lines*, December 15, 2000. www.arc.org/C_Lines/CLArchive/story_web00_04.html

on the southern edge of Bethlehem – welcomes clergy from all over the world. When Tantur opened in 1971, it overlooked Bethlehem on one side and the spacious Judean hills on the other. Now the center is crammed in between the two large Israeli settlements of Gilo and Har Homa. At the time of my visit Israel had declared Bethlehem a closed military zone whose Palestinian residents were under total curfew.

Bethlehem is located approximately five miles south of Jerusalem. It is the birthplace of Jesus Christ, and the Church of the Nativity ranks among the most important holy places throughout the Christian world. Half of Bethlehem's 27,000 residents are Christian. The Dheisheh refugee camp adjacent to Bethlehem – where many Palestinian Christians were forced to resettle in 1948 – was visited by Pope John Paul II in 2000.

Throughout Israel and the occupied territories, the Catholic Church operates 151 institutions, which include thirty-three parishes, seven hospitals, eleven dispensaries, eight orphanages, five homes for the elderly, seven homes for the handicapped, seventy schools, five theological seminaries and five institutions of higher learning. In recent years both the Catholic Church and the other religious institutions have been forced to curtail their activities because Israel now routinely refuses to issue visas to staff members operating these facilities.

Catholic Relief Services, the Mennonite Central Committee and Lutheran World Federation have enjoyed tax exemption agreements for over fifty years with the Israeli government. Israel recently announced its intention to back out of these agreements. This will create economic hardships for these organizations, and could lead to closing the Lutheran World Federation's Augusta Victoria Hospital on the Mount of Olives, which serves the Palestinian community.

The Israeli government's Security Fence, part of which slices through a large section of Bethlehem, damages Christian institutions and the daily livelihood of individual Christians. The Fence separates families from each other, students from their schools, workers from their jobs, farmers from their land, doctors and patients from their hospitals – and most symbolically, Bethlehem from Jerusalem. The fence cuts off access to holy sites for Christians world-wide. If the Israeli government continues to build the Fence, the endangered indigenous Christians of the Holy Land could very well disappear.[26]

After discussing the fate of Bethlehem's Christians over lunch with B.D. and some of his colleagues, B.D. gave me a tour of Tantur. When we got to the roof, I took out my camera and began photographing the two Israeli settlements. I heard a gun shot coming from the direction of the Israeli checkpoint, but I did not realize the bullet was directed at me. As a second bullet raced past my head, I understood. A veteran of the civil war in Beirut, I threw myself on the floor, and yelled at B.D. to do the same. Huddled behind the wall, I knew that if the Israeli soldier had wanted to kill me he could have. He fired a warning shot, which I respected. We crawled off the roof on our hands and knees. I finished taking my photos of the Israeli settlements from the relative safety of an inside corridor.

. . .

One afternoon I took a taxi to Emek Refaim Street in West Jerusalem, where a suicide bomber had recently turned a neighborhood pizza parlor into twisted metal and burning flesh, killing scores of young Israelis. One of the women who worked at Bat Shalom agreed to see me. This organization, under the umbrella of The Jerusalem Link, is one of two important women's peace movements in Israel. Bat Shalom represents the Israeli side; the Jerusalem Center for Women, the Palestinian side. These two groups strive for the recognition of the right to self-determination of both peoples, through the establishment of a Palestinian state alongside Israel on the June 4, 1967, boundaries. "A peaceful solution to the

---

26   Bethlehem, City of Jesus website, www.bethlehem.org

Palestinian-Israeli conflict, and Israeli withdrawal from all occupied Arab territory, are prerequisites for a just and comprehensive peace."[27]

After hearing such overly optimistic goals which, in my opinion were unattainable – at least under the Sharon government – I came back to the reality of the street. As I walked along Emek Refaim Street looking for a taxi, my heart nearly stopped every time a bus approached. The Palestinian suicide bombers favored buses crowded with students and commuters. Their weapons were jammed with metal parts which lodged shards in necks and ripped open skulls on impact. I remembered the naked fear of walking down a street in Beirut during the civil war, only there it was car bombs not buses. The result was the same: the tragic loss of innocent life.

My heart went out to the Israeli mother who was obliged to send her children off to school each morning wondering as she waved good-bye if she would ever see them again. I knew that sinking-heart feeling, too, because I had to put my children on a bus every morning in the midst of civil war.

Every Israeli had reason to fear for his life. They were targets, whether they were strolling arm-in-arm down a street with friends, or taking their dogs for daily walks around the neighborhood or waiting for a bus along a busy street in Tel Aviv, Natanya or West Jerusalem. Parents who reluctantly allowed their teenagers to go out with friends to a movie or to a pizza parlor lived in fear of a phone call from the city morgue asking them to come collect their children's body parts.

. . .

I visited the Jerusalem Center for Women with Christa. That was where I met and interviewed Yasmine, a survivor of the Deir Yassin massacre in 1948, when members of the *Irgun* and Stern Gangs

---

27   Jerusalem Link website, www.batshalom.org/jlink_principles.php

– led by Ariel Sharon and Menahem Begin – killed 120 Palestinians in the village of Deir Yassin. Yasmine spoke at length about
this incident and its impact on Palestinians in nearby villages. She
talked about the daily frustrations that came with working in Jerusalem, a journey she was often obliged to make on foot. Most of all
she feared her neighborhood in Ramallah: she and her mother live
across the street from Psagot, the Israeli settlement.

Christa also directed me to the offices of *HaMoked*, Center
for the Defense of the Individual, one of the few Israeli organizations which defends Palestinians and monitors infringements on
human rights in the occupied territories. I introduced myself to C.,
the Director. I asked if he could spare me a few minutes, and he
invited me into his office.

"The Israeli Army is arresting thousands of men, all ages, on
suspicion of terrorist activities, or because they suspect that in the
future, they may commit hostile acts against Israel," he explained.
"We have the impossible task of trying to keep track of all these
men."

"Given the number of attacks aren't the arrests warranted?" I
asked.

"There are 1.4 million Palestinians living in Gaza, and 2.3
million living on the West Bank. Between September, 2000, and
March, 2002, 440 Israelis have been killed in approximately
seventy-two suicide bombings. Compare the population figures
with the number of suicide bombings and decide for yourself if
they warrant all those arrests."

According to the Israeli Ministry of Foreign Affairs website – as
of September 5, 2005 – there have been sixty-eight suicide bombings through August, 2005, killing 587 Israelis. An additional 500
Israeli soldiers and settlers have been killed. Twelve of the suicide
attacks were prior to the current *Intifada* which began in September, 2000.

"Well, what about *Hamas*, Islamic Jihad and the al-Aqsa Martyrs Brigade?" I asked. "Aren't they a threat?"

"Absolutely! Islamic Jihad has tens of thousands of members. So does *Hamas* and they readily admit they want to destroy Israel and create an Islamic State in its place. These groups also have the moral support of many Palestinians. The al-Aqsa Martyrs Brigade, a sub-group of Arafat's *Fatah* organization, also has thousands of members."

C. went on to say that the Israeli Settler Movement has approximately 300,000 members, and their aim is to drive every Palestinian into exile. 'Transfer' is the word they use. They, too, are a threat to the stability of Israel.

. . .

The following morning Christa called.

"Cathy, you are not hearing from a lot of people on the far right. You need that voice in your interviews."

"I agree. What do you suggest I do? I hope you are not going to propose dropping me off at that settlement full of Russian immigrants we drove through the other day," I said, laughing. "I don't think they'd want to talk to me."

"No, I am proposing that you go to the Wailing Wall."

"What? Just like that? Walk into the Wailing Wall area? And what would you have me do once I get there?"

"Find some women, go up to them and introduce yourself. Ask them if they would agree to talk to you."

"That sounds easy enough. I can do that. And I'll call you when I return. Better still. How about dinner tonight? Let's meet in the garden of the Jerusalem Hotel around eight."

"Okay."

. . .

It was late afternoon when I walked through the Damascus Gate and into the Muslim Quarter, where shopkeepers were busy boxing up unsold produce and sweeping out their stores. Young boys, supposed to be helping their fathers, instead were playing tag with their friends, jumping in and out of the shadows along the narrow cobblestone alleyway.

I walked the length of *Al Wad Road* until I came to the end of the Muslim Quarter. As I entered the covered arched walkway leading to the Jewish Quarter, I came across four young Palestinians boys sitting on the stone pavement playing marbles. I approached the desk manned by several young Jewish men. I asked if I could visit the Western Wall.

"Are you Jewish?" asked one.

"No," I replied.

"Then why do you want to visit our holy place?"

"I have lots of Jewish friends in America. I would like to tell them I visited the Wailing Wall."

After explaining it was my artificial metal knees that kept their metal detector beeping, I was given permission to pass. The remains of the *Cardo Maximus* – a 6th Century Byzantine Street which once served as Jerusalem's main market and processional thoroughfare – were under the covered stone alleyway through which I passed. Archeologists believe it was built by the Roman Emperor Hadrian (117–38 CE). A small area of road has been preserved along with some of the original Byzantine columns. Beyond the columns is an underground mall with Jewish stores and art galleries.

The Western Wall was formerly called the Wailing Wall by European Jews because for centuries Jews had come here to bewail the loss of their temple. This Wall is the holiest of Jewish sites, built by King Herod just before the time of Jesus, to shore up the western side of the Temple Mount and the vast, artificial ceremonial plaza Herod created there, now part of the forty-acre complex that houses the Al-Aqsa Mosque and the Dome of the Rock.

For centuries the wall stood sixty feet high and ninety-one feet long, towering over a narrow alley twelve feet wide which could accommodate only a few hundred densely packed worshipers. Immediately after the June, 1967, war, Israeli bulldozers razed the

Moroccan Arab neighborhood facing the wall and created the spacious plaza into which I walked when I exited the alleyway.

I did not know what to expect when I entered the plaza in front of the Wailing Wall: perhaps thousands of devout Orthodox Jews would be standing at the Wall, the men on one side, segregated from the women on the other, each group chanting and swaying in prayer.

The plaza was nearly empty. Tourism throughout the city was at an all-time low. Except for a few faithful praying at the Wall, I saw no one I could talk to. I saw a young soldier walking in my direction, and in an instant I knew what I had to do.

"Excuse me," I said. "I am an American. I am visiting Jerusalem for the first time. I'm very interested in learning about the Israeli-Palestinian conflict. Would you have time to talk to me?"

We sat across from the Wailing Wall on a stone bench. One of his buddies, another soldier, joined us and we talked for about forty-five minutes. Pretending ignorance of the conflict limited my questions. The soldiers professed an absolute conviction that they were fighting a just war against an Arab enemy that wanted to push them into the sea. According to them, the enemy refused to accept and acknowledge the existence and rights of Jews in Israel and so they were justified in defending themselves. They resented the fact that some countries called them occupiers. We talked about the 1967 war, the Israeli invasion of Lebanon, and how suicide bombers were affecting their social lives.

. . .

For my fifty-ninth birthday Christa invited me to join her for lunch at her favorite restaurant, and it was not *Al Buraq*.

"Meet me in the Muslim Quarter, in front of the Austrian Hostel, at 11:30. That will give us plenty of time to get seated in the restaurant before the end of Prayer. It's Friday, and when the service is finished, everyone rushes to the restaurants in the Old City."

We turned right into the Christian Quarter at the same junction as before in the Old City, where the Muslim Quarter meets the

Jewish Quarter, and began a slow ascent up the long, wide steps of the sunlit *Souq Khan al-Zeit,* usually the busiest shopping street in the Old City. We entered a little one-room restaurant to the left of the steps. Within a few minutes, we were seated at a corner table.

"They make the very best hummus in all of Jerusalem here," Christa assured me.

She was right. We scooped up every last savory morsel of the chickpea and tahini dip with warm flat bread, washing it down with strong mint tea.

After lunch, Christa gave me a tour of the Christian quarter. As we were about to turn left at the top of the stairs to head toward the Church of the Holy Sepulcher, Christa stopped dead in her tracks. Inside a small prayer room, we saw two Israeli soldiers leaning lazily against the altar. A third, reloading his gun, had strewn the bullets across the altar. Christa marched to the door.

"How dare you! Get out this instant. You are forbidden to enter any Christian place of worship."

I was taken aback by her audacity. I wondered how the soldiers would respond. They mumbled something about not doing anything wrong. She crossed her arms and glared at them, standing her ground, until they walked away.

"Boy, it's a good thing you're a foreigner, Christa. Otherwise I'd probably have to spend the afternoon trying to get you out of jail."

She shrugged.

In order to reach the Church of the Holy Sepulcher we walked along a dimly-lit covered bazaar crowded with souvenir shops offering everything from statues of saints to rosaries to Bibles to copper and bronze replicas of ancient vases and jugs.

Along the rather narrow street, we encountered two soldiers escorting six Israeli school children.

"Is that really necessary?" I asked. "Can't those kids walk through the Christian Quarter by themselves?"

"Of course they can, but they won't. They're afraid. They've been taught that the Arabs want to kill them."

We finally arrived at Christianity's holiest site, the Church of the

Holy Sepulcher, built by Emperor Constantine's mother, Helen, in the 4th century on the site of a Roman pagan temple. 12th century French Crusaders – perhaps the same warriors who built the stronghold in Ramallah – constructed the building, which still stands today. Evidence of the Crusaders is everywhere in the Holy Land, but nowhere more so than at the Church of the Holy Sepulcher. As we crossed the threshold of the church, Christa pointed to the columns on either side of the massive wooden doors.

"Crusader markings," she said, showing me the crosses etched in the wood.

The sand-colored stone church is unkempt and run down, with a few broken windowpanes and sections of stone façade chipped away. Unlike many other buildings in Jerusalem which assume a rich honey glow at sunset – particularly lovely in the high desert light – this dull structure undergoes no such transformation. Once inside you are in a huge, cavernous stone edifice with multiple levels. From a distance – apparently coming from many levels below our feet – I heard a voice of such beauty and clarity it sounded as if it could have been an angel. When we descended to the lowest level of the church, I found the angel: perhaps from North Africa, a woman sat alone in an unlit chapel chanting her prayer to God.

The church contains the last five Stations of the Cross, the Chapel of Golgotha where Jesus was crucified, the Sepulcher where Jesus was buried and from which He arose, and the Chapel of Mary Magdalene, where the risen Christ first revealed himself. Three religious communities administer the church: the Greek Orthodox, the Roman Franciscans and the Armenian Orthodox. Like everything else in the Holy Land, they constantly dispute.

It is almost as if the Turkish Sultan, Abdul Majid, knew back in 1852 that arguments over the Holy Places were inevitable. To try to ease the tensions, he officially established the principle of Status Quo, which defines, regulates, and maintains without change the proprietary rights of the Holy Places, granted exclusively to the three major Christian rites: Greek, Armenian and Roman Catholic, making the Armenian church equal in importance to the Catholic and Greek Orthodox Churches despite its relatively small size. Under the principle of the Status Quo, the cadre of guards and caretakers called *Kawasses* are Muslim, a choice inspired by Abdul Majid's logic. Not being Christian, they can impartially administer any Holy Place, eliminating points of contention between the three major Christian rites.[28]

Eight centuries ago the key to the church was entrusted to two Muslim families, one named Nuseibeh, the other Joudeh. The ten-inch metal key is still safeguarded in the house of the Joudeh family. Every morning at dawn, Wajeeh Nuseibeh – who took over the job of door keeper from his father twenty years ago – picks up the key and opens the massive wooden church doors. Every night at 8:00 PM he returns to shut and lock them.[29]

The Armenian Quarter in the Old City is the smallest, even though Armenians claim to have had a presence in Jerusalem since the first century. They adopted Christianity as their official religion in 286 CE, and have been living in Jerusalem for the last 1,700 years. The Armenian Quarter was established in the 14th Century; approximately 2,500 Armenians live in Jerusalem and another 1,500 elsewhere in Israel.[30] The Armenians of Jerusalem are famous for their beautiful hand-made ceramics. The shop and factory are located on Nablus Road across from America's East Jerusalem Consulate.

· · ·

That evening we were invited to the house of Christa's friends, Fouad, a businessman and his wife, Hannah, a physician. Their

---

28 Frommer's "Jerusalem" (the Jewish Quarter), www.frommers.com/destinations/jerusalem/0088030405.html

29 Frommer's "Jerusalem" (the Western Wall), www.frommers.com/destinations/jerusalem/0088030406.html

30 Armenian Patriarchate of St. James, Jerusalem, www.armenian-patriarchate.org

son, Adam, was home for a visit. Also invited were lifelong friends B., his wife, Dorothy, and their daughter, who had just returned from a year abroad.

"I am sad for my country," Adam said. "I am an Israeli citizen. I have spent my whole life here. My Israel was built on the values of humanism and pluralism. Unfortunately, it is being lost. I am going to the States for the rest of my studies, and do not plan to return. Most of my friends are doing the same thing."

We spent about four hours discussing politics. B., 55, formerly an officer in the Israeli Army and now a prominent Jerusalem businessman, explained the many aspects of Israeli policy toward the Arabs. I told him of my experience crossing from Ramallah, how I had climbed a fence in plain view of Israeli soldiers.

He laughed.

"Haven't you figured it out yet? Israel is not worried about its security. We have one of the most powerful armies in the world. The Israeli government wants to humiliate the Palestinians. It wants to break their will to resist."

B.'s father had begun his political life as a right-winger but eventually changed his views.

"My father disagreed with Ben-Gurion's hawkish policies. He was convinced that there was a better way to get on with our Arab neighbors. If people like my father and Moshe Sharett had prevailed, instead of Ben-Gurion, we would have a different kind of Israel today. And we would be at peace with our neighbors."

B.'s father was a member of the Israeli delegation who went to Tunisia to negotiate with Arafat. After his expulsion from Beirut in 1982, Arafat had taken refuge there. In B's opinion Arafat was a decent man, committed to creating a Palestinian state for his people.

We went on to discuss the Christian Evangelical movement in the US and the adoption of Zionism as a core element of its religious doctrine. While B. agreed that it was a highly unusual alliance, he admitted the Israeli government was not particular about who supported it financially just as long as the money continued to pour in.

Since my visit to Israel/Palestine in 2002, it has become increasingly clear that Christian Zionists in the US have formed an alliance with pro-Israeli lobbies and neo-conservative elements in the Republican Party enabling them to put sufficient pressure on both the President and Congress to support Israel.[31]

Christian Zionism is a theology developed in the nineteenth century by Evangelical Protestants in England and the United States. It affirms that the election of Israel by God continues in the Jewish people today. This people must return to the Promised Land and re-found Israel as a nation. This return signifies the redemption of the world in the last days. It must be expressed by the rebuilding of the Jewish temple in Jerusalem – only possible by destroying the present Muslim edifices, the Dome of the Rock and the Al-Aqsa Mosque. Christ will then return and select a number of Jews, who will be converted to Christianity. Together with true-believing Christians – a category which excludes most Christians: Catholics, the Greek Orthodox and liberal Protestants – these believers will be raptured to heaven while God purges the earth of unbelievers in the battle of Armageddon. Then the believers will return to live in a redeemed earth.[32]

This is an astonishingly cynical bargain even by Middle Eastern standards.

. . .

Several people suggested I send my interview tapes home either by mail or DHL. Sylvaine was the most adamant.

"You will have spent two weeks here doing valuable work. Why risk having your things confiscated? I guarantee you the Israelis will go through everything in your luggage at Ben-Gurion Airport."

---

31 Ruether, Rosemary Radford. "Challenging Christian Zionism." *Cornerstone*, Issue 33, Summer 2004. www.sabeel.org/old/news/cstone33/Rosemary%20R%20Reuther-Christian%20Zionism.htm

32 *Ibid.*

Since this happened to her every time she left the country, I think she assumed everyone else was treated the same way.

But B.D. agreed with her. "Do not let them suspect for one minute that you were ever in the West Bank. You came to Israel to visit your Jewish friends. Name a few, and leave it at that."

After weighing the risks, I decided to send my interview tapes, my notes and the Palestinian textbooks I hauled back from Ramallah via DHL.

That evening I met Mary in the hotel lobby for the stiff drink we had promised ourselves before leaving for Tel Aviv. We had ordered our taxi for 9:30, giving us ample time to reach the airport before our midnight departure. Fortunately I had no trouble going through Israeli security. Shortly before midnight, we boarded our plane for the eleven-hour flight back to Toronto.

HOMECOMING

I STOOD FOR OVER AN HOUR TO CLEAR CUSTOMS AT THE Toronto airport. When I finally got through, I had to walk a quarter of a mile to stand in another line, this time to pass through American customs. I made a comment to Mary about the inconvenience of having to wait in such long lines.

She leaned toward me and whispered, "The Palestinians have to do this all the time."

I nodded. "Yes ... how could I have forgotten so quickly!"

After two additional security checks, we boarded a bus for another terminal. Mary was going to Chapel Hill, I to Minneapolis.

I had a window seat for my hour and a half flight. It was a perfect day to fly. Aside from the occasional puff of cloud, the sky was a brilliant deep blue. As we flew across miles of old-growth forests and great lakes with no sign of human life, I was struck by the sublime, almost spiritual peacefulness. I had just returned from a city supposed to be sacred, in a place called the Holy Land. I wondered how a place could be "holy" when millions of people lived under occupation. And what was "holy" about suicide bombers killing innocent Israelis, or a state using its military might to violate people's most basic human rights? Is a place "holy" where innocent civilians are blown to shreds by extremists, and where pregnant women are denied access by soldiers to a medical facility?

I took a much greater appreciation for many things in my life, particularly my freedom, away from this experience. Unlike the Palestinians, I can travel anywhere I please without a special permit. I will not be taken off a plane because I am Palestinian. When I return to my country, I am not asked humiliating questions. At the airport I can get into my car and drive on highways without soldiers stopping me at checkpoints. I have no reason to fear a suicide bomber or car bomb exploding nearby. I can cross from Minnesota into Wisconsin without having to show ID.

I have also taken many hours of insightful conversations with Israelis and Palestinians from this troubled land, the kinds of people who rarely, if ever, get heard in America. Theirs are the voices seeking a just peace which addresses the Palestinian right of self-determination. They are the ones mindful of Israeli concerns for security and regional integration. They are the ones who stand for equality, human rights, democracy and peaceful coexistence.

A conversation you will not find in the Interview section is the one I would have liked to have had with the Israeli Security agent at Ben-Gurion Airport. I would have asked him why he decided to detain one of my DHL boxes for ten days and, when he finally released it, found it perfectly acceptable to confiscate three of my interview tapes. I do not know what his reasoning was, why he chose those particular ones, what possible significance they could have had. Then again, he could have been sending me a message, reminding me of something I had seemingly forgotten: who is in charge!

INTERVIEWS

MANY OF THESE INTERVIEWS WERE TAPE-RECORDED DURING MY visit to Jerusalem and the West Bank in March, 2002. Conducted in English, they were transcribed verbatim except for minor editing for clarity.

This second edition includes interviews with Israelis from both the peace camp and the extreme right wing of Israel's Likud Party, as well as conversations with Israeli Arabs and Palestinians living in the West Bank, and presents a much more thorough discussion of the Israeli-Palestinian problem. The new interviews, indicated by an asterisk (*), were conducted by phone between October 22, and November 8, 2005.

I am grateful to those who agreed to be interviewed by phone. This could not have occurred without the help of an incredible network of friends both here and in Israel.

Elias: A history teacher teaching at a Catholic high school in Ramallah

Ronen: A Philosophy major at Hebrew University*

Sam B.: A businessman who lives in al-Bireh, a suburb of Ramallah

Eliyahu: An Israeli member of Jerusalem Peace Makers*

Huwaida: Co-founder of the International Solidarity Movement

Judy B.: A right-wing Israeli who opposed the Gaza withdrawal*

Hanna: An Israeli peace activist

Tali: A single Israeli woman

Maise: A documentary film producer who works for the Palestinian Authority

Seham: A Palestinian midwife living in the al-Amari refugee camp in Ramallah

Maha: An actress who works with Palestinian children

Um Walid: A "48 Arab" (a Palestinian who refused to leave in 1948)

Carmen: A Palestinian and recent graduate of BirZeit University

Amira: A Palestinian employed by Hebrew University

Yasmine: A Palestinian survivor of the Deir Yassin massacre

Omar: A Palestinian who teaches Arabic at Hebrew University

Shira: An Israeli professor at Hebrew University

Rabbi Cohen: A Chaplain, United States Air Force*

Two Israeli Soldiers patrolling the Western Wall

Three Palestinian Teenage Girls, ages 14 to 16

ELIAS

HISTORY TEACHER

Elias and I sat on a stone bench on the edge of the playground at a Ramallah high school. It was a perfect spring day, the cloudless sky intensely blue. I could hear a lively concert of birds on a nearby tree and as I leaned forward to listen, the sun warmed my neck and shoulders, and I momentarily forgot that I was in Ramallah where no one took notice of such days. Here, residents are routinely awakened to the nerve-shattering noise of F16s zigzagging across the morning sky, breaking the sound barrier, shattering glass somewhere nearby. After that wake-up call, they spend the rest of the day terrified of the ever-present Apache gunships, their metallic blades thrashing, their motors churning furiously overhead.

The anxiety is no less intense in Israel proper, where Israelis cautiously go about their daily business acutely aware that a crazed suicide bomber might board one of their buses or enter the restaurant where they are dining with friends. The bomber's intention is to kill as many Israelis as possible.

In this electric atmosphere forty-year-old Elias, a Greek Orthodox Christian history teacher, has to raise his two young girls. In spite of these hardships, I was struck by his compassion for others, even for the Israelis who had put him in jail for throwing stones at their tanks.

ELIAS: Last weekend, my brother got engaged. His fiancée lives in Beit Shahour, a village near Bethlehem which is not far from Ramallah. Because of the checkpoints, it took him five hours to get there. Absent the checkpoints it takes forty-five minutes.

The Israelis built a road for Israeli use only which leads to the settlement of Nokim, the home of one of Sharon's cabinet members. To do this, the Israeli government changed the route of the road from Ramallah to Jerusalem, and from Jerusalem through Bethlehem to Beit Shahour.

My mother and brothers could not accompany my brother to his engagement party. Only my father received the requisite travel permit to leave with him. While they were in Beit Shahour a Palestinian killed an Israeli man on the road. The Israeli Army closed the road and my brother and father were unable to return to Ramallah.

These closures harm all of us. Many people cannot get to their jobs. There is major unemployment. Even *Ha'aretz*, the Israeli newspaper, says that three-quarters of the people living in the occupied territories now live on two dollars a day or less. This is extreme poverty.

Do you know how many Palestinians live in the West Bank and Gaza? There are approximately 3.4 million.

The Israelis say that one Israeli was killed on the road from Beit Shahour to Bethlehem. Is that a reason to cut off the road for hundreds of thousands of people and forbid them to pass?

There is a road from Ramallah to Hebron. It is closed. It is the only road between these two cities. The Israelis cut it. No Palestinian is allowed to use the road.

The only way to access Hebron is through West Jerusalem and, of course, we are not allowed into West Jerusalem. We can't even leave Ramallah. We need a travel permit to leave and the Israelis won't issue us one.

CATHY: If you had to travel, where would you obtain your permit?

ELIAS: Before the *Intifada*, we went to the Palestinian civilian ministry in Ramallah. They then took our ID cards to the Israelis who checked our names against their computer list. If you weren't on their list, you were issued a travel permit.

Now, everything has changed. Even people who have never had a problem with the Israelis are denied a travel permit.

CATHY: Tell me about the checkpoints.

ELIAS: The checkpoints were put in place during the first *Intifada*. Before that, we could go anywhere, even into Israel proper.

By the end of the first *Intifada*, Israel had installed checkpoints throughout the entire West Bank. This includes al-Ram, the checkpoint between Jerusalem and Qalandya, the checkpoint at the entrance to Ramallah. This entire area used to be Arab neighborhoods before Israel confiscated the land and built thousands of Israeli settlements

CATHY: Why did Palestinians start the first *Intifada*?

ELIAS: The first *Intifada* began in 1987. When Israeli soldiers killed six Palestinian children, youngsters across the territories reacted. Eventually people of all ages started throwing stones at Israeli soldiers as a way of protesting Israeli violence and oppression. It became known, at least among us, as the Palestinian peoples' *Intifada*. The Israeli Army did not use as much force against Palestinian population centers as they do now. Instead, then Prime Minister Rabin's approach was to break the bones of stone-throwers.

Of course it is a shame that any Palestinian ever resorted to violence, but it was just as wrong for the Israeli Army to break arms. All these years later, here we are still fighting to end the occupation. Except now our circle is getting smaller and smaller and we are stuck in the middle with no exit. These small enclaves or cantons make the Palestinians feel like they live in a jail.

Easter is approaching. We won't be allowed to go to Bethlehem. At Christmas, we couldn't get to the Church of the Nativity. We are prisoners and Israel is our jailer.

On the Ramallah–Bir Zeit road, the Israelis stop people from reaching BirZeit University. They dig ditches in the road and throw up huge cement barriers, both of which make driving there impossible. University students have been stopped, beaten, humiliated and made to sit in the dirt for hours before being released.

Recently, they put two barricades in front of the university's two entrances, some two kilometers apart. Some days they close the road off completely isolating some thirty-five villages north of Ramallah.

What is the solution? What is our future? As a Palestinian, I don't see a future unless there is an end to the occupation. We want, like any people in the world, to live in peace, to live on and safeguard our land. We would like to raise our children in a safe environment.

We know America will never come to our aid. There is no political payoff, no oil. More than oil, there is the Jewish influence in America which turns a blind eye to the Zionists stealing our land for settlements. Sharon's ideas of expansionism are old Zionist ideas: this is Jewish land; transfer the Palestinians to other Arab countries.

CATHY: Could this happen?

ELIAS: Sharon will have to kill all of us first. The people will refuse to leave but it is becoming more and more difficult to live like this. Look at what is happening in Palestinian neighborhoods across East Jerusalem.

Remember when Clinton said, "Where there are Palestinians, there will be Palestinian sovereignty; wherever there are Jews, there will be Israeli sovereignty?"

Israeli settlers are trying to penetrate Palestinian houses to establish themselves in every neighborhood. The point is endless fragmentation of the land so it cannot be divided. Israel's ultimate goal is to minimize the Palestinian population in East Jerusalem.

In principle, land ownership by Palestinians is recognized in Jerusalem but Israel has declared fifty-five percent of the land open green space. This means that this land is off-limits to Palestinians. These spaces are then rezoned because Israel controls the zoning process. As a result, Palestinian land is expropriated for Israeli public purposes, meaning it will never be used for Palestinian public purposes.

According to Israeli law, this practice is legal. Of course it is really a way to control and disperse Palestinians. Look at the Israeli settlement in the West Bank. This was all land previously owned by Palestinians. Israel declared these areas open green spaces, calling them nature preserves. A short while later, the Israeli bulldozers turned up. The Arab homes were destroyed and the 300-year-old olive trees were uprooted, effectively erasing any evidence of a Palestinian presence. Massive settlement projects took their place.

Four hundred twenty Israeli settlers live in Hebron and 1,200 Israeli soldiers guard them. Some 120,000 Palestinians live in Hebron too but, for most of the week, they must live under strict military curfew. They are allowed to leave their homes for three hours every other day to get what they need to eat and survive. The settlers have even insisted that the traditional call to prayer from the minarets be discontinued because it disturbs their peace.

I asked my father one day why he left his village in 1948. "We left by force, my son. The Jews killed many, many people in Ladd, Haifa, Jaffa and Lydia. They told us to leave if we did not want to meet the same fate. They told us we could return once the fighting stopped. We believed them, and here we are fifty-three years later."

The refugee problem is a big problem. UN resolution 194 says refugees must be allowed to return. To where? To their towns and villages that don't exist anymore? Israel destroyed 450 of our villages and towns. Every single structure was torn down. Every tree dug up. Everything bulldozed to make the land flat.

Now Israel, "Look, there were never any Palestinians here."

In spite of these difficulties, we still hope that our children will be able to live in peace on this land some day.

If Sharon continues to declare war on us, this will not happen. Security without peace means no security for them or us. Peace for us means peace for them. Israel took seventy-eight percent of Palestinian land. Our future Palestinian state will only be twenty-two percent of the original Palestine.

This is unworkable, at least at the present time, because the West Bank and Gaza, our so-called 'future Palestinian state,' is full of Israeli settlers. We don't even have a road connecting the West Bank to Gaza or from the West Bank to Jordan. There are borders between the West Bank and Jordan, between Gaza and Egypt. We want an independent state. That doesn't mean closed borders between Palestinian villages. It doesn't mean having to get a travel permit if I want to go visit my sister in the next village.

If only Sharon would act like French President Charles De Gaulle, who gave the Algerians their independence, we could solve the problem very easily. For now we say to Sharon: "Go from our land to our past land, our '48 land, and leave us alone."

We Palestinians pray that Sharon will become a sensible and reasonable man and take his soldiers and settlers from the West Bank. If he did this, all our problems would be solved immediately.

CATHY: The Israeli government gives no indication of ending the occupation.

ELIAS: This is true about Sharon, but look at former Prime Minister Rabin. He was a military man like Ariel Sharon yet he signed the Oslo Accords with Yasser Arafat.

CATHY: Were the Oslo Accords favorable to the Palestinians?

ELIAS: No, not particularly, but it was a step in the right direction. It was a beginning, an interim agreement. If we look at history, there were many agreements. Some failed, some succeeded.

CATHY: Americans believe Israelis are victims of Palestinian terror. Do you think you have any allies in America?

ELIAS: Apparently not. Worse are the twenty-two Arab countries which do nothing to help us. They have the money and oil to threaten America yet they do nothing.

CATHY: You have some allies on the Israeli side. Even in America, many Jewish groups like Jewish Voice for Peace are working toward a just settlement. In 1982, when then-Defense Minister Sharon and his army bombed Beirut, 250,000 Israelis marched in the streets of Tel Aviv to protest their government's actions.

ELIAS: Let me tell you something. The war between Israel and the Palestinians is not with the Jewish people. We know them. We respect them. Our enemy is political Zionism.

Our problem is Ariel Sharon who is very pro-Zionist. Our problem is America's support of political Zionism. It is the Arab leaders' self-interests because they want to stay in power and since they rely on America to keep them in power they do America's bidding.

CATHY: What do you think of King Abdallah's peace proposal?

ELIAS: I don't accept it. There is no mention of right of return. By not mentioning this, the Abdallah plan gives Sharon a gift.

CATHY: Suppose someone said to you: "Yes, I agree the Oslo Accords are not favorable to the Palestinians but the Palestinian leadership says it a step in the right direction." Why can't Abdallah's plan be seen in the same light?

ELIAS: Arafat at Camp David [with Clinton and Barak] could have agreed to the unfair demands of Barak. He refused. Do you know why? Many things were never put on the table. Jerusalem was one; the right of return was the other.

Israel said they might let 1,000–2,000 Palestinians over the age of fifty come back. What kind of logic is that? It is like Israel demanding that we end the violence before it will agree to talk to us. Sharon says, "Palestinians must stop the violence before we accept to negotiate."

The Palestinians agree and stop the violence but still there is no talk. If we do what Sharon asks, he then asks for more. Even if we were to talk to the Israelis, what would we talk about? Would we talk about negotiations over the West Bank and Gaza? Isn't seventy-eight percent of Palestine enough for the Israelis?

We have given up all our old villages: Ramle, Haifa, Jaffa, all the beautiful coastline. The most important land they have taken from us, and they still want to come here and take our twenty-two percent and turn it into Israeli settlements?

CATHY: You're a history teacher. What do you teach your students about Palestinian history?

ELIAS: The Palestinians do not have their own history books. I cannot teach them anything about 1948. The Jordanians write our history because we lived on the West Bank which belonged, before

1967, to Jordan. Egypt writes the history of Gaza as it belonged to Egypt.

CATHY: You mean Palestinian children are growing up without any knowledge of their own history?

ELIAS: The only way they get their history is through oral tradition. Of course, they know their flag, certain national celebrations, but this is all taught orally. Oslo finally gave us permission to write our own history books. Next year, in certain classes, we will begin teaching it for the first time.

CATHY: In America, the media suggests that Palestinian mothers send their children to the checkpoints to be killed by Israeli soldiers.

ELIAS: This is ridiculous. If you have a child, you would never allow him to go to the checkpoints. I am a parent. I love my children very much. I don't allow them out of the house. They are terrified of the Israeli soldiers.

CATHY: Why don't Israelis come to the Territories to see for themselves what's happening? If they came and saw, I think they would demand a change in government policy.

ELIAS: Yes. If they came, they would see the misery, the villages in and around Jenin that don't even have enough food, the women who have to deliver babies at checkpoints.

But no Israeli is allowed to pass an Israeli checkpoint. They are told it is for their own protection. Journalists, when they come, have to walk around back roads, and sneak into our towns and villages. Why?

Because the Israeli government doesn't want the world to see what they are doing to us. Most of us don't have guns. We don't have Apache gunships. We don't fly F16s and bomb Israelis.

Last week, a man tried to take his wife to the hospital. She was about to deliver a baby. The Israelis killed her husband. I saw it on television. And she got hit with a bullet, too.

If the Israeli people saw the terrible conditions in the refugee camps in Gaza, they wouldn't believe their eyes. I met an Israeli woman one time during a teachers' convention. She told me, "We know nothing about your lives in the occupied territories."

Sharon, in my opinion, has a failed policy. His government is on the verge of falling so he has to appear to be doing something. We Palestinians are such easy targets for him. Israelis are asking, "Where is the security you promised?" According to Sharon, "Security equals peace." If he wants peace, we can make peace. Even King Hussein said, "Land for peace."

That is what we want. If Israel wants security, they have to make peace with the Palestinians. Stop Israeli violence, and we can talk. Let our children, on both sides, live in peace. My children were not born in Lebanon or Jordan, or Russia or Eastern Europe. They were born on this land. Let them live here in peace.

When there is an explosion in Tel Aviv, Israelis immediately blame all of us for one or two crazy people. They do not even know us, yet they blame us collectively.

CATHY: Do you condone the suicide bombings?

ELIAS: Of course I don't, but we are human beings and we want to act like human beings. You have to ask yourself why certain individuals would be willing to blow themselves up. I say individuals because there are not tens of hundreds or even thousands who commit these hideous acts.

The Israelis have driven them to such acts. These bombers have seen their land confiscated, their fathers killed, their mothers held up at checkpoints where they bleed to death. They go berserk. They think they have no other recourse. If Israel stopped treating us like terrorists, stopped killing us, and stealing our land, the Israeli people would never see a suicide bomber.

There is a saying in Palestine now, "Squeeze a cat into a corner and it will become a lion." Let me remind you of one very important thing. Before Ariel Sharon came to power, there had only been a dozen suicide bombings inside Israel. When he became Prime Minister, and implemented his extremist policies in the West Bank and Gaza, suicide bombers began to strike in greater numbers.

CATHY: In America, Jewish peace groups are asking the Palestinians to practice nonviolent resistance to the Israeli occupation. How do you respond to that?

ELIAS: I understand what they are saying, and I think that is a reasonable demand. However, here in Palestine, it is not so easy to lie down in front of an Israeli tank. In practice, it is very difficult.

Back in '48, Begin and Shamir used terrorist attacks to scare Palestinians out of their towns and villages. In Iraq, the Israelis put bombs in the synagogues so Jews would flee. They did the same thing in Beirut in '82. If we review history, and looked at what the Zionists did to the Palestinians, maybe people would blame the Palestinians less for their resistance. The way to stop the violence is to take away the reason for the violence. End the occupation.

Now in March, 2002, the whole world is telling Ariel Sharon to let Yasser Arafat leave Ramallah to attend the Arab Summit in Beirut. Sharon said he could go if he arrested the men who assassinated the Israeli minister. He arrested the men responsible yet Sharon did not let him leave. Arafat cannot go to the corner to buy a newspaper. How is he supposed to do all the things Sharon asks of him?

We do not like to kill innocent people but Sharon must see that suicide bombers are a direct result of his harsh policies against the Palestinian people.

CATHY: You're essentially condoning an eye for an eye. Is it possible to change this way of thinking?

ELIAS: For twenty-four days we were peaceful. We didn't attack any Israelis. There was no violence. *Hamas* and Islamic Jihad sent no suicide bombers.

What did Sharon do? He assassinated an important Palestinian leader to provoke a response from our extremist groups. Sadly, it worked, and we are still paying the consequences of an eye for an eye.

Let me tell you something very important about your nonviolent approach. At the beginning of the current *Intifada*, there was a group of prominent Palestinians who proposed nonviolence to Israeli aggression. Sharon had them physically expelled from the country.

Sharon could not have carried out his policies if we had all placed our bodies in the streets in front of tanks. If we had acted nonviolently, Sharon would not have had any terrorists to attack. So, of course, he had to get rid of the voices calling for nonviolent resistance.

Sharon said, "I demand seven days of peace before I will negotiate with Arafat." We gave him twenty-four days of peace.

CATHY: Does Sharon have a long-term strategy to end the conflict?

ELIAS: No, because he has no intention of negotiating with the Palestinians. His plan is to constantly stir up the radical movements because he knows he can count on them to retaliate. As long as they retaliate, he has his excuse to go after the terrorists.

CATHY: Does his government support his policies?

ELIAS: Of course. Haven't you heard his ministers speak out? Lieberman wants all Palestinians transferred to Jordan. Some of the other ministers claim he is being too tolerant. Sharon has the full backing of his government. If he were to make any kind of compromise, one that could be construed as being lenient on Arafat, his government would fall.

CATHY: Would Netanyahu replace Sharon if he fell? If so, will his policies be worse?

ELIAS: How do you define worse?

Look, we aren't afraid of Sharon or Netanyahu, or any other

Israeli government official. This is our land we are fighting for. This gives us courage and a degree of power that Sharon cannot eliminate.

And, as long as we are suffering, the Israelis are suffering, too.

What is the future? We don't know. Earlier you asked me about the Abdallah agreement. Sharon answered Abdallah's call for peace and recognition by going into the Palestinian camps and destroying them. Sharon doesn't care what anyone says. He doesn't need them. He is strong, and he knows he has President Bush's blessing.

Look, America can stop the violence in the Middle East with three words, end the occupation.

RONEN

PHILOSOPHY MAJOR AT HEBREW UNIVERSITY

Ronen Shoval is a 25-year-old Philosophy major at Hebrew University. He resides in a wealthy Tel Aviv neighborhood. He identifies himself as a right-wing Zionist with a very strong ideology. On his mother's side he is a seventh generation Israeli. His father made aliya *from Argentina.*

RONEN: Do you know what *aliya* means?

CATHY: No, explain it.

RONEN: First, let me say that *aliya* has a special meaning for Jews. Second, it is not to be confused with immigration which is a very ordinary event. Other people immigrate from place to place but the Jewish people make *aliya* to *Eretz Yisrael*. *Aliya* means to go to a higher place. In Israel, we say, "up to Jerusalem," or "up to the Western Wall."

CATHY: Did you support Ariel Sharon's Gaza withdrawal?

RONEN: I am the spokesperson for the Students in Orange Organization. We were opposed to the Gaza withdrawal. I personally organized 4,000 students from forty-six Israeli campuses to protest the withdrawal. We demonstrated in front of Tel Aviv University. We carried out a hunger strike which lasted twelve days. Our President [Moshe Katsav] personally came and asked us to end the strike because it was becoming dangerous for our health.

CATHY: Did he commend you for what you were doing or scold you?

RONEN: In our private conversations he was very sympathetic to our cause. However, publicly he was obliged to support his Prime Minister.

CATHY: What was the reaction of the Israeli public to the Gaza withdrawal?

RONEN: Fifty percent supported the withdrawal; fifty percent were against it.

To those who supported the withdrawal, I have some advice. Francis Fukiyama, a Harvard professor who wrote *The End of History*, claims we are ushering in the rise of democratic capitalism at the expense of our ideologies. He is wrong and those who supported withdrawal were wrong.

You Americans are a cautious people. You don't have strong ideologies. Your president told you he was going to war with Iraq. You went along with his plan even though his decisions to go to war were not based on any specific ideology. Those of us who opposed the Gaza withdrawal have a strong ideology and we will do whatever is necessary to preserve it.

Let me explain.

The ideology of the Palestinians exists only since the PLO was created in '64. Yet, they claim Palestine belongs to them and not to the Jews. By this they imply that the Jews don't have a legitimate right to be in Israel when in fact the Palestinians never exercised national sovereignty in the country in which they lived.

I have every right to be in Israel. I was born here. My people were thrown out by the Romans and exiled so my people have the right to return to Israel. Everywhere you go in Israel you will find Jewish roots. Dig anywhere and you will find them. Compare this long history to that of the Palestinians who were nothing until '64. They didn't even have a national identity.

Do you know who Golda Meir was?

CATHY: She was Prime Minister of Israel in the '60s.

RONEN: Yes, and she was born in Israel.

CATHY: Actually, she was born in Russia then emigrated to Milwaukee, Wisconsin.

RONEN: That's not important. Do you know what she said about the Palestinians?

CATHY: No.

RONEN: She said, "There is no such thing as Palestinians. They never existed as a nationality. Before 1948, we were the Palestinians."

> [**Authors Note**: Golda Meir went on to say: "The British chose to call the land they mandated Palestine and the Arabs picked it up as their nation's supposed ancient name though they couldn't even pronounce it correctly and turned it into *Falastin*, a fictional entity."[33]]

CATHY: What will happen now that the Gaza withdrawal is completed?

RONEN: Israel will continue to struggle. The Palestinians do not want peace. Nothing has changed since Arafat refused Barak's offer at Camp David.

CATHY: What should Israel do?

RONEN: Give the Palestinians two options: a monetary incentive to move to Jordan, Lebanon or Syria; or, if they choose to stay, they can continue to reside, as they currently do, in their enclaves. They can vote for their local officials but they will otherwise have no other rights. Their status will be similar to that of students who go to the US on student visas. They can attend school but otherwise have no rights.

CATHY: I don't see this as a viable solution.

RONEN: Look, the problem is really not so serious. Let me explain. In America you just went through two hurricanes. Several cities were destroyed but those who lost their homes can count on government assistance to rebuild them. If help doesn't come you can blame the government. Here in Israel, we count on no one. We trust no one. Eisenhower refused to bomb the Nazi concentration camps; Britain wouldn't either. We trust only ourselves to fight to have a better life.

The only other option would be to run and I refuse to do that.

---

33   Honig, Sarah. *The Jerusalem Post*, November 25, 1995.

There is every reason to suppose we have at least fifty more years of fighting ahead of us.

CATHY: You're only twenty-five years old. Isn't there another way?

RONEN: I've already suggested what those Palestinians who wish to remain here can do. Otherwise, the Palestinian problem, as people call it, is really not a problem. Lebanon, Syria and Jordan can give them all citizenship and the question of refugees and rights will resolve itself. Yes, we Israelis can live with those Palestinians who wish to remain if they let us live in security and not in fear of our lives.

CATHY: Can we talk about Ariel Sharon's Security Wall?

RONEN: First of all, it is not a wall. It is a fence and only four percent has been completed thus far.

Look, if Israel is making an occupation, as people accuse us of doing, and if certain Palestinians want to kill themselves then let them go into their own town squares and ignite themselves to prove they are willing to do anything to get their own state. Just don't go into Israeli cities and kill innocent people. If they can't do that, then a wall is absolutely necessary.

CATHY: Are you an optimist or a pessimist, Ronen?

RONEN: In the Middle East a pessimist is an optimist with experience.

SAM B.

BUSINESSMAN AND WRITER

Sam B. is an American-born Palestinian who moved to Ramallah from America in 1995 to start his own business. He is co-author of Home Land: Oral Histories of Palestine and Palestinians, *and a frequent contributor to* Counter Punch, *an online newsletter. One of his articles appeared in Rabbi Michael Lerner's November/December, 2002, issue of* Tikkun.

CATHY: Do Israelis know what is going on in the occupied territories?

SAM: Most of them have no knowledge of the occupation, particularly if they have not served in the army in either the West Bank or Gaza.

On the whole, they are not even engaged in the political debate at large. Yes, they see checkpoints on the news. They hear about Israeli security and think this is a good thing. They want to believe that these checkpoints protect them, that they aid Israel's security in general.

This is absurd. Any Israeli can at least walk to a checkpoint. They will not be allowed through, but they can stand on the Israeli side and observe the way Palestinians are treated at checkpoints.

Better still, they can observe the number of people who walk around the checkpoints over back roads. You do not have to be a genius to know that these checkpoints have nothing to do with Israeli security. It is a façade, and the Israeli society has bought into it.

CATHY: It is an easy enough thing to believe, especially if you've been taught that the Palestinian is a bad person. Given that environment, given America's inability to do anything constructive, how will things ever change?

SAM: Once the Israeli and American governments agree to end the occupation, to have open borders, and freedom on both sides,

I think there will be more protection for both Israelis and Palestinians. There will be accountability on both sides.

Now, the Israeli government hides under the mantle of occupation and does what it wants. If you end the occupation, you make everyone responsible for maintaining law and order. If there is freedom on both sides, and if there is any negative action taken on either side, it can be brought under control. Everyone will be accountable for keeping the peace. There will be no scapegoats.

Over the last seven years, the Palestinian Authority in Ramallah has not been able to accomplish much. They have not been given the wherewithal to address problems, or take initiatives to solve them. They are completely and totally dependent on the Israelis for everything they do.

Of course, these are things we desperately need to address. What ends up happening is that everyone blames the occupation for everything that does not work. A stalemate results, and we are unable to move forward. In reality, we are not permitted to inch forward. We are in a stalemate. This is where Israel wants to keep us.

CATHY: How has the *Intifada* affected Israel?

SAM: It has been a disaster for the Israeli economy. It is crippling the Israeli society but, of course, it is doing the same thing to ours.

The Israeli government owes us half a billion dollars for taxes collected on goods imported into the PA from Israel. Where is that money?

CATHY: Was Oslo bad for the Palestinians?

SAM: Yes, America's so-called "peace initiative" did only one thing. It moved the stick one notch lower. Once you agree to lower the notch, the stick eventually breaks.

CATHY: According to Rabbi Michael Lerner of *Tikkun*, Arafat did everything he was asked to do in the Oslo Accords. Lerner even said that Arafat did a better job of guaranteeing security than Israel, and that if Israel claimed any success, it was all due to Arafat's tight control over his people. Do you agree?

SAM: Let me get back to Oslo for a minute, and then I'll address the security issue.

Today in the paper, there was an excellent article which said that Oslo was wrong. Oslo equipped the Palestinians with very minor automatic weapons. However, for nine years those weapons were not used. What Oslo gave the Palestinians was the moral and political justification to use those weapons. When you create that kind of groundwork, a broomstick or a stone becomes a weapon. And that is what is happening. Do not blame it on the guns. Blame it on the political and military environment Israel created by allowing the Palestinians to revolt.

This is not to say that I agree with suicide bombers and the killing of innocent civilians, but for eighteen months the Palestinians have seen their people die in the hundreds. How do you expect them to keep watching without reacting? No matter how much Arafat guarantees Israel's security.

And yes, I agree with Rabbi Lerner. No matter how much the CIA was involved in training Arafat's men in security enforcement, the violence will not stop until Israeli violence stops.

CATHY: Certain journalists in America say that the Palestinians, with their suicide bombers, are losing support for their cause. How do you respond?

SAM: I am aware of what the American press is saying. I know, too, that people are expecting us to react nonviolently to Israeli aggression. It is not going to happen. As long as there are Apache gunships over our cities every day, terrorizing our people, shooting at unarmed civilians in the refugee camps, assassinating alleged terrorists, it is not going to happen.

I personally think that the Palestinian-Israeli conflict has gone beyond all reasonableness. Public opinion was on our side in the first *Intifada*. In fact, when was public opinion not on our side, except perhaps in America?

The international mechanisms that influence public opinion act when there is a crisis. Yet, it has never obliged a leader to take action to end the Israeli occupation. Why? Because the structure of the American veto power [in the UN], and its support for Israel, has stopped any action. If the Palestinians are in a struggle for public opinion, that's a nice way of saying, 'Eliminate yourselves over the years while you struggle in your right to statehood.' We do not want a last martyr who proclaims that he was right. We are a people who just want to live free of Israeli occupation.

Look at the American Indians. They had a great cause, but where do they live today? On reservations, in miserable conditions, on land no one else wants. We do not want to end up like them.

On the issue of public opinion, America has failed miserably. I thought when Secretary of State Powell spoke in Kentucky about a new policy recently that things would change. Regardless of everything he glossed over: the refugee problem, the water issue, he knew that the occupation had to end. What he did not do was issue a policy statement on the need to end the occupation.

CATHY: Why did the Americans not follow through on this?

SAM: That is a good question. Personally, I think it is because we have a non-elected American president who cannot afford to alienate AIPAC (American-Israeli Political Action Committee), the most influential pro-Israeli lobby in America, or his Christian fundamentalist constituents. Do not forget that Bush's father lost an election when he criticized Israel and threatened to withhold financial aid if it didn't curtail settlement activity. George W. is looking for a second term, and will not do anything to jeopardize his chances. American politics are historically short-term politics.

Things could have changed after 9/11, particularly since Sharon had already declared Oslo dead. That was a unique opportunity for Bush, contrary to any other American president, to see in a breakdown the potential for a positive political upward swing. He had the moral power after 9/11 to do whatever he wanted.

One of those endeavors could have been to support the end of Israeli occupation, and give the Palestinians their own state. He blew away a wonderful opportunity to end the crisis. Instead, he was totally preoccupied with Afghanistan and his war on terror.

CATHY: With Bush's war on terrorism, some pundits in America argue that he has given the green light to Sharon to continue his war against the Palestinians. Do you agree?

SAM: Of course, for all the reasons I have already stated. In my opinion, the Palestinians have also failed in their resistance movement against the Israelis. They were always looking for the Americans to come in and save them. At the end of the day, it is up to us to convince our neighbors that there is something worth living together for. We desperately need to do this. For thirty-five years, not to mention since '48, the Palestinian struggle has been going on.

Our inability to speak in Hebrew to the Israeli public, our inability to get media coverage in Hebrew-language newspapers, is hindering our ability to reach out to the Israeli people, to talk directly with them, so that everything we say is not distorted by Israeli government officials. Only when we decide to sit down together, to speak the same language, can we begin to make progress toward peace.

CATHY: Do you see any hint of that happening?

SAM: Yes, I do. I think we are moving forward slowly. However, it is just the beginning.

I think we are finally realizing that it is not enough to write an opinion peace for the *New York Times*. We can no longer wait for the white horse to ride in and save us. We must begin to speak directly to the Israeli people if we are ever going to get to the finish line together.

CATHY: Many Israelis blame the Palestinians for helping to get Sharon elected. How do you respond to this?

SAM: They are wrong. Their public opinion is not based on strategic analysis; it is based on emotions. I blame the Israeli political establishment for not seeing the need to end the occupation. They said that there were no sacred dates in the Oslo Accord. There were, and the Israeli government should have been more honest.

According to the Oslo Agreement, the Israelis should have already been out of the West Bank and Gaza, effectively ending thirty-five years of occupation.

CATHY: Does Israeli intransigence have anything to do with the Zionist dream of conquering all of Judea and Samaria for Israel?

SAM: Personally, I don't think, in 2002, that mainstream Israelis view themselves as pioneers for the State of Israel. Rather, they see themselves as working in an Israeli community.

Sharon, when asked by a reporter shortly after his election if he had changed his political views since '82, responded, "I have not changed anything except for one thing. I used to say Jordan is Palestine. Now I do not say that."

If this is indeed his agenda, 'a land without people for a people without land,' it will be one of extreme right-wing, which means that nothing will change. So far, Sharon has achieved nothing. His is a bankrupt government. Under these conditions, he is more likely to provoke a major event to try to get out of this crisis. He is a warrior, not a statesman. He knows nothing but how to wage war. Members of his Cabinet use words like 'transfer,' 'liquidation,' 'resettlement.'

What does this mean?

If a political route were to be acknowledged, like the Abdallah peace plan, a political route might be followed.

Recently, President Hosni Mubarak of Egypt tried to create another political route by requesting an emergency summit of the Arab League to discuss recognition of Israel and international borders. The response from Sharon and Netanyahu was that establishing international borders would endanger the State of Israel. Netanyahu was even more extreme. He said that Saudi Arabia has no moral high ground on anything because they support terrorism.

The Israeli government does not have a reason, an incentive, for existing in a peaceful environment. Something has to bring the Israelis to their knees.

CATHY: What happens next?

SAM: I see the current situation lasting another year or two. I think the Israelis need to elect a new leader. I do not know who that will be. However, there has to be a political platform.

The Americans cannot keep repeating that there are two parties, the occupier and the occupied. The bank robber and the bank employee cannot sit down at a table and solve their problems. There is an urgent need for an external third party.

America is far from being the neutral third party. However, given that they are the only superpower in the world, they should be able to neutralize themselves to play an active, more evenhanded role. I do not see anyone in the Bush Administration willing to do that.

CATHY: What must the Palestinians do?

SAM: I do not think the Palestinians need to do anything. Everything has been put on the table. When talks begin again, the Palestinian leadership can start talking about some of the Palestinian pillars of the struggle in a more flexible manner, whether it be refugees or transfer of land to make an equation that works best for Israeli security.

If the Palestinians should find themselves in a situation where there is a real chance for a breakthrough, I am certain the Palestinians will show flexibility in every single pillar of their struggle.

So far, there has not been any political thrust forward. There is not much more that America or Israel can ask of them, other than perhaps relieving themselves of being Palestinian!

No matter how it is discussed, the focal point will have to be how to end the occupation. That is the best security buffer that Israel could ever hope to have. Building walls and barbed wire does not work. We are past the Berlin Wall days. Security comes with a peaceful relationship. Perhaps we will never want to kiss each other every morning, but we need to have normal relations with each other. Otherwise, peace will not work.

There are many countries in the world that hate each other, but they do not shoot one another on their respective borders every day. The longer this conflict drags on, the longer it will take us to have normal relations. If occupation ended tomorrow, we could have normal relations the next day.

CATHY: With George W. Bush in the White House is this likely to happen?

SAM: I do not think an individual creates government policy. The institution is only able to succeed in its policy agenda if it does not jeopardize the electability of the president-at-hand. If you have a strong president, the establishment that creates policy moves forward without fear that their policies might jeopardize the president.

When you have a president who is on the verge of non-election, then any policy outside the lobby groups becomes a policy that has the potential to affect an election next time around.

I think that is exactly where we are today. There are so many pressures on President Bush: the military establishment, Israel and AIPAC, the Christian fundamentalists. The best thing he can do for himself is to do nothing. Wave the flags of patriotism, especially after 9/11, declare a war on terrorism, and hope that rides him all the way to the next election. Anything else just sets him up for an election loss next time around.

This is the opposite of Sharon, who was elected by a landslide.

As a result, he can throw F16s at Nablus without fear because (1) he doesn't want to be reelected. He is at the end of his political career; and (2) the establishment in Israel that creates policy did not go out of its way to create new policy when Sharon started bombing cities, going into refugee camps and demolishing homes.

None of these actions directly affects Sharon, who had a solid victory. However, if Israel keeps losing its citizens, his actions may ultimately affect him politically. I really feel that once you are well-established in a political position as an individual, you are free to do many things.

In American political short-term thinking, your only goal is the next election.

CATHY: According to Israel Shahak, it is the military establishment in any given government that determines long-term policy, not elected officials. Do you agree?

SAM: I agree with what he says. This is certainly what sets leaders apart. There are those who follow on the charted path. Then there are real leaders who actually change the course of history. Arafat, as bad as he may be as a modern leader, changed the path of the entire Palestinian movement at Oslo. He could have just fallen into the same old traditional role, but he did not.

CATHY: Arafat essentially gave away the house at Oslo. Why do the Palestinians stand behind him?

SAM: It is very complicated, internal politics. If you pressed anyone in the PA, pre-*Intifada*, you would hear that this was an interim agreement with some tradeoffs. At the end of the day, this is what is going to create a future for the Palestinian people, because it will end the occupation.

Camp David broke down because no matter what was in the details of the political discussion, there was a fine print that said 'this ends the conflict.' I don't think that Arafat, who had already given everything he could possibly give, was willing to sign-off on a statement that said, 'this ends the conflict,' unless all the pieces had been worked out.

Was he supposed to forget the refugees altogether?

How could Barak and Clinton have expected Arafat to sign off on that statement?

Arafat may as well have shot himself in the head if he had signed that document. This is the kind of thing that sets leaders apart. Rabin was also a leader, even though he promoted breaking Palestinian bones in the first *Intifada*. He took his country on a different path. It was a clash with the military internally, but that was what set him apart. Being elected is not being a leader; it is simply being a politician.

CATHY: Are any of our world leaders today willing to walk a different path?

SAM: It's an international problem and I don't have an answer.

CATHY: Is the current American administration aware of what is happening in Israel?

SAM: Of course, Arafat opened his doors to the CIA. It came in and looked at everything, yet, knowing what it knew, the American administration refused to reflect that knowledge in current policy decisions, for all the reasons we have already discussed.

ELIYAHU

MEMBER OF JERUSALEM PEACE MAKERS

Eliyahu is a 36-year-old Israeli. I spoke with him by phone from his home in Jerusalem in early October, 2005, shortly after the successful Gaza withdrawal.

CATHY: What are your views on the Gaza pullout?

ELIYAHU: I am relieved that it all went so smoothly.

CATHY: Was the pullout carried out for demographic reasons?

ELIYAHU: That may have been one of Prime Minister Sharon's considerations but the moral cost of occupying 1.4 million Palestinians outweighed, in my opinion, all other considerations.

CATHY: There has been a dramatic reduction in suicide bombings. Tourism is on the rise and life appears to have returned to normal for the Israelis. Does this give rise to hope for a more stable and secure future?

ELIYAHU: The Israeli people have consistently shown a resiliency against all odds. Yes, we are cautiously hopeful. In fact, I would venture to say that approximately sixty to seventy percent of Israelis are optimistic. And there are many positive things happening. Have you ever heard of *Sulha*?

CATHY: No

ELIYAHU: Its full name is the *Sulha* Peace Project and in July of this year over 4,000 Israelis and Palestinians met in a park not far from Tel Aviv for three days of peacemaking.

Sulha in Arabic means reconciliation. The Hebrew word *Slicha* means the same thing. The theme of this project was forgiveness between people. The park was divided into different areas which included the Tent of Hagar and Sarah, the Tent of Adam and Eve, the Tent of the Children of the Prophets, the children's camp (600 children participated), the food tent, the camping area and the main stage. For three days everywhere you walked around the grounds people milled about, walking, sitting, eating, sleeping and talking in Hebrew, Arabic and English, or some combination thereof. Even some Jordanians attended the event.

Between Israelis and Palestinians there is a strong grassroots effort toward reconciliation. For Rosh Hashanah and Ramadan (October 3rd and 4th) this year, Israelis and Palestinians met inside the New Gate of the Old City to honor each others' religious traditions.

In Nazareth, the *Imams* (Muslim clergy) have begun teaching tolerant Islam and are encouraging inter-faith dialogues. Both peoples are tired of this conflict. The Palestinians are fed up with *Hamas* and Islamic Jihad. Because the Palestinian leadership is weak, there is growing frustration within the Palestinian community. This will not disappear until a strong leadership emerges, one that will confront and disarm the radicals.

I believe the best way to confront the extremists like *Hamas* is to invite them into the political process. If *Hamas* wants to participate in the upcoming Palestinian elections, something they say they want, then putting them on the ballot will force them to become more moderate. If they decide to return to violence they will lose any support they may have garnered with the people.

One thing I will say about *Hamas* is that they are not corrupt like the Palestinian Authority. Their organization is transparent. They also have a huge social network that provides medical clinics, schools, food and shelter for hundreds of thousands of needy Palestinians. If we Israelis are not careful, we may also have to confront a growing Islamic political movement within Israeli Arab society. They are beginning to talk about self-reliance. They complain of the inequality in funding education, sewage and housing.

There is a move toward radical Islam within the Israeli Arab population. The numbers are still small but it is growing in influence. I mentioned the *Imam* in Nazareth who was taking a stand against radical Islam and that is a hopeful sign. However, this trend toward radical Islam is a concern.

Some members of the Likud government recognize this and argue that the Sharon government needs to address the inequalities and complaints of its Arab citizens. In so doing, they argue, the Israeli Arabs will become more loyal to the State of Israel and less likely to turn to radical Islam.

CATHY: Do Israeli Arabs have the same rights as Israelis?

ELIYAHU: Both Israeli Arabs and Palestinians in Israel have more rights than they do in any Arab country. They have freedom to practice their religion; they can work. Israeli Arabs can circulate within Israel proper. They can attend any university. Look at the Palestinians in Lebanon. Only in 2005 did the Lebanese government finally agree to let them work outside their camps.

CATHY: Do all Likud Party members feel the need to address Israeli Arab complaints?

ELIYAHU: The members from places like Haifa and Tel Aviv are pretty reasonable when it comes to the Palestinian question. It is the religious and right-wing Israelis from Jerusalem in particular who want to transfer all Palestinians out of Israel.

These people are fanatics and they are a huge problem for Israel.

As someone who works toward reconciliation I constantly ask myself, how do we engage those fanatic voices from both sides in dialogue without giving them legitimacy while not marginalizing them, in which case they will turn to violence?

It is a seemingly impossible task but we must find language within the world of Islam and Judaism that they understand so as to engage them in conversation. This can be accomplished in a number of ways: honoring their devotion to their religion, preparing Ramadan meals together, applauding their passion for the land while at the same time showing that the other has the same passion. In other words, creating a safe space where diverging ideologies can come together and be acknowledged.

CATHY: What will happen in Gaza if the Palestinian Authority cannot establish calm?

ELIYAHU: That is a good question and a worrisome one. Do you know who Nasser Youssef is?

CATHY: I've never heard of him.

ELIYAHU: He is currently the PA Interior Minister but at the time of the Gaza pullout he was head of the PA security forces in Gaza. An Israeli journalist by the name of Yossi Halevi from *The Jerusalem Post* met with him in Gaza. During their conversation Yossi asked Nasser what his vision was of relations between a Jewish state and a Palestinian one after a peace agreement was signed.

Yossi suggested the following scenario: Israel withdraws to the '67 borders, uproots the settlements and redefines Jerusalem. What happens then? Nasser said that once the refugees returned and gravitated to those areas in Israel where they once lived we would then see no need for an artificial border between Israel and Palestine. The two states would then merge into one.

Yossi at this point asked if the negotiations weren't over a two-state solution. Nasser agreed but said that was only an interim step.

This kind of talk is worrisome to many of us. An Israeli moderate recognizes the conflict as a struggle between two legitimate national narratives. It would appear that a Palestinian moderate, like Nasser, has another agenda. Yes, he opposes the destruction of Israel through terror and war but he advocates the disappearance of Israel through a one-state solution.

I don't believe any Israeli would accept that.

[**Authors Note**: Yossi Klein Halevi's article "Letter to Palestinians" appeared in *The Jerusalem Post*, September 28, 2005.]

HUWAIDA ARRAF

CO-FOUNDER OF THE INTERNATIONAL SOLIDARITY MOVEMENT

Huwaida Arraf is co-founder of the International Solidarity Movement. Huwaida is joined in her work by her husband, Adam Shapiro, who directed the Seeds of Peace program in Jerusalem for a number of years. ISM is an organization of international volunteers committed to nonviolent resistance to Israeli occupation and aggression.

I interviewed this American-born Palestinian in her apartment next to the Ramallah Hospital in early March, 2002. Several members of the Christian Peacemaker Team were staying with her at the time and I was able to interview them as well.

HUWAIDA: Last evening Apache gunships attacked the al-Amari refugee camp here in Ramallah. Israeli troops entered the camp and rounded up all males between the ages of sixteen to sixty. The prisoners were forced to remove their shirts and trousers before being blindfolded, handcuffed and led away.

When we got to the camp the next morning, the refugees were still in a state of panic. The Apache gunships, still hovering overhead, only added to the tension. The women were panicked. One ran up to me, pleading. "Help us please, can you tell us where our men are?"

Another said, "They took my husband and son, I don't know what to do."

A boy, maybe 15, told me the soldiers demanded that all men report to the school. "They forced us to strip down to our underwear," he said. "After questioning, we were led into the school yard, where we remained with our hands tied above our heads. I was there from 11 AM to 7 PM. I started to cry. I felt like I was going to pass out. I was cold and hungry. I pleaded with the soldiers earlier in the day, telling them I was just a child. It wasn't until midnight, when I broke down crying again, that they let me go home. I don't know where they took the others."

A few days ago, Israeli troops invaded the Balata refugee camp, in Nablus, too, where 22,000 refugees live in squalid conditions. The same kind of assault also occurred in the Jenin refugee camp. It was precisely because of this pattern of behavior that we were afraid for the al-Amari refugees. In circumstances such as these, it is our goal to place internationals inside these camps to act as human shields against the Israeli Army.

CATHY: How many foreigners did you actually place inside each camp?

HUWAIDA: Fifteen, if possible. Their presence is primarily to put pressure on the Israelis not to attack again. Their presence is also intended to attract media attention. This sometimes acts as a deterrent to Israeli aggression.

We are essentially telling the Israelis, "We'll be watching what you do, and if you do strike, it will get noticed by the international community." If the Israelis were to kill an American citizen, it would cause a stir in the international community. Obviously, we don't want anyone killed, but we do want the Israelis to know that we are watching what they do. It also serves as an incentive to the international community to pay a little more attention to the fact that these are civilian areas being attacked.

CATHY: Who are the internationals?

HUWAIDA: We have a lot of Americans here right now, but they come from many countries.

CATHY: Are they here representing a specific organization in the States?

HUWAIDA: No, they are here for many different reasons, often working for human rights organizations. Some are here on vacation, and contact us when they arrive to offer their assistance. A lot of the people who are active, who do take a stand, are fed up with their own government's inaction and biased policies. They want their presence to show that Americans care, regardless of what their government does.

Yesterday, myself and four other Americans headed up to the Balata refugee camp near Nablus, where Israeli troops were again poised to attack. The Israelis claimed that they were after terrorists. Before I left Ramallah, I sent out an alert for more internationals to show up at the camp, to be able to report on what was happening, to serve as eyewitnesses to any human rights abuses that might occur once the Israelis entered the camp.

Nablus is only forty kilometers north of Ramallah. With the Israeli checkpoints, it took us three hours to get there even with our foreign passports. I generally don't show my American passport to bypass the long line of Palestinians waiting to cross at a checkpoint, but yesterday we felt it was urgent we reached Nablus before dark. Without our foreign passports yesterday, our trip would have taken anywhere from five to nine hours.

When we arrived in the Balata refugee camp, people were clearing away debris and rubble from the shelling and tank fire the previous day. We felt, at this point, that the most helpful thing we could do was to show our solidarity and moral support, and more than anything, record their stories and take pictures, so we could get their story out to the media. We went from home to home, inspecting the destruction. All had large holes in their walls. The actual camp has 22,000 refugees. At best, the structures are tin-roof hovels. Instead of roads, there are alleyways.

The camp is unbelievably crammed as you can imagine. In some places, my body couldn't fit between the houses. Even the alleyways are very narrow. Homes are often separated only by a wall; others are attached one to the other. The army's method, when they come into these camps, is to bust through the walls. Each home had a huge gaping hole.

CATHY: How did the Israelis accomplish this?

HUWAIDA: The families were not sure because they were all locked into one room. They just heard explosions. What actually caused the damage, what made the holes into the walls, they didn't know.

The holes were large enough for the soldiers to walk through.

In one instance, an entire wall had crumbled; in another, the entire house. The soldiers must have started at one end of a row of houses throwing an explosive against a wall then another until, in the end, they had a row of houses each one with a gaping hole right in the middle, like a symmetrical line of large donut holes.

CATHY: Sounds like this was a well-planned assault.

HUWAIDA: The Israelis attacked the camp with about 1,500 troops, Apache gunships, tanks and bulldozers. It was a major operation.

CATHY: How do people in the refugee camps perceive you? Were they reluctant to tell you their stories?

HUWAIDA: Actually, they were eager to tell us their stories. They understand that the international community, in general, pays them little attention. Palestinians are amazed at how the world can see this wanton destruction on television and not react with outrage. They asked us where we were from. When they learned that we're Americans, they said, "Your president says that we are the terrorists. What kind of people attack women and old men who have lost everything twice. Why are we the terrorists?"

The Israelis justify these actions by saying that they are after terrorists. In my opinion they want to intimidate the Palestinians, humiliate them, wear down their resistance so they will pack up and leave their land. Most Palestinians will tell you, "I did that in 1948. Never again. The Israelis will have to kill me on my land. I will never move."

What I find incredible is that the international community, at least for the most part, buys into Israel's claims that it must enter these camps to flush out terrorists in order to insure its own security.

Does this mean then that the same international community expects the Palestinians to accept their oppression? Does this mean that Palestinians should not resist in any way when their rights are taken away; when their lands are occupied and their sons are killed? Palestinians, for the most part, are not using terrorist means to resist Israeli aggression.

Of course, I very much disagree with the suicide bombers attacking civilians inside Israel. I vehemently oppose those types of actions. I understand why they happen, but I certainly do not condone them. I can assure you that the majority of the people resisting the occupation do not approve of the use of suicide bombers.

My point is this: Palestinians do not have the right to resist. If they resist, Israel calls them terrorists, and hunts them down like animals inside the camps. What would you do if someone came and took your land, and locked you in a room? Would you not try to resist? Would you not be outraged if, because you resisted, you were labeled a terrorist?

As internationals here, I feel one of our obligations is to unify the message of the Palestinian people that the occupation is the root cause of the violence. Lots of times, when Arafat calls for a cease fire, and we actually see for ourselves what is happening, we are shocked that he would demand such a thing and acquiesce to the Israelis.

We see Arafat asking his people not to resist Israeli occupation, even when the Israelis attack. We then see Sharon put every imaginable obstacle in their way, so that there will be no way for the Palestinians to come to the negotiating table. Arafat actually said, "I demand a complete cease fire. Do not fire, even if you are fired upon." I heard him say these words.

How many journalists reported on that incredible statement?

Believe it or not, Arafat's order actually put an end to the fighting until Sharon assassinated another PLO member, thereby provoking a reaction from one of the more radical elements of the Palestinian resistance.

During that three-week lull, there was actually an increase in Israeli attacks on Palestinians at checkpoints. We saw this with our own eyes. Yet, the Israelis claimed that they were only stopping terrorists from attacking innocent Israeli lives. In fact, during that three-week period, the media reported that it was calm in the territories when, in fact, thirty-two Palestinians died at the hands of Israeli soldiers.

In other words, even if the Palestinians do nothing, even if they passively resist occupation, even if they do not respond to Israeli provocation by firing on Israeli troops, Palestinians continue to be threatened, harassed, killed and otherwise treated as terrorists who threaten the security of Israel.

I assure you that Palestinians, for the most part, are trying passive resistance to occupation. How long must they continue to do this, when Ariel Sharon is not interested in sitting down to negotiate? Sharon places obstacle after obstacle in their path. And when they still do not respond, he orders another assassination of some prominent Palestinian, sparks a reaction, then announces to the whole world that he is dealing with terrorists, and has no choice but to wipe them out.

CATHY: Why the concentrated attacks on specific refugee camps?

HUWAIDA: In certain places, it is to clear away the people and their houses to make room for more Israeli settlements. In others, it is a question of beating the Palestinians down, breaking their resistance, their will to survive. Then, sitting down to negotiate with them on Israeli terms, to accept whatever Israel decides to generously offer. In general, Israel just wants the land for more settlements.

CATHY: You're an American. Over the last two years you've been a witness to what is happening in the territories. Who listens to what you have to say?

HUWAIDA: A lot of the correspondents have a good idea of what happens here. Even some of the larger network correspondents do a good job of reporting the truth. Unfortunately, once their stories hit the States, they are either edited to death, or thrown into the trash basket.

Our work gets shown to smaller organizations, like Amnesty International and church groups. It is at the grassroots level that we hope to raise awareness of what is happening in the occupied territories.

CATHY: Do Israelis know what goes on in the territories?

HUWAIDA: Israelis aren't even allowed into the territories. They're told it's for their own safety. Daniel Barenboim wanted to perform in Ramallah this week. The Israeli government wouldn't let him cross the Qalandya checkpoint. He had to cancel his concert.

CATHY: How ironic that in America it is Jewish organizations who are at the forefront of the peace movement. Rabbi Michael Lerner is actively seeking a withdrawal of US aid to Israel until it complies with UN Resolution 242.

HUWAIDA: Here, too, there are certain groups, like *Bat Shalom*, *Gush Shalom*, and Peace Now who organize peace demonstrations and rallies.

CATHY: What brought you here?

HUWAIDA: Two years ago, I came here with Seeds of Peace, an American NGO. However, we were not allowed to take a stand or become actively involved. I could not abide by those rules, so I quit. I needed the freedom to do more for the Palestinian cause, so I helped form the International Solidarity Movement. Our main goal is to get as many internationals as possible to come to Palestine and stand with the Palestinians. Back home these internationals talk to groups about what they have learned and seen.

Basically, when you have a Palestinian demonstration protesting a checkpoint closing, nothing happens. If Israeli troops put down a demonstration violently when internationals are present, you get press coverage. Otherwise, the suppression of a Palestinians demonstration is reported as, "A Palestinian uprising forced Israeli troops to open fire today …"

CATHY: Do the Palestinians ever get discouraged?

HUWAIDA: Surprisingly not! You would think that every Palestinian would be disheartened and discouraged, but they aren't. They realize the importance of never giving up hope. Of course, they're very grateful for the international presence, and recognize that presence protects them from the really harsh violence they are generally subjected to.

From personal experience, I can tell you that when internationals are present at a demonstration, the Israelis do not fire live ammunition.

CATHY: Internationals were present last month at a demonstration in front of Arafat's house. I believe the Israelis responded by firing tear gas into the crowd?

HUWAIDA: Yes, I forgot about that incident. They used tear gas and sound grenades. In the civilized world, there needs to be a valid reason to fire tear gas into a crowd. Not here.

CATHY: Last December, Dr. Barghouti, a Physicians for Human Rights activist, was beaten in front of internationals as he was holding a press conference. One of his knee caps was shattered. I seem to recall there was an Italian member of the European Parliament among the internationals.

HUWAIDA: Yes, that's right. It would appear that, at times, the Israelis do not care who is watching. Imagine what would have happened to Dr. Barghouti if the internationals had not been there.

At least in Europe, these types of attacks, in full view of internationals, get press attention; it makes the nightly news. I hope eventually this sort of thing will happen in America.

CATHY: How do you attract internationals to your cause?

HUWAIDA: By our actions mostly, and world of mouth. We're working on nonviolent direct action to combat the occupation and that is an approach people accept and respect. I believe it can be successful and I work hard to expand that idea in every Palestinian town and village.

Internationals, when they come here, are willing to stand up in front of Israeli soldiers alongside Palestinians. This awes the Palestinians. If they hate the US government for its support of the Israelis, they are very grateful that individual Americans are so willing to put their lives on the line for them.

Believe me, when Palestinians feel like no one else in the world is listening, this kind of courageous act gives them a tremendous boost of moral confidence and support. More importantly, it makes them feel that they are not alone.

So far, we have had successful campaigns with the participation of large numbers of internationals. We hope to continue increasing the number by having them return to their hometowns with their own personal stories. That is how our nonviolent resistance movement is going to work. This is how we will eventually turn the tide of support against Israel, and put pressure on our own government to change its Middle East policy. It is called "people power."

If the international community is not willing to provide protection for Palestinians, as they are bound to do by international law, then individuals must do it.

I believe that when the US government sees its citizens standing up for justice in the Middle East, they will be obliged to rethink their policy.

CATHY: Have you or any of your internationals ever been arrested?

HUWAIDA: I have not, but Brian almost did. [Brian, a Christian Peacemaker, was staying with Huwaida at the time of this interview]. He got shoved into an Israeli personnel carrier recently and stayed there for five hours. We called the American consulate, but, as usual, they were not willing to do anything. Eventually the Israelis let Brian go.

CATHY: Have you seen the new Palestinian history books?

HUWAIDA: I haven't, but I know that in the States there has been a lot of controversy over them. President Clinton drew attention to the issue when he addressed the Israel Policy Forum in New York. He actually demanded that the Palestinians change the culture of violence and the culture of incitement that, since Oslo, has gone unchecked. He insisted that young Palestinians are still being educated to believe in confrontation with Israel. Senator Hillary Clinton denounced the hateful, anti-Israel rhetoric in official Palestinian schoolbooks.

Their information came from a report issued by the Center for Monitoring the Impact of Peace (CMIP), a Jewish-American NGO, whose research director, Itamar Marcus, is an Israeli settler living in the West Bank settlement of Efrat.

Marcus' report claims that Palestinian children have been learning to identify Israel as the evil colonialist enemy who stole their land. He claims that the new PA textbooks fail to teach their children to see Israel as a neighbor with whom peaceful relations are expected. They do not teach acceptance of Israel's existence on the national level, nor do they impart tolerance of individual Jews on the personal level.

[**Authors Note**: I spoke with several people in the Palestinian Authority about this charge and was assured that the textbooks avoid dealing with unresolved political issues. The books do not provide a map of Israel because the latter has yet to define its borders. Nor do the new textbooks provide a map of Palestine either, because its borders remain to be negotiated. The texts do, however, reflect the Palestinian narrative which is basically that of the native in conflict with a settler-colonial movement. President Clinton and his wife, Hillary, endorsed the allegation, but never bothered to have the report's claims checked against the actual texts.

In fact, the new PA textbooks have made a special effort to promote tolerance, openness, and democratic values. Dr. Ruth Firer, head of a research team from the Harry S. Truman Research Institute for the Advancement of Peace, made a statement saying that Israeli educators were surprised to find how moderate the anger

directed towards Israelis in the Palestinian textbooks was, compared to the Palestinian predicament and suffering. This surprise
is doubled when the Palestinian books are compared to Israeli
ones which mention gentiles solely in the context of pogroms
and the Holocaust. Dr. Firer directed some stern words at CMIP,
charging that they have neither educational nor methodological
skills, and only want to prove it is impossible to achieve peace with
the Palestinians.

Two professors from Hebrew University said that the new Palestinian textbooks were actually less provocative than the Israeli
ones, and that they were a hundred percent improvement over the
Jordanian history taught previously in the Palestinian schools. In
Israeli textbooks, the map of Israel shows settlements not as settlements, but as established Israeli cities and villages. There is no
mention of a Palestinian village like Ramallah, Bethlehem, Nablus
or Jenin. In fact, there is no mention of an occupied West Bank. It
is referred to as Judea and Samaria.]

CATHY: Yesterday I spent the day at a local school. I spoke to several
of the classes. I was amazed at their lack of hatred toward Israelis.

HUWAIDA: I remember one time in Gaza. We met with a representative from the Palestinian Authority whose job it was to coordinate security with the Israelis. One day, without any warning, he
heard an Apache gunship overheard. The next minute, it was firing
a missile into his building. He escaped just in time.

Do you know what this PA representative said to me when I
walked into his office? Instead of blaming someone for almost killing him, he calmly said, "Welcome, I am glad you have come to see
for yourselves what we endure."

For its geographic size, Gaza is the worst hellhole on earth. It
has seen more destruction and more refugee displacement, and all
because of military hardware supplied courtesy of the US government. At all times, I feel completely safe walking anywhere in the
West Bank or Gaza because the Palestinians know the difference
between the American people and their government.

Sometimes, if we are in a new area, little kids think we are Israelis. They call out, "Shalom, Shalom," which means 'welcome' in Hebrew. Imagine, they think we might be Israelis, yet they don't show us any hostility. I find that remarkable.

Yes, for people who have no freedom, cannot travel from one village to another, cannot visit family members in a nearby town, who live under constant fear of Apache gunships, and whose children may never know what it is like to splash in water at the beach, play in the sand or ride the waves, even though they live along the sea in Gaza, there is an amazing lack of hostility in their hearts.

JUDY B.

RIGHT-WING ISRAELI

Judy is originally from Seattle, Washington. She was raised in a Zionist home and was active in the Zionist youth movement. Nine years ago she and her son moved to Israel, settled in a kibbutz and learned Hebrew. She is a right-wing Israeli and opposed the Gaza withdrawal.

CATHY: Why were you opposed to the Gaza withdrawal?

JUDY: It was not a democratically taken decision. When we elected Sharon he said he would never do such a thing. No one knows why he changed his mind. He never explained why we had to withdraw. He never even went to Gaza to meet with the settlers there.

Every cabinet member who opposed his plan was thrown out of government. I know this because I work for the Ministry of Tourism. There was never even a referendum.

Sharon's withdrawal sent a wrong message to *Hamas* and other terrorist groups. "Perpetuate violence and we will give in and run." That's the message Sharon sent by withdrawing.

CATHY: Was it American pressure that forced Sharon's hand?

JUDY: Sharon's political advisor, Dov Weisglass, said in a press conference last summer that Sharon did it to get the international community off Israel's back and that by doing what he did Sharon poured formaldehyde on the peace process.

CATHY: What did he mean by that statement?

JUDY: Look, the world thinks Sharon did a great thing by leaving Gaza. For the foreseeable future no one is going to ask Israel to make any more concessions. That means that for the foreseeable future the peace process is in deep-freeze.

CATHY: If that is the case then why is there so much discontent over the withdrawal?

JUDY: I worked closely with the settlers in Gaza. They were the cream of the crop of Israeli settlers. They literally turned sand dunes into communities. They were doing hydroponics agriculture and exporting their products to Europe. They were a very tightly knit community with zero crime rate. They had good schools. These communities were like the old kibbutz-era ones.

Their forced evacuation was a totally traumatic event. It is deceptive to think that Israeli soldiers were gentle to the settlers. People may disagree but Jews feel a kinship with fellow Jews. It was extremely painful for the settlers to be literally pulled out of their homes by fellow Jews for no reason.

And of course the scenes which followed post-withdrawal with the Palestinians rioting and tearing down greenhouses and synagogues was not pretty.

As for the Palestinians, they were employed by these settlers and now they have no jobs.

Twelve weeks have passed since the withdrawal and the Palestinians still have no jobs.

As for the poor settlers, eighty-seven percent of them have yet to see a penny in compensation. They are living in tent cities in the border crossing with Gaza, and according to the Israeli government it will take two years before they receive their compensation package.

In elections next spring people will remember this and vote their disgust with Sharon. And in Israel, believe me, everyone pays close attention to politics because it affects our lives in very tangible ways.

Here it is different from the States where people vote on one issue or don't vote at all. In Israel we are very attached to our politics and yes, it is probably because we are such a small country.

CATHY: Will Benjamin Netanyahu run against Sharon in the next election?

JUDY: In America Netanyahu is glorified to super-star status, but not in Israel. Here he is seen as too opportunistic. When he was in office he turned his back on too many people and the right wing will never forgive him for giving away part of Hebron.

CATHY: What happened in Hebron?

JUDY: In '96 Netanyahu signed the Wye Accord which gave joint control of the Tomb of the Patriarch, where Abraham and Sarah are buried, to both Israelis and Palestinians. Now Jews have certain days when they can come to worship and the Arabs have the other days. This is totally unacceptable.

Even though Netanyahu was against the Gaza withdrawal he stayed in the government until the last minute. If he had departed sooner he could have led other politicians out. He claimed it was because he was Finance Minister and had a responsibility to the country. At the moment in Israel there is very limited political leadership.

Let me say something else about the Gaza withdrawal. What Sharon has created is a slippery slope. The moment you give away Gaza and the principle of never giving in has been abrogated and you quite literally throw Jews out on the street, you have lost the trust of your people.

CATHY: Sharon put up the security wall. Wasn't that fact appreciated by the Israeli public?

JUDY: Yes, and we do need defensible borders. Terrorist attacks have stopped in the north because of the wall. Apparently attacks are down ninety percent. If a wall is what we need to stop attacks on our lives, then so be it. The wall makes it difficult to circulate in Jerusalem, however. Yesterday I found it almost impossible to get where I needed to go because of the wall. The bottom line is this. If there was no terror there would be no need for a wall.

CATHY: Is there a solution to the conflict?

JUDY: I don't pretend to have solutions to this crisis. I don't think there is one. Frankly, some problems just don't have solutions.

We have been successful. We Israelis have shown that we aren't going to curl up and go away. We essentially crushed the leadership of *Hamas*. The fact that we have had success in stamping out a five-year *Intifada* makes Sharon's Gaza withdrawal all that more perplexing. I just don't get it.

An astonishing number of tourists are coming to Israel now. People are finally realizing that terror happens everywhere. It has become a fact of life. Our tourists are not just Jewish. We have a lot of Christians who want to make a pilgrimage to the Holy Land. And since I work for the Tourism Ministry I can attest to the fact that we are pushing the agenda that Israel is safe.

Yearly we have approximately 50,000 Jews from the US, Western Europe and Canada immigrating to Israel. This is certainly an indication of how Jews feel about Israel. I came because I wanted my children to have a real childhood. In the States I couldn't even let them go out of the house because it wasn't safe.

CATHY: You still have the fear of suicide bombers here. Mothers still have to put their children on school buses.

JUDY: Yes, the bombings happen and will probably continue to happen, but statistically it will happen less and less and that is how we Israelis think.

On Sunday mornings we never use the buses. That is the day Israeli soldiers are returning to their bases and when suicide bombers are more likely to strike. Again, it is all about statistics.

Look, kids in Israel have been living like this for fifty or sixty years. They aren't going to start living under glass for security reasons.

CATHY: Do you know any Palestinians?

JUDY: Sure I know some but in general there is a tremendous distrust between us and them. Truthfully, I feel sorry for any Palestinian who has to live under the Palestinian Authority. They truly suffer from poor leadership.

We Israelis in fifty-seven years have built Israel into a first-rate country. The Arabs live in abject poverty. They lived under a despot when Arafat was alive. This is a tragedy for them because they have the potential to do great things.

Their problems are not, however, our responsibility. The Israeli-Palestinian conflict is a regional problem and requires a regional solution. We have done our share. Now it is up to the international community to play its role. Look, Jordan has a seventy percent Palestinian population. They should be the ones proposing a solution.

Israeli Arabs, on the other hand, do very well in Israeli society. Three Arab parties and eight ministers represent them in the *Knesset*. There is an Arabic press. Arab Israelis live as Israelis and they are quite content because they see how the Arabs have to live under the Palestinian Authority.

Admittedly we have a way to go in terms of equality toward Arab Israelis, as do most Western countries when it comes to treatment of minorities. I think, in the whole scope of things, that progress is being made in the right direction. I think Israel sets a wonderful example of how Arabs and Jews can live together.

CATHY: Arabs and Jews lived peacefully side by side in Beirut, Baghdad and Damascus for centuries.

JUDY: Oh, but they were treated as second-class citizens and those countries were not sovereign nations.

CATHY: I lived in Lebanon for fourteen years, so I can speak to the Jews in that country. Lebanon, by the way, is a sovereign nation with a duly elected parliament. When I arrived in Beirut in '69 Beirut had a thriving Jewish community. One of my husband's closest friends in medical school was Jewish. Many people I knew went to a certain Dr. Israeli near Bab Edriss. Albeit in a state of disrepair, Beirut's synagogue still stands in the city center not far from the Phoenicia Hotel.

JUDY: I don't know anything about how Jews lived in Beirut, but

Arab Israelis live in Israel as equals. They have the right to vote. They have access to good health care and education. We live together as a sovereign nation even if it is on land stolen from the Arabs. Things aren't perfect, obviously, but its the way things are.

In the meantime, we will continue to build our society and try to be a beacon of tolerance.

HANNA

ISRAELI PEACE ACTIVIST

I waited for Hanna outside a popular restaurant in West Jerusalem. The afternoon was fading and, as in any desert climate at sunset, the air was very quickly turning chilly. When she finally arrived, some ten minutes late, I was cold and in need of a warm drink.

She took me by surprise. I did not expect a blond-haired woman with a crew cut and heavy makeup, which she did not need. She had a beautiful face.

CATHY: Some Israeli journalists write critically of Sharon and his policies in the West Bank and Gaza. This surprises me.

HANNA: Why? Those of us who have our eyes open are not afraid to criticize Sharon and his policies.

CATHY: In Ramallah, the Palestinians I met were not critical of Arafat.

HANNA: Sure, even less so now since he has been confined to his compound basement. Do not forget that he has also gotten more sympathy from abroad in the past few months.

CATHY: Does Sharon understand that he is contributing to Arafat's popularity?

HANNA: He does not care. The only purpose in keeping Arafat under house arrest, destroying his helicopters, ruining his airstrip, shooting up his police stations and killing his policemen, is to humiliate him. There is a long-standing vendetta between these two men and Sharon aims to win.

CATHY: Is it hard to be a peace activist in Israel?

HANNA: I think it is hard to be a peace activist anywhere. What is so amazing is that the authorities, both in the US and Israel, find us so intimidating and dangerous. It is the same kind of logic that has maintained an embargo on Cuba all these years and killed a democratically-elected Allende in Chile.

It is the same system that arrests human rights workers and holds them in administrative detention, and targets medical personnel and journalists in the occupied territories.

It is extremely frustrating for us Israeli peace activists because we are not given credit for all the hard work we do to promote a just solution. We are constantly in action on the streets, together with our Palestinian partners. There are dozens of conscientious objectors in military prison. There are ongoing protest demonstrations, newspaper ads, and joint activities of all kinds.

CATHY: What can you tell me about the attack on the gambling hall in Rishon Lezion. Was it a suicide bomber?

HANNA: Let me answer your question this way. It would have been extremely difficult for a Palestinian to walk up three flights of stairs in an illegal gambling club frequented by a large number of retired people, all of whom were Israeli.

I was suspicious of the story as it was told by official sources. The attack could have come from an extremist Israeli group opposed to gambling, especially if they thought they could get away with it. At any rate, the attack certainly gave Sharon another excuse to destroy more Palestinian towns and houses to make way for more settlements.

CATHY: Is it true that the Israeli government makes it difficult for anyone pro-Palestinian to get into the country?

HANNA: This is true. Do you know who Michael Tarazi is?

CATHY: No.

HANNA: He is an American citizen who lives in Ramallah. He works as a legal advisor to the PLO peace negotiating team and he promotes nonviolent resistance to the occupation. Recently, he was refused entry at Ben-Gurion Airport. He was put in detention and expelled.

Preventing this man from entering Israel is part of a war, not against terrorism as Sharon says, but against those peace-seeking Palestinians who prove, by their actions, that there is a partner for peace. As such, he constitutes a danger for the Israeli propaganda machine. He is someone the Israeli government considers extremely dangerous.

CATHY: What can you tell me about the recent English translation of Moshe Sharett's *Diary*?

HANNA: I am pleased to see them [sic] translated. I have always felt that if Moshe Sharett had been given more power for decision making as foreign minister, and later as prime minister in the early 1950's, that Israel's history would have been very different and much more to my liking.

It was unfortunate for Israel that Ben-Gurion was in charge during its formative years and so unwilling to diverge from his hawkish agenda. The translation of Sharett's diary is a treasure for anyone seeking the truth about Israel's birth.

Some day, when honest historians research the period of the occupation and the current *Intifada*, they will prove to have been among the most immoral and criminal in Israel's history.

They are certainly not the only years in which Israel acted immorally, however. Consider how they destroyed 400–500 Arab villages in 1948, to create the refugee problem, or how Ariel Sharon led attacks into Jordan and masterminded the massacre in Qibyia in the 1950s.

Without a doubt, the past two years have certainly been among the worst. If we do not change the current government and its ideology of a Greater Israel at all costs, toward a non-militaristic government willing to live within the 1967 borders, and also compromise in other areas, this country will become morally polluted and will give impetus to an even greater increase in the most fanatic elements in the Middle East. Anyone who says that Turkey will not and cannot revert to the pre-Ataturk era, should remember Iran.

Just how long Israel will be able to exist in a highly fundamentalist Middle East is a question all of us should and must ponder.

TALI

A SINGLE ISRAELI WOMAN

Tali is in her early forties. She lives alone on the top floor of a four-story walkup in what was, before the June '67 war, a low-end Palestinian neighborhood. After the war, all Palestinians were forced to move elsewhere. The buildings are identical, drab, gray square blocks lined up along both sides of the street. Except for an occasional play area in front of a few of the buildings, there are no distinguishing characteristics. Little has been done in the way of improvements since 1967. Her apartment, though small, is sunny and colorfully decorated. We sat on a narrow balcony off her living room, with her laundry blowing in the light breeze from a clothesline just below eye level.

TALI: I'm employed by an Israeli organization that promotes tolerance between us and the Palestinians.

CATHY: Does this mean that you work with the Palestinians directly?

TALI: Yes.

CATHY: Are they responsive to your initiatives?

TALI: It is difficult these days to get anything done between our two groups.

CATHY: Was there better coordination before the current *Intifada*?

TALI: Yes, of course, much better. Now, it is next to impossible. The Jewish groups organize a conference, and the Arabs cannot get through the checkpoints to get here. Certain members of our group get very frustrated after making a tremendous effort to get a conference together. They make comments like, "Look at the Arabs. Why don't they make more of an effort?"

Reasonable heads prevail and respond, "Look here, they cannot even get to the store to buy a loaf of bread. You want them to show up at one of our meetings?"

CATHY: How does the government explain its actions in the Palestinian towns and villages?

TALI: They say that the army is looking for wanted, armed people. They assure the Israeli public that they do not harm the civilians. When civilians get hurt, it is called a mistake.

Ariel Sharon tells the Israelis, "We are only going after people who threaten Israel's security. We are collecting ammunition and weapons so they will not be used on Israelis."

CATHY: I understand why people would want to believe that. When you are scared, you want to believe that your government is doing the right thing. This is a normal, human reaction.

TALI: Yes, I was chatting with the cleaning lady in our office, who happens to be Jewish. She emphatically insisted that Israel would never harm innocent people. She is less educated, more emotional, and more apt to believe what her government tells her. She said, "The Palestinians are killing so many of us. For every Israeli they kill, we will just have to kill that many more of them."

CATHY: Is she a Russian immigrant?

TALI: No, she is of Oriental origin.

CATHY: Do the Russian immigrants speak Hebrew?

TALI: Some do, some do not.

CATHY: If they watched Israeli television, would they understand the news in Hebrew?

TALI: Some of them would. However, Russian immigrants have their own radio and television stations. They even have their own newspapers.

CATHY: That makes it easy to censor any news they get.

TALI: Yes, indeed.

CATHY: Many of the Palestinians I've interviewed in Jerusalem speak Hebrew. In Ramallah, Hebrew is not taught in the schools. Is that a mistake?

TALI: Yes, because anyone who works at a university or Israeli business, or has to have any interchange with Israelis, must know Hebrew.

The Oriental [Sephardic] Jews speak Arabic, or at least the local dialect of their original countries. We have a lot of Moroccan and Algerian Jews.

CATHY: You consider yourself a centrist. Are you a minority in Israel?

TALI: Most definitely. For the record, I am actually left-wing. I support the *Intifada*, so that definitely puts me in the left-wing camp.

CATHY: How do you get the Israeli public to understand that if the Palestinians are allowed to have their twenty-two percent of the original Palestine, they will have a chance at peace?

TALI: Even I do not believe that by giving the Palestinians twenty-two percent it would guarantee peace. There will not be peace with Ariel Sharon. It is that simple. We need a good leader to steer us toward peace. If we ever found such a person, the Israeli public would follow him. Of that, I have no doubt.

This is obviously an optimistic point of view: that Israel will some day have a good leader. The pessimistic point of view is that until the Palestinians kill more Israelis, no one will ever talk of making peace.

CATHY: Excuse me, but are you suggesting that there should be more suicide bombers?

TALI: Listen, in war, people carry out horrific acts. Until more Israelis die, we will never begin to talk about peace. That is the sad and honest truth. The Palestinians are having a very deep effect on our society. Israelis are really scared. They are in awe that the Palestinians can do this to them. Of course, they react like this because most Israelis do not know what is happening in the territories.

Israel is humiliating a whole people, and they hate us for what we do to them. Too many Israelis are ignoring this fact.

Look, the worst case scenario would be to keep Sharon in power another two years, or until the end of his mandate. He will do his best to throw the Arabs right into the sea, like he pretends they want to do to the Jews.

Sadly, if there were elections today, the right-wing would win. Sharon and his cabinet would try to convince the nation that the only way to guarantee security for Israelis would be to declare war on Palestinian terrorism.

I think right now there are more right-wing than left in this country, and Sharon would have no problem carrying out his plan. All he has to do is blame Israel's economic crisis on the *Intifada*, and most Israelis would agree with him. They would much rather blame the crisis on the Palestinians than blame it on what the Israeli government is doing to the Palestinians.

CATHY: I saw a group of religious Jews, adults and children, were being escorted through the Christian Quarter by armed guards with M16s draped across their chests. They looked like they feared for their lives. Was this truly fear?

TALI: Israelis are taught at a very young age that Palestinians are such bad people that they need armed bodyguards to escort them anywhere there are Arabs. On top of that, the ultra-Orthodox Jews wear costumes and flaunt themselves, and their bodyguards carry M16s as a reminder of their power. Their children grow up to fear, to distrust, to denigrate and detest the Arabs.

CATHY: What will happen when these children become adults?

TALI: That's what is so awful. They will be the ones to incite the next *Intifada* and perpetuate this crisis. It is like a long-standing family feud at its ugliest.

CATHY: Why do you think the Israeli Army puts up the barricades? It is that same arrogance of power?

TALI: They want to show the Palestinians who is boss. They want to humiliate them at every occasion. It is an ugly game, and it has nothing to do with security.

CATHY: When I crossed back into Jerusalem a few days ago, I was surprised at how porous the al-Ram checkpoint was. A suicide bomber could have been in our van, or walked alongside me, and the Israelis would never have known.

TALI: Oh, but occasionally the Israeli soldiers catch a suicide bomber, when they are lucky, and they make a big publicity about it. They say how important the checkpoints are for Israeli security.

The Israeli government does not think past these acts of humiliation. They do not think about the resentment the Palestinian feels as he or she passes through on foot, or waits hours in line to have his car inspected, and has to repeat this every single day. They do not seem to realize that it sends a very strong message to the Palestinians that we hate you, and want to stamp you out. Of course, in reality, Ariel Sharon does hate the Palestinians, and does want them to know that he wishes to push all of them out.

CATHY: Tell me something about Israeli society. Is there friction between the Ashkenazi [East European] Jews and the Oriental Jews?

TALI: It is more of a class issue: rich versus poor, educated versus uneducated. There are, of course, a lot of cultural differences between the two groups. There are many working class people, and with that comes a lot of discrimination.

Look at the Ethiopian Jews who came here several years ago. They have not been integrated into Israeli society. For the most part, they do not speak Hebrew, yet they serve in the army. The same is true of the Russian Jews. Many of them do not speak Hebrew.

Don't forget that the original settlers, in the late 1800s and early 1900s, were from Eastern Europe, and that they have very peculiar cultural customs which, for the most part, have not changed.

I honestly think that the only reason we have such diverse groups living here is so we can fill Israel with as many Jews as possible. The government does not really care where they come from, as long as they come. And they should care.

I have since learned that there are, in fact, four levels of citizenship in Israel, the first four being various categories of Jews. The Ashkenazi, the white European Jews, are at the top of the pyramid. On the next level down are the Mizrachi or Sephardic Jews who are from the Arab countries. They form the largest component of Israeli Jews. Next to the bottom are the Ethiopian Jews who are black and who live in the poorest neighborhoods of West Jerusalem. They, however, fare somewhat better than the Yemeni Jews who were transported to Israel involuntarily, held in primitive camps and had many of their babies stolen or given up for adoption to Ashkenazi families. The Palestinians are beneath all these layers of Jews.

CATHY: According to Israel Shahak, the most influential and richest Jews in the world are Oriental: mostly Egyptian and Syrian. Is this true?

TALI: Yes, that is true. However, they are not Israeli citizens. And yes, they will do anything for Israel to the point of donating any amount of money the government needs for a particular project. They are always ready to open their checkbooks. You mention the word "donate" in Israel and everyone listens. It is the operative word here. Did you know that Israel gets a lot of donations from the Christian conservatives in America?

CATHY: Yes, Shahak mentions that connection in his book, *Jewish Fundamentalism*.

TALI: The Israeli government is always looking for money and they are not particular about whom they take it from.

Even though the Christian conservatives believe that a strong Israel will bring about the Second Coming of the Messiah and that, in the end, the Jews who do not convert will perish, the Israeli government says, "Sure, whatever … Just show us your money and support."

CATHY: Aside from the Palestinian problem and a weak economy, does Israel have other problems?

TALI: We have an incredibly high accident rate. More Israelis have died in road accidents than were killed by the Palestinians in the two *Intifadas* combined. Last year alone, 500 Israelis died in car crashes.

CATHY: Were the numbers always that high?

TALI: No, not at all. The Israeli public has changed. They were always rude people, but now they are even worse.

In my opinion, the Ashkenazi are the worst. For example, they come to pick someone up in a neighborhood late at night. Instead of using their cell phone to call the person, to tell them that they are waiting for them in their car, they honk their horns, even if it is in the middle of the night. I think this new level of rudeness comes from being frightened and nervous all the time. However, it is not an excuse to forget how to be civil with other people. I guess, too, like anywhere else, when you have power you become arrogant.

CATHY: What do you mean by that?

TALI: Take an army reservist. He is put in a position of power. He knows that he can treat the Palestinians any way he wants, and that no one will say anything to him. That is the arrogance of power. The problem is that you can get used to treating people like that.

CATHY: Do you know any reservists?

TALI: Sure, all the men in my family are reservists.

CATHY: When they come back from serving in the territories, do they talk about what they did or saw?

TALI: My brother refuses to talk about his tours of duty in the territories. He is a very sensitive guy, and probably does not want to relive what he was asked to do. My cousin tells me that when you are on a job long enough, you lose your sensitivity. The situation turns you into someone you are not in real life.

CATHY: Is this because of fear?

TALI: No, it is because of the power you suddenly have. Nice guys, like my brother and cousin, have to serve with men who are, by nature, rude and big bullies. My brother and cousin watch what these bullies do, and pretty soon they are doing the same things. Slowly, you get used to your new power, and you use it more and more.

CATHY: Many of these young reservists are only twenty-two years old. Why do they hate Palestinians?

TALI: They are taught growing up that there is a class distinction between them and the Palestinians, and that they are better than the Arabs. Most Israeli families hire Arabs as domestic help. You do not mix with a hired hand. You may be courteous or civil to them, but you certainly do not consider them your equal. The simple fact that you can hire them, as a maid or gardener, automatically means that you have more money than they do, and that you are more educated. Also, in school, students are taught that Arabs hate Jews and that they want to throw them into the sea.

So, it's a combination of instilled fear from an early age, class difference and the arrogance that comes with the power they have over the Palestinians.

CATHY: What do Israelis think of the "new historians" revised interpretations of the birth of Israel? I am thinking of Israel Shahak, Simha Flapan and Benny Morris in particular.

TALI: Many Israelis call these authors Jew-haters.

CATHY: Even though they are Israeli Jews?

TALI: Look, the best way to be an anti-Semite is to be a Jew. The only person in the world who is entitled to be anti-Semitic is a Jew. Let me give you an example of what I mean. If you are fat, you are the only one who is allowed to make a joke about fat people. Otherwise, you cannot say a thing.

For myself, I find that these historians have very interesting things to say. However, I do not agree with everything they say.

CATHY: There are many truths.

TALI: Exactly, and those who find these historians threatening are the ones calling them Jew-haters. Look, it is really very simple. Do the Palestinians have a right to their own country? If they do, what are we doing settling on their land?

CATHY: Do you believe there can be a two-state solution?

TALI: There has to be. There is no other way.

MAISE

DOCUMENTARY FILM PRODUCER

Maise, a woman in her early fifties, is employed as a documentary film-maker for the Palestinian Authority. She has faced many challenges, suffered many losses in her life, yet conveys a sense of immense tranquility through her generous and gentle spirit. She lives in a small house, a stone's throw from Yasser Arafat's compound. Her neighborhood is routinely bombarded. Apache gunships hover overhead daily. More times than not she and her neighbors are placed under military curfew. They go days, sometimes weeks, without water or electricity. In spite of these hardships, it is evident that her humble abode – where she writes, paints, does needlework and costume design – is her refuge from the madness outside her door.

CATHY: People who have experienced great sorrows in their lives often become very ugly. How have so many Palestinians managed to remain so meek after fifty-three years as refugees?

MAISE: Our collective tragedy has taught us the importance of staying closely connected and supportive of one another. When my twenty-six-year-old brother was killed by the Israelis, it also killed my mother, who was only sixty-two at the time. She was a strong woman, in perfect health, but after his death she died of a broken heart. It was a very tragic year for me. I could not have survived without my community of friends.

CATHY: Where are your other brothers now?

MAISE: One of them is here. He is a cinema director. The other is a writer who lives in Jordan with his family. My father died three years ago. After my mother died, I lived with him for twelve years before coming here. During that time, I refused to marry because my father needed someone to stay with him. I have four sisters. All of them are married.

After twelve years in Amman, I had a strong desire to return to Palestine. I dreamed for years that I would go back to my homeland. When the opportunity arose, I went to my father and said,

"Please father, I have to go. It is something bigger than me. Please give me your blessing."

I spent one month here, then two weeks in Jordan. This went on for two years, until he died.

I would like to go back to something you said earlier about people turning ugly. In 1972, the Israeli government gave my sister and I permission to visit our village. When we arrived at the house we once owned, we found an Israeli family living there. When we asked if we could visit our family house, the woman said, "No, this is our house now." My sister pleaded, "This is the house where my sisters and I were born."

The Israeli answered, "No, this house is now our house."

My sister asked, "Could we at least drink the water from the well that my father dug, and that my mother and my whole family drank from?"

The lady smiled, "Yes, you can go and drink from the well."

When my sister went to the well, she discovered that it had been turned into a sewer. She closed the top and started crying.

The Jewish woman picked up a gun and said, "You leave right this minute, or else I am going to kill you and your sister. I will throw your bodies in the well and no one will ever know that you were here."

My sister and I left, of course. We were very sad to think that this Israeli could not find it in her heart to be courteous toward us.

CATHY: When you came to Palestine, how did you support yourself?

MAISE: I was working for the PLO information office in Jordan. However, when I arrived in Palestine their office was in Gaza. I could not go there, because the Israelis would not give me a travel permit. At that time, we had no office yet in Ramallah. After a few months, the PA opened one here.

CATHY: Yesterday I visited Dr. Moughrabi at the Qattan Center for Educational Research and Development. He helped me obtain copies of the new Palestinian textbooks. He explained that the Oslo Accords gave the Palestinians permission to write their own history.

MAISE: And not like they would have wanted, only as the Oslo Agreement dictated.

CATHY: Did the Oslo Agreement actually tell the Palestinians what they could write?

MAISE: Yes, the Palestinians were obliged to write only what they were told to write. For example, I am not from Ramallah. I am from a village near Jerusalem. My mother and father, my grandmother and grandfather, were all born and raised there.

No one in this book can say such a thing. According to Oslo, my village is part of Israel now. It was never Palestinian. The history we have just written is very limited. We were not allowed to speak of historical Palestine. We could only talk of the area under the Palestinian Authority.

CATHY: Are you allowed to speak of pre-'67 Palestine, or at least talk about the West Bank and Gaza?

MAISE: Yes, we can talk about these places. It is just the land that was occupied by the Israelis in 1948 that we are forbidden to mention. Now, we are allowed to talk about just the twenty-two percent of the original Palestine.

CATHY: Did Oslo forbid you to mention things like the Deir Yassin massacre of 1948?

MAISE: Of course. If we talk of these things, we are labeled terrorist. We are accused of wanting to destroy Israel, of wanting to throw the Israelis into the sea. You see, these places all belong to Israel now, so we have no right to talk about them.

CATHY: Does Arafat have any authority over the *Hamas* and Islamic Jihad movements?

MAISE: Sometimes yes, sometimes no. It depends on what is going on. If there is Israeli aggression, like assaults on the camps, *Hamas* and the others do not listen to anyone.

CATHY: Do you consider the people in these movements Israeli collaborators?

MAISE: It would appear this way, particularly when they know that any terrorist attack, any infiltration into a settlement, will mean an invasion into a camp with many innocent people dying. Yes, they do play into the hands of Sharon.

I am against any operation that targets civilians. I cannot imagine killing innocent people, and the majority of Palestinians would agree with me. We should never act like the Nazis acted toward the Jews. We should act like human beings, and treat everyone with dignity.

CATHY: When you were thrown out of your village, how did you survive?

MAISE: My parents moved from place to place around the Bethlehem area until my father found a job in Amman. He returned to see us every month, for two days. He brought us some money and food. In the meantime, my mother worked nights as a seamstress. Every morning, she collected vegetables grown by the villagers. She piled them on a large basket, placed it on her head, and walked to Jerusalem's center, some twelve kilometers away. If she sold something, she was able to buy things we needed, like food. She returned on foot, too.

She did this so her family could survive, so we would never have to live in a refugee camp.

CATHY: What is your job in the PA?

MAISE: I produce television programs, both cultural and political. For example, the Australians wanted us to make a film about democracy in Palestine. At the beginning of the *Intifada*, the PA Council decided we would do a program for them every month; one about the West Bank, the other about Gaza. They were going to give me $1,000 every month for this project. I was so happy because I was going to be able to put money aside to buy a house. But when the *Intifada* started, the project fell through.

CATHY: Why didn't the Australians want a film about the *Intifada*?

MAISE: This particular NGO wanted something about democracy, not fighting.

CATHY: Is it not hard to talk about democracy when you live under occupation?

MAISE: Democracy is a Western idea.

CATHY: Exactly my point. It is a Western idea and, at the present time, it does not apply to Palestine.

MAISE: No one wants to examine the essential problems here. If they did, they would have to talk to the Israelis who occupy our land. America does not want to do that. America wants the Palestinians to behave like puppets. Play democracy, play government.

CATHY: Israel is a democracy.

MAISE: If you are Jewish, it is a democracy.

CATHY: In America, people want to see the Palestinians practice nonviolent resistance to the occupation. They feel that their cause would be seen much more favorably.

MAISE: Yes, this sounds very well and good but you have to live here to understand the situation better. The people in the camps live with Israeli aggression all day, every day. Their homes are demolished, their camps are bulldozed, their loved ones are killed, their household possessions are stolen.

If there were some balance inside our society, some small recognition of our humanity, there would not be such terrible acts perpetrated against the Israeli people. Our civilians are killed indiscriminately by Israelis. Now, Israelis are killed in the same way. Both sides are afraid. This is unfair to both Israelis and Palestinians.

SEHAM

PALESTINIAN MIDWIFE

Seham is 43 years old. She has been a widow since 1989, when Israeli soldiers shot and killed her husband. She is a midwife by profession. However, she is currently unemployed, as are most Palestinians under closure and curfew. She has six children, three daughters (twenty-two, twenty-one and twenty) and three sons (a sixteeen-year-old and twelve-year-old twins).

She receives 700 shekels every month from the Palestinian Authority. This money pays for her electricity, water and telephone. Food comes exclusively from donations by neighbors and UNRW, *a UN relief agency. Second-hand clothes are donated, too. She alters them to suit her children's needs.*

Her children attend a school in the refugee camp. During Israeli incursions, they are forced to stay at home, unable even to open a window.

SEHAM: How are we to defend ourselves against the Israelis? If there has to be constant war, at least give us tanks, Apaches and F16s, too. Now, it is only our hearts which are exploding.

I forbid my children to throw stones at Israeli tanks. It is not that they do not deserve to have stones thrown at them, but I fear for my children's safety. If they did such a thing, the Israelis would not hesitate to kill them like they killed my husband.

The bottom line is that I would do anything to protect my children. If I caught them throwing even one stone, I would beat them severely.

CATHY: Do you think your life will improve some day?

SEHAM: I know, as a Palestinian, that I do not have a good future in this country. Only when I find that my home is safe, that my life is safe, and that my children can walk outside without fear of being shot by an Israeli soldier, will I believe there is hope for a better future. Not before.

CATHY: Do you agree with the suicide bombers?

SEHAM: I do not agree with the suicide bombers at all. And contrary to some news reports, here in the camps the children do not talk about them all the time.

And the poor parents of suicide bombers. They do not know ahead of time that their children are going to blow themselves up.

Believe me, it is awful, and I only wish they would stop. These bombers also put our lives in danger every time they kill Israelis. It must stop.

CATHY: Where do you get the courage to get out of bed each day?

SEHAM: Let me tell you, there are bad days, and less bad days, but I cry every single day.

CATHY: Do you have a message you wish me to convey to Americans?

SEHAM: Indeed I do. Please come and change places with us. See for yourselves how awful our lives are. You must really see what is going on, see how we are forced to live. Then, you will understand better.

You Americans see only one side of the story, the Israeli side. We Palestinians are human beings, too. We also have a story.

If you Americans could do one thing, I would ask you to increase your political activism and encourage your politicians to find a middle ground. Only then, will you have a more balanced approach to solving our crisis.

Please ask your government to stop selling arms to Israel. We have no army, no weapons, no tanks, no Apaches or F16s. We are defenseless against such powerful weapons.

MAHA

ACTRESS WHO WORKS WITH CHILDREN

Maha is director of Ashta, an acting troupe which works with Palestinian children, teaching them to express themselves, to let loose of their fears and emotions, and to reinterpret them into positive modes of self-expression. Ashta is the only institution in the occupied territories that works with children in the realm of drama. It does not have enough staff or actors to go into the individual schools, but is fortunate to have its own studio, which was donated. The children come to Ashta after school and on weekends.

CATHY: Is *Ashta's* goal primarily to teach children how to cope with the current crisis?

MAHA: To some extent, yes. However, it was started as an activity, like in many other parts of the world. Here, as elsewhere, people learn to express themselves, to build self-esteem. Drama is a wonderful and necessary art form. It is essential, especially during times like this, to intensify our work in order to help the maximum number of children. We are in the process of training more people so that we can reach more children, especially in more remote, less fortunate areas.

CATHY: Who funds your work?

MAHA: *Ashta* is a non-governmental organization. We apply for a grant, like any other NGO, and receive, or don't, depending on funds available. We're lucky. We are finding more and more people interested in our work. Drama is an excellent way to convince and affect attitudes, to express feelings. These things ultimately help our children. This has been proven time and time again. As a result, more and more institutions are willing to help us in our work.

CATHY: How many children participate in your program?

MAHA: In each club, we have approximately twelve to fifteen. Sometimes we have smaller groups of eight to ten. Frankly, we try to avoid larger groups. We believe we can produce more effective results with smaller ones.

CATHY: Do you suggest a subject or topic to the students? Do they write their own scripts?

MAHA: It differs. We usually do not start with a play. We like to start with games. We do not like to push the children into some stressful activity such as having to learn lines. We want them to relax and have fun and, in the process, come up with their own sketches. This is a great way to build self-esteem. If a group stays together for at least a year, the children eventually develop better, more sophisticated techniques. At that time, they are ready to study lines for a play.

Unfortunately, every time there is a crisis, we seem to return to zero. Of course, in order to carry out this program, there is a lot of networking and coordination, often involving Israeli entities. When there is fighting, like now, everything seems to fall apart.

These past two years have been very hard for us. Unfortunately, we have become quite cynical about our relationship with the Israelis. They make things very difficult for us.

I used to have to travel every day from Jerusalem, where I am a resident, to get to Ramallah. Now, my husband and I have moved our family here.

When we first came to Ramallah, my children asked me, every time we passed an Israeli checkpoint, why the soldiers were so mean. My son used to joke, "Perhaps we should give the Israelis part of our lunch to make them like us better, or maybe invite them to our house and share what we have with them." Finally, I had to tell them some of the Palestinian history because, of course, this is something they do not get from their textbooks.

Now, my children have lost their rationale. Now, they live under continuous bombing. They see the Apache gunships hovering overhead. They see them shoot their missiles. They are totally confused.

On weekends and holidays we return to Jerusalem. Unlike West Bank residents, we are allowed to travel freely. On one of our treks into Jerusalem, when the checkpoints were closed to everyone, we had to pass through very rough roads, climbing up and down hills and narrow dirt paths with nothing but the fear of an Israeli soldier spotting us and shooting at us.

We are only ten to fifteen minutes from Jerusalem, but this walk took us an hour and a half. The people all around us were trying, just like us, to survive, to get where it was they had to go. Sometimes they bring sandwiches along because they know they might have to wait or walk for hours. It is all so confusing, so deeply disruptive to our lives.

This is not normal living, but we are trying to adapt to the situation. We have to accept, for now, but we shouldn't get too comfortable in our acceptance. Otherwise, we might lose our will to change things. We risk becoming too complacent in our misery. Maybe this is what the Israelis want after all.

CATHY: What do the Israelis say at a checkpoint?

MAHA: Say? They don't speak. They yell, "Your papers," or "This checkpoint is closed, go home." There is no human interaction with the soldiers. They act like robots, programmed to be nasty with us.

Although I am an actress, and I know how to control my breathing, every time I am at a checkpoint my breathing begins to accelerate and my heart starts pumping very rapidly. I cannot help myself. I get irritated for as long as I am obliged to stand before an Israeli soldier. Checkpoints are the extreme humiliation and Palestinians are forced to do this every day.

CATHY: What are some of the other consequences of occupation?

MAHA: Even during this so-called peace process, after Oslo, we have had trouble with the food supply. Many times the Israelis brought expired food into the territories. They re-labeled it, so that we would not know. Another time, lots of people died from what the doctors thought was food poisoning. It turned out that the Israelis had put rat poison in some of the food. This created a huge scandal.

[**Authors Note**: I could not independently verify this.]

The polluting of water resources is another terrible problem we faced. Our wells are being polluted with sewage from the settlements.

CATHY: Don't the settlers have their own wells?

MAHA: Yes, of course, but they, nonetheless, deposit their sewage in our springs and streams. As a result, many of our villages have no water for weeks at a time. This was a terrible hardship on our poor villagers.

CATHY: Why would Israeli settlers behave like this?

MAHA: So Palestinians will get fed up and leave and the settlers can claim our lands and build more settlements. This is how they operate in many parts of the occupied territories.

According to the Oslo Accords, the Israeli military was supposed to leave Zone A, the land under PA control. They never left even though they claimed to have officially handed over the land to the Palestinian Authority.

The Israelis treat us like we are animals in a zoo. They are really only expanding the cage by setting up these Zones. When they gave us the first cage, Zone A, we were not allowed to go from one part of Zone A to another part of Zone A without a travel permit.

The Israeli government says that they are giving us our land back. If this is true, how is it that every day the West Bank is shrinking in size? Every day, during the past ten years of the so-called peace process, the West Bank has been shrinking because settlements have been growing.

America and Israel say that we refused the Clinton–Barak proposals at Camp David, and that Barak was willing to give us ninety-one percent. No one in the media bothered to complete the whole sentence so the world only heard ninety-one percent. They didn't hear the second half of the sentence: out of the seventy percent of the total West Bank territory. Now, the world wants to know why the Palestinians refused ninety-one percent of the West Bank.

Barak and Clinton have made us look like the bad people, the ones who were refusing peace with the Israelis. This is not right.

You want more ways that the occupation is hard on us? Assassinations of so-called terrorists. Who says they are terrorists? The Israelis? Why does everyone take their word for everything that happens here?

Settlers and soldiers come into our villages; they uproot our olive trees, sometimes 300-year-old trees, so that the settlers can build their homes. The army says it is to clear the way so snipers cannot shoot. This is not true. It is to clear the land to make way for settlements.

So, I ask you, what kind of peace is this? What kind of peace are we talking about? What kind of negotiations are we talking about? These are not negotiations. These are demands for concessions from the Palestinians who get nothing in return.

CATHY: Do you have a message for the American public?

MAHA: America is a colonialist country; Israel is the same. Like the real Native Americans, we are the real Palestinians, and we are going to stay in Palestine.

Americans need to know that their tax dollars supply the Israeli Army with tanks, Apache gunships and F16s, which come into our towns and villages to kill us. Every single person in the States is indirectly killing each of us here.

The American public has the power to stop this. America says it is a democratic country. What does this mean? That if you are not with us, you are against us, and therefore a terrorist?

George W. Bush wants us to think that he is right and that the rest of the world is wrong. You no longer have a democracy in America. You have a plutocracy of powerful people who run your government and their big corporations. In a sense, the American public is in the same situation as we are here: powerless.

CATHY: They don't realize this.

MAHA: Because they don't want to, because it is easier not to ask the hard questions. Life is relatively easy for most Americans so, as you say in America, why rock the boat? Why ask questions? Why change things?

CATHY: Do you think the Israeli society is ignorant of what goes on in the territories?

MAHA: For the most part, yes. They are quite willing to believe what they hear on Israeli television. It is so easy to become complacent in situations like this. It is a comfort to hear that the Israeli Army is protecting you and your family. So why ask questions?

The Israeli public is paranoid about their safety and their existence so why not go after the bad Palestinians who are trying to hurt them? When you are paranoid about your safety, you do not ask a lot of questions. You only want to be protected.

The Israeli government says, "If we don't take action, there will be dire consequences."

Does this kind of comment need additional explanations? I don't think so. This is self-defense against Palestinians who want to throw Israelis into the sea.

It is very easy to manipulate the Israeli public. They want to be pacified into believing that they will be safe. Up till now, they have bought into this. With the suicide bombers, they are even more terrified, and do not know what to think.

CATHY: Since 9/11, this same mentality prevails in America. People have been lulled into believing that we had to attack the Afghans, that we had to go after Saddam Hussein.

MAHA: It is only by a grassroots effort that things will change in the world. The Internet has been the best tool available for the *Intifada*. More people are informed about what is happening in Palestine, thanks to the news they get off the web. No government can censor that news; no government can stop its flow.

CATHY: When I meet Israelis next week in Jerusalem, what would you like me to say to them?

MAHA: Come and live among us, visit our refugee camps, our hospitals, watch what goes on at the checkpoints. Try to cross the checkpoints without saying who you are.

Do this for yourself, for your fellow Israelis. I think, then, you will understand why we are so frustrated and weary, and desperate enough to go blow ourselves up, taking innocent Israelis with us.

UM WALID

A '48 ARAB

I interviewed Um Walid, a '48 Arab, in her home in Ramallah. She is 85 years old, speaks fluent French, Arabic and English. She is very well-educated and has traveled extensively. We sat in her living room – cluttered with comfortable, overstuffed furniture – one entire wall given over to a ceiling-to-floor bookcase crammed with hundreds of books. The overflow sat in piles on the floor. Her other loves were obviously movies and music, because she had an impressive selection of both at arm's reach.

CATHY: What does the future hold for Palestinians?

UM WALID: I see the Israelis living in their part of Israel, and us living in our small part. The Israelis will never have our part of the original Palestine.

CATHY: What will stop the Israelis from taking all the land?

UM WALID: The Palestinian people, the other Arab countries.

CATHY: So far, the other Arab countries haven't lifted a finger to help you.

UM WALID: They cannot sit by forever. They will eventually break off their friendship with America. There will come a time when they will no longer be willing to help America. Why would any Arab government want to be friendly with America? Look at what they do. If one Israeli is killed, they get excited, and say, "What a tragedy."

Hundreds of Palestinians die, and what do they say? Nothing! Did the Americans say they were sorry that the Israelis killed thirty-six Palestinians today?

It is terrible what is happening. It is old men and women, even children. The Israelis think we are animals. We are human beings who only want to live in peace. We want Israel to leave our small piece of Palestine. We will never accept to be transferred. If we want to leave and go elsewhere, that is our business, but we will not be forced out as we were in '48.

Give us a hand in friendship, and we are willing to be friends. Shelling, Apache gunships and F16s are not a way to initiate a friendship. The Israelis are even pulling our trees out of their roots. Did you know that some of these trees take thirty years before they bear a single fruit? The Israelis tear them out with bulldozers. It is not just olive trees; it is also mangos, figs, lemons and almonds; all the trees that are plentiful in our country.

The Israeli soldiers also cut the electricity in the villages, they dig up the water mains, shoot bullets in our water reservoirs. In the fields, where the cattle eat, they put poison on the ground, so the livestock will die. What kind of behavior is that?

Look at the way the American government is letting Sharon do whatever he wants. Why doesn't your president stop him? Why do our people have to suffer?

We have stones, not weapons. We do not have planes or tanks or anything to fight them. Why should they be allowed to use these heavy arms against unarmed civilians, when we cannot defend ourselves?

Every day, there are ten to twelve people killed, sometimes more. Yesterday, there were fourteen. Today, thirty-six were killed in Beit Gela, Nablus, Gaza and Bethlehem. Imagine hurting Bethlehem where Jesus Christ was born. This town is holy for the entire world. In the face of such outrageous acts, how does America stay silent? I don't understand.

CATHY: Special interest groups make it difficult for the administration to act.

UM WALID: My goodness, what is the percentage of these people to the entire American population? Do you mean to tell me that a few can keep silent a whole nation?

CATHY: That is not difficult when the general public is uninformed.

UM WALID: You're right. Not many people in America know about our struggle. They know only about Israel.

I have a nephew who works at the UN. On one of my trips to New York, he had just returned from China. On the occasion of my arrival, and his, my nephew's neighbors came to say hello. One man kept asking me questions about communism and the Russians, until I finally told him that the Russians were the first foreign country to come to our aid when the Turks were against the Christians in Palestine. The Russians were very critical of the Turks for their harsh treatment of the Christians. They were not even allowed to ring their church bells. When a Christian died, the people were not allowed to carry the body on their shoulders. They had to pull the corpse along the ground.

My mother told me that her father was a well-known man in Acre, a village in the north. He was a good friend of the Greek Orthodox Patriarch. He asked the Patriarch to open schools for boys and schools for girls because he wanted his children to attend such schools. The Patriarch responded by saying, "We will teach your children Russian."

My grandfather replied, "No, you will not teach them Russian. They will learn either French or English."

My mother died in 1970. She was eighty-four years old, and she spoke perfect French. All of this with the help of the Russians. Imagine, they even opened schools in the small villages. There is a village, near Acre, in the uppermost section of Palestine, near the Lebanese border. Mostly, Christians lived there along with a few Druze. The Russians even opened a school there. They saw what we needed and they gave it to us.

The Americans are not interested in us. George (W.) Bush talks like a silly boy. So what are we to do? Suffer because of this half-wit of a man?

When Saddam Hussein invaded Kuwait, America was quick to force him out so they could get their hands on the oil fields. Unfortunately, we have nothing that interests America.

The UN ruled that Israel should move off our land which they have occupied since '67. Why don't the Israelis leave? Why don't they obey the UN particularly when all the nations, except America, agree that they should? Isn't America ashamed to be the only nation that stands with Israel?

CATHY: Before the current *Intifada*, was Ramallah ever under total siege?

UM WALID: I used to travel alone from Ramallah to Jerusalem, spend the day there and come back. At that time, anyone could travel freely to Jerusalem.

CATHY: Tell me something about yourself.

UM WALID: My husband and I lived in Haifa. He worked in the Customs office. In 1947, the Jews started killing Arabs. It got to be very dangerous in Haifa. My son, my third child, was one year old. My oldest was eight. They were very frightened of the explosions and gunfire so my father-in-law came to Haifa and took the children and me to his village near the Jordan River, north of Tiberius, not far from the Lebanese border.

At that time much of this area belonged to wealthy Lebanese families who rented out their land to the local villagers who grew cash crops, mostly olive and fruit trees. Olives, as you know, were a very lucrative business. My father-in-law had his own lands and was very well-to-do. He was the most important Christian in this mostly Muslim area.

CATHY: After '48 and the creation of the State of Israel, what was the percentage of Christians in Palestine?

UM WALID: Probably about twenty percent of the population. Today, there are even less. The rest is in the Diaspora. We are of many creeds: Latins, Greek Catholics, Protestants and, of course, Greek Orthodox. We even had a Mormon church in Acre.

CATHY: Were there any Jews in Acre?

UM WALID: Yes, there was even a synagogue.

CATHY: When you left with your father-in-law, did you think you would return one day?

UM WALID: Of course, my husband stayed behind. We were only going for a short visit. In fact, after we left, he actually rented a larger house thinking we would live there when we returned to Haifa. I never saw it, of course. After we left, the entire region was closed to us, and we could not return.

Eventually, my husband and I did sneak back into the village and into our house. All our furniture, everything, was gone. We ended up staying with my in-laws for one and a half years.

In the end, I could not stay any longer. My husband asked me where we should go. I suggested Damascus. My youngest son was born there. He lives in Houston now. From there, we moved to Beirut, where we lived for twenty years. Our house was in the Masra neighborhood, near the Abdel Nasser Mosque. During the Lebanese civil war, four rockets hit our house.

My husband died in Beirut in 1982. From the church to the cemetery to bury him, we had to drive under Israeli bombing. After that, we left for America. Two of my sons now live in Ramallah. This is why I came back.

CARMEN

RECENT GRADUATE OF BIRZEIT UNIVERSITY

When I reached the offices of al-Quds University, located off the dimly-lit souk which leads to the Dome of the Rock in the Muslim Quarter of the Old City, I met twenty-year-old Carmen. I was so taken by her delicately sculptured face, her long, black, wavy hair and impeccable dress that I momentarily forgot why I had come. At first, she refused my request for an interview. When I assured her that I would not use her real name, she still resisted. "What's the point? Who in America cares what happens to us."

"Americans rarely, if ever, hear from Palestinians," I said. "This is your opportunity to speak out."

Her office overlooked a small, sun-lit courtyard. In one corner lay the remains of several Roman columns, a stark reminder that this place has seen constant turmoil for thousands of years.

CARMEN: Last night, no one could get anywhere near the Qalandya checkpoint, which is right near my house. We knew something terrible was taking place because we heard explosions all night long.

By 5:00 AM I was wide awake, trying to figure out what had happened. What is so bizarre about our lives now is that we talk about these things as though they are normal. A suicide bombing here; an Apache gunship missile strike there. How sad that these words have seeped into our everyday vocabulary.

CATHY: Did the Israeli Army also enter Ramallah a few months ago?

CARMEN: Yes.

CATHY: Why did they eventually leave?

CARMEN: No one knows. We actually took it as a sign of hope that things were getting better. In light of this massive invasion, it would appear that Sharon was saving Ramallah for special treatment.

CATHY: Last week, when the Israeli government told all internationals to leave Ramallah, the residents got quite worried. They anticipated something awful. What is actually going on in Ramallah?

CARMEN: There have been a lot of assassinations using Apache gunships. The city is under total curfew. All the shops are closed, as are all the schools. The Israeli Army went into the al-Amari refugee camp and arrested all the men.

CATHY: What happens to these men?

CARMEN: Who knows? Once they are taken away, you rarely learn what happens to them. They can be held in military detention for up to six months, without ever being charged with a crime. They can be put in solitary confinement even longer.

Months later, the Israelis will send a notice to a family announcing that their husband, father or brother died in prison. I cannot even begin to imagine how these men are treated in Israeli prisons.

Sometimes I ask myself, "are we humans?" If so, and I think we are, why are the Israelis treating us like this?

Of course, it is bad on both sides. You watch the news and see the suicide bombing. But is this the solution? Is this how we are going to solve our problems?

If you had asked me a few months ago what I thought of suicide bombers, I would have said it was awful. Right now, when I see how they treat us, I'm confused. I don't know anymore. If I lived in the Deheishe refugee camp near Bethlehem, and saw how the Israelis treated my father, brother or husband, I might, for one split second, think of becoming a suicide bomber.

I live in a pretty calm area of East Jerusalem. And even though I am an Israeli Arab, I'm often held up at an Israeli checkpoint for over an hour. I know they are doing this just to humiliate me, to remind me that they are in control, and rule my life. In the long run, how is this going to affect me?

How can I be a supporter of peace and negotiations with all that is going on now in Ramallah? Sometimes, I think this whole thing is a game that Sharon and Arafat are playing.

CATHY: Tell me more.

CARMEN: I think it is a game of passion to see who will break first. I'm afraid it is the people who will break first.

CATHY: A leader is supposed to be, first and foremost, working for his people.

CARMEN: Yes, that is true. But look at what Sharon is doing to Arafat. Anything that hurts Arafat only makes Sharon appear stronger.

CATHY: What are Palestinians able to do against Sharon?

CARMEN: Not much, except resist. We can refuse to give in to daily humiliations, refuse to bend to the Israelis, refuse to leave our land, to abandon our homes, unless, of course, we are bulldozed out.

It is a matter of self-pride. Sharon wants to see us all cower in a corner. We refuse. This is our weapon against Sharon.

Our press is not very effective, even inside Israel, and the international press hardly pays any attention to us. If they do, it is to tell the world that the Palestinians are terrorists.

Photojournalists show the world the aftermath of a suicide bombing. They rarely show a refugee camp after heavy bombardment, or bulldozers demolishing homes and uprooting 300-year-old olive trees to make way for more settlements.

CATHY: Let's talk about the future.

CARMEN: A future? We don't have a future. If our young people are allowed to grow up, the only thing they will have learned is how to throw stones at Israeli soldiers at checkpoints. They certainly will not be going to school because that is the first thing the Israelis close. They will not have a park to swing in, either, or a clean, safe neighborhood where they can ride their bikes.

What is the future of a child who grows up knowing that his father, brother or uncle was killed by an Israeli bullet? Will he be able to erase all those images that haunt him, or will he find it impossible to pretend they never happened?

CATHY: Suppose that Arafat and Sharon declared a truce and entered into peace negotiations. Would you be able to put aside your differences if it meant peace?

CARMEN: I would certainly try. However, a two-state solution is not the answer. We need one open state where we can all live together.

Look, we Palestinians will not be able to forget what the Israelis did to us any more than they will be able to forget our suicide bombers. They, too, live in fear. Their children are growing up knowing the misery that we, our parents and grandparents, have known for fifty-three years.

So, separating everyone will not be the right solution. We need to heal together. If we are separated, a person, one day might attack his neighbor for no apparent reason, and it will all start again. If we live together, everyone will be obliged to make peace work.

CATHY: Do you know any Israelis? Have you ever talked politics with them?

CARMEN: Yes, most of them are left of center and pro-Palestinian. We often talk about coexistence and living in one big, open society, where we both have equal rights, where we are both treated like human beings.

There are also times when we Palestinians sit in dialogue groups with right-wing Israelis who want to see us deported, thrown into the sea, or put on buses and sent to other Arab countries.

This kind of talk is commonly heard. The radio talk shows are full of such hateful discourse.

CATHY: How are your pro-Palestinian friends handling this current crisis?

CARMEN: They are very depressed. They constantly call us to check on our well-being, especially if they have heard that one of us has been hurt, or is in trouble. We have a wonderful network of friends on the other side. I actually think it is harder on them than it is on us. They cannot openly express their views, for fear of being attacked.

CATHY: From the extreme right?

CARMEN: Yes, because most Israelis wear blinders. They can't see an alternative.

Israelis are scared. You just have to watch how they walk down a street. They are always looking around, suspicious of the person next to them. They are fearful of parked cars, of objects on the ground. Their children also watch the news. They know what's happening.

CATHY: If Israelis are getting killed by suicide bombers, why are they still supporting Sharon's brutal policies?

CARMEN: Most Israelis are happy with what their soldiers are doing in Ramallah. This proves that their government is doing something.

They actually believe Sharon when he says, "By making this operation in Ramallah, I am stopping terrorism."

The right-wing loves this kind of military action, too. It makes them feel good. Instead of sitting there 24/7, someone is doing something to make them less scared. This someone is Sharon.

CATHY: Don't they realize that these brutal responses will only lead to more suicide bombings?

CARMEN: This is how you and I think. This is how most Palestinians think. Apparently, Israelis think, "I am scared. I want a quick fix. Sharon is giving me one. I'm satisfied with that."

Violence is a circle that does not stop unless you take a scissor and cut it. If you do not find a way to stop, it continues to go round and round. Unfortunately, most people under pressure do not think clearly. All they know is that they want some sense of security to hold onto.

This is what the Palestinian people are doing. They're scared. They feel that they have no other choice but to hold onto Arafat. They stand behind him. Even if they don't agree with him they think, "At least its something, and something is better than nothing."

This is all so crazy. It crawls into my psyche and won't go away.

I am only twenty years old. I am not even supposed to be a woman yet. Look at me sitting here, talking to you about politics as if I were at least thirty-five.

I just finished my studies at BirZeit University, located a few kilometers north of Ramallah. Every day, I used to cross the checkpoints at al-Ram and Qalandya.

CATHY: How long did it take you to cross?

CARMEN: In normal times, from my home to BirZeit, it used to take about forty minutes. Now, with the checkpoints, forty minutes has turned into two and a half hours each way.

Here is how it went: After waking up and getting dressed, and taking public transportation to the checkpoint, I had to line up like an animal waiting to be inspected. This was both mentally and spiritually draining.

I was constantly watched. And even if I tried to think of something happy, in order to get through the checkpoint with my sanity intact, it was almost impossible because wherever I looked a soldier was pointing a gun at me.

The Israelis have many other ways of making our lives difficult, too. They prepare open holes in the ground so that you stumble and fall while walking through their checkpoint. Then, they fill these pot holes with water so that your clothes get splashed and covered in dirt.

What I have just described was only the al-Ram checkpoint. After that, there was Qalandya, and after that, a kilometer walk before I finally reached my university.

Seated in class, finally, I tried to concentrate. I wanted to take a deep breath but it was impossible because my lungs were filled with the smell of exhaust from Israeli tanks at the checkpoints. I tried to shut these thoughts out but suddenly my teacher says something about a checkpoint and my mind flashes back there again.

At the end of the day, when I finally arrive home, all I could do is sit and read a fantasy book, or watch a movie, then go to bed. Sleep is the only way to forget but even this is difficult. Israeli tanks and soldiers have a way of creeping into dreams.

With all my complaining, I am a very fortunate young lady. I just came back from a vacation. Frankly, if I did not leave the country every once in a while, I would go mad.

CATHY: How do you get out? Through Ben-Gurion Airport?

CARMEN: That is a good question. If you decide to go to Europe or the States, you must go through Ben-Gurion Airport. As a Jerusalem resident, I am allowed to use that airport.

To do that is a hassle. Let us say my flight is at 6:00 PM, I must leave my house at 6:00 AM. Because of the security checks, I need about six hours to have my clothes scanned by laser, piece by piece, and that includes my socks.

CATHY: Are you made to get undressed?

CARMEN: Of course, but first, Israeli security makes an attempt to be civilized. They have you walk through the scanner. Of course, every time you do, you beep. So, they begin by making you take every piece of metal off. Then, it is your shoes, and finally, a complete body search, for your own safety, of course, and theirs.

After that, you can proceed to your gate. All the while, you have a very special escort because you are Palestinian. You are even escorted to your seat. And if you buy something before boarding the plane, you are in serious trouble.

CATHY: Why?

CARMEN: Because they have to take your purchase and scan it to make sure there is not a bomb inside. Mind you, that purchase was made in their own duty-free shop.

CATHY: If you returned through Amman, Jordan, could you avoid this kind of hassle?

CARMEN: You cannot return through Amman if you have not

departed from Amman. And if you leave from Amman, the Israelis will keep your ID with them. This way, if you don't come back through Amman, or if you stay out longer than you are permitted, they will tell you bye-bye when you try to return.

CATHY: Even if you are a Jerusalem resident and an Israeli citizen?

CARMEN: They have this rule that if you do not come back after two years, you automatically lose your ID and your right to reside in Jerusalem.

CATHY: When you leave from Ben-Gurion airport, do the Israelis also keep your ID?

CARMEN: No, they issue you a travel document, which is not really a passport. It just looks like one. It is good for one year, so it is very important that you go and come back within that time frame, if you want to keep your residency.

CATHY: Where do you obtain your travel document?

CARMEN: We have to line up in front of the Population Ministry on Nablus Street, next to the Jerusalem Hotel. Usually, this takes at least a day. Any Palestinian who wishes to leave has to go to that office and request a travel permit.

Of course, it is up to the Israelis as to whether or not they honor your request. It is torture to do this thing. The Israelis make everything very hard.

CATHY: How does the system work?

CARMEN: Well, on a normal day, to go to this office, you have to wake up at three in the morning to be there by four or five, at the latest.

There, you join the line with the hundreds of other people who were there before you. By the time you get to the guard at the door, to get your number, he has usually already closed for the day.

However, if you are lucky enough to get a number, even if you have to return the next day, you are at least assured of getting inside the building. Once there, you still have to wait four to five hours for your turn.

The Israelis will then make you run back and forth and up and down, to get all sorts of documents to prove that you have paid your taxes, your electricity and water bills, and that you have the proper school certificate. It is a deadly process.

If I want to renew my travel document, which is valid for only one year, and I know that I will be traveling next January, and it is already March, I will start the process immediately so I will be sure to have my travel permit in time to get a visa for the country I plan to visit.

CATHY: You mean you still have to go to a Consulate and apply for a visa?

CARMEN: Yes. Personally, this time I didn't have a problem when I went to the American Consulate. I was going with an Israeli-Palestinian dialogue group. As far as the American Consulate was concerned, I was going to America to be brainwashed, so I got my visas on the spot.

People who are less fortunate have to bring proof that they have been living here for the last fifty years. You have to show that you are returning to a job. You must have written proof that your employer has given you permission to travel for a certain number of days. You have to show that you are leaving a son or daughter behind, or that you have a house.

Then, the Consulate runs a background check to make sure you are not involved in any political activities. In the end, there is no guarantee that you will get your visa to study in the States, to visit family, or be allowed to travel like a normal tourist.

I know that when I wanted to visit the UK, I had to ask my school to send a fax to prove that I was still a student. I had to get a letter from the people who were going to be my hosts, affirming that they would be in charge of all my activities while I was in the UK, and would supervise the places I visited, even how I spent my money.

The British Consulate wanted to know who was providing the money for me to travel, why I was going and why I chose the UK. I got my visa because I was still a student at BirZeit University and could prove that I was coming back.

CATHY: Tell me about this dialogue group you participated in.

CARMEN: (Laughter) It was called Building Bridges for Peace. It was primarily a youth group of Israelis and Palestinians. We lived together in a camp for three weeks. We were taught communication skills and games, all having to do with getting along with the other side.

CATHY: Tell me more.

CARMEN: One side would talk, and we would have to repeat what the other side said in order to show that we were actually listening.

The funny part was that when we finished our meeting, we would sit and have lunch together, participate in sports and even sing together. When it came to politics we ended up fighting. It was quite funny because you would see us in the discussion groups screaming our heads off, and later you would find us hugging and dancing together.

CATHY: Give me an example of how a dialogue went.

CARMEN: Two people were chosen from each group. They would go up on stage. One side started, then the other side took its turn.

If it was my turn, I would say something like, "The Israelis are killing Palestinian children at checkpoints."

The Israeli girl would have to mirror what I said, repeating it back to me, word for word.

Then, it would be her turn, and she would say, "Palestinians are killing my friends in suicide bombings." I would then repeat what she said, taking a few minutes to respond.

The rest of the group would then have their turn saying things back and forth, but it had to constantly be a mirror. You could not just hear what they were saying and respond without mirroring back what the other side had said. If you did, it wouldn't count and the counselor would call for a time-out and oblige you to repeat what the other side had said.

At times, we made some headway. We were sympathizing with the Israelis, and they with us. But then, someone would get a letter from back home saying that such and such happened, and all our progress would evaporate.

The American moderators at the camp were supposed to be there to ease the tensions. Of course, part of the struggle was to win the Americans over to one side. The Israelis were always trying to get them to take their side. This was easy because the moderators were already pro-Israeli. They didn't know anything about Palestine. Most Americans, when they hear the word "Palestine," think we're saying "Pakistan." They don't even know where Palestine is. If you say "Jerusalem," they immediately say, "Oh sure, you mean Israel."

Even if I didn't manage to change their way of thinking, the Americans, at least, will not forget me. I am still in touch with some of them, in fact. They know, now, when they hear in the news that all Palestinians are terrorists, to say, "No, that isn't true. I met a girl who was really nice. Her name is Carmen, and she is not a terrorist."

AMIRA

EMPLOYED AT HEBREW UNIVERSITY

Amira, an Israeli Arab, works at Hebrew University on the French Hill, on the northern edge of East Jerusalem. After I introduced myself, she invited me in very articulate English to follow her to her office.

I had a hard time keeping up with this attractive, slim woman in her early forties. With short black hair, she was dressed very stylishly in a navy and red silk dress and heels. By the time we arrived at her corner office, four flights later, I was relieved to be able to fall into the nearest chair, while she rushed to answer the telephone.

CATHY: You're an Israeli Arab. What does that mean?

AMIRA: First, there is a difference between being a citizen and having Israeli nationality, so please don't get confused.

I'm an Israeli Arab and, therefore, have citizenship in the State of Israel, but only Jews have Israeli nationality. This is a very important distinction because you can purchase land in Israel only if you are Jewish.

Sometimes, I think of myself as an Arab woman but, of course, my identity is really mixed. I am both Palestinian and Israeli. This makes my life very complicated. As a woman in an Arab society, I have always tried to be equal to my brothers, to my husband and to the other men in my family.

This is not easy. On top of this, I am supposed to be Israeli. I feel that I am in a constant struggle. It is very frustrating.

I was born in Akbara but this was not my family's village. In 1948, they were thrown out of their village in the north. My parents were in their twenties when this happened.

CATHY: I hear the phrase '48 Arab used often. Who are they?

AMIRA: Fearless people, like my parents, who refused to leave Palestine when they were thrown out of their villages.

CATHY: Why did some leave and some stay?

AMIRA: Some people were frightened and left the country. They were terrorized by what happened in their villages and cities in '47–'48. In some villages, like Lydia and Deir Yassin, there were terrible slaughters of innocent people.

Some were kicked out by force from their towns and villages, like my father-in-law, but he refused to stay out of his country. He brought his family back to Palestine, while many in his family chose to stay in Lebanon and live as refugees.

My parents decided not to leave. However, their lives were made very difficult by the Zionists who threw them out of one village after another. I was a small child while this was happening.

CATHY: As a child, did you attend school with Israeli children?

AMIRA: No, they attend Jewish-only schools.

CATHY: Are their schools still that way today?

AMIRA: Yes, from first grade to the end of high school.

CATHY: Can an Arab attend Hebrew University?

AMIRA: If they pass the entrance exam, any Arab can attend school here.

CATHY: Do you mean only Israeli Arabs?

AMIRA: No, Palestinians attend classes here, too. Can you imagine how the Israeli image would suffer in the world if people thought that Palestinians were forbidden to attend Israeli universities?

This way, you see, they can claim to be an open and free society and say, "Look at what we offer the Palestinians."

CATHY: What is the percentage of Palestinian students who attend Hebrew University?

AMIRA: Approximately a quarter.

CATHY: Did you grow up learning Hebrew?

AMIRA: In school, we were taught in Arabic. However, my parents insisted we learn Hebrew. They knew we would not qualify for any job in Israel if we didn't speak Hebrew. And, as we are Israeli Arabs, I agree that we should speak Hebrew and try to fit into the Israeli culture. Unfortunately, we are a long way from achieving that end.

Look at the Palestinian primary and secondary school system in Israel. Israeli Arabs must pay the same taxes as Israelis, but our schools are not adequately staffed. They are overcrowded, badly built and in need of major repairs. Jewish schools have computer labs, libraries, science labs and space for recreational activities.

CATHY: There is a language barrier between Israelis and Palestinians in the occupied territories. I just spent at week in Ramallah and was surprised to learn that none of the schools there teach Hebrew. A dialogue has to begin between these two peoples if peace is to be achieved. Will that barrier ever be lowered?

AMIRA: The hatred is very strong on both sides, so this will not be an easy thing to accomplish. I guess that if there is ever an opportunity for peace in the future, such language barriers could be overcome. But right now, the willingness is not there, at least not on the part of the Palestinians.

To the Israelis, I would say, "Show us your willingness to end the occupation, and we will learn your language."

By the way, I doubt many Israelis speak Arabic. To be honest, aside from a mild case of cynicism, I do try to keep a balance for myself particularly in my work here at the university.

CATHY: Do the Israeli professors and staff here make any effort to find common ground with you and your Palestinian colleagues?

AMIRA: On a professional level, everyone is very civilized and polite. On a social level, there is no interaction. In the course of a conversation, now and again, we might say, "We should get together sometime and have lunch," but it does not happen.

You see, many on the staff here are settlers so there really is not much common ground.

CATHY: Do you teach here?

AMIRA: No, I work as a coordinator for early childhood programs in the Arab sector. This is a program spearheaded by Hebrew University. I was hired for my cultural background and Arabic language skills.

Very few people on the staff speak Arabic. Everything is published in Hebrew, and if you do not know the language, you are out of luck. There is little tolerance for other languages. Sometimes this attitude makes me feel like a second-class citizen.

CATHY: Do you pay the same taxes as Israelis?

AMIRA: Yes, but there is something very important I want to tell you first. Every Arab who can afford it, likes to have his or her own house, but there are no building projects permitted in East Jerusalem for Arabs, because we are not allowed to buy land.

CATHY: Is a Palestinian ever granted a construction permit?

AMIRA: It is very, very rare. It is also a very long and expensive process. This is why so many people build without permit. It is next to impossible for a Palestinian to obtain a permit. Sometimes it takes years to get permission. Who wants to wait that long when you are in need of a house?

By contrast, the government pays for and constructs Israeli housing on confiscated Arab land. On top of that we often pay more taxes than Israelis do.

CATHY: Tell me more about the taxes you pay.

AMIRA: My house is large. According to Israeli law, if it is more than 120 meters it is considered a big house so we must pay more taxes. Compared to an Israeli living on the French Hill in a very nice, comfortable neighborhood on Mt. Scopus overlooking Jerusalem, we also pay the double in taxes.

We have nothing to show for all the taxes we pay. As Israeli citizens, we are not even guaranteed social services and family programs, such as daycare. It is only for Israelis.

CATHY: Is the French Hill part of the pre-'67 border?

AMIRA: Yes, the area around the French Hill and Hebrew University used to be full of Arab houses. Of course, with settlement construction and the university expansion, our land was confiscated.

CATHY: The Palestinians are asking for a state on twenty-two percent of the original Palestine. Why won't the Israeli government give it to them?

AMIRA: I don't have an answer. They are frightened perhaps and think that if they hold onto more land, they will feel more secure. According to the latest newspaper polls, forty-six percent of Israelis want the Palestinians transferred somewhere else.

CATHY: In 1914, Chaim Weizman called this "a land without people for a people without land." Is that still the prevailing attitude?

AMIRA: I have heard tour guides talk as though nobody ever lived here before the Zionists arrived. It is beyond me how they can still so blatantly deny the existence of the Palestinians.

Sometimes, when we go to Arab villages, I hear it said that the Arabs sold the land and moved away. I want to scream, "What are you talking about? Why would any Palestinian sell his land? Why is the Israeli version of history the correct one?"

There are many other ways we are made to feel inferior. Take military service. We are not entitled to serve in the army but if we do not serve, we don't qualify for many of the social services. Here, every Israeli is supposed to get a stipend for child support. We are Israeli Arabs. We are considered Israeli. The government collects our taxes as if we were citizens of this state. However, because we are not allowed to serve in the army, we do not qualify for child support.

CATHY: Does every Israeli have to perform military service?

AMIRA: No, the religious people do not have to serve in the army. In fact, they have more rights than most Israelis because they go to religious schools.

The Druze are the only Arabs who serve in the army.

CATHY: How did that come about?

AMIRA: In 1948, their leaders signed an agreement to serve in the Israeli Army in exchange for social services.

CATHY: Do you know any Druze?

AMIRA: Yes, of course. The Israelis claim they are different from the Palestinian Arabs. They lavish praise on them, calling them great warriors but it is just a way of buying their loyalty. These are poor people who would otherwise not find employment. And the pay is not anywhere near what an Israeli gets for serving in the army.

CATHY: Do you feel discriminated against as an Arab woman?

AMIRA: Yes, sometimes. I can feel it in the street while walking about doing my shopping, particularly since the *Intifada* began. There is a store where I used to buy my groceries. Since they discovered that I was an Arab, they do not even address me anymore. As long as they thought I was an Israeli, I was a good customer. Now, I am not even welcome there. I have known these people for a long time, and now I am an untouchable to them? I was very hurt. I do not feel myself less than anyone else and I resent any kind of discrimination.

CATHY: Does your husband feel this kind of discrimination in his work?

AMIRA: He has his own business and is responsible for his staff, so he is in a very different environment.

CATHY: Are West Bank and Gaza realities shown on Israeli television?

AMIRA: Israelis see some things. In general, they ignore what goes on in the West Bank. All they want to know is why we Palestinians are killing them. They don't want to know about the reality and hardships of the occupation.

Israelis think they're more civilized than we are. They live in beautiful neighborhoods with lovely gardens and playgrounds.

They think, because we live in less well-kept neighborhoods, that we are less than them.

I will take you on a tour of my neighborhood near Hebrew University. You'll see for yourself the difference between our two neighborhoods.

We pay the same taxes as Israelis. Our roads are not paved; theirs are. We have dirt fields; they have gardens and secure playgrounds for their children.

Yes, I have a beautiful house because my husband makes a good living. However, the neighborhood around my building is run down. Our local schools are poorly equipped. Our children have no playgrounds to play on after school or at recess. I can afford to send my children to private school so I cannot complain. But those who can't, what are they to do?

> [**Authors Note:** After our interview, Amira took me on a tour of the French Hill, a beautiful neighborhood in East Jerusalem, full of Israeli settlements with well-groomed lawns, gardens and well-paved roads. Her neighborhood was as she had described it. Despite being lovely homes they were surrounded by vacant lots strewn with garbage. The Israeli government does not provide garbage collection in her neighborhood, either. Across the street in the Jewish neighborhood garbage is collected on a regular basis. Both neighborhoods pay the same taxes. Amira drove me around East Jerusalem. She showed me the by-pass, Israeli-only roads and the bulldozed streets in Arab neighborhoods that are closed to traffic.]

CATHY: Why are there so many bulldozed streets in the Arab neighborhoods?

AMIRA: The Israelis like to make the Arab driver's trek to work harder by forcing him or her to take a longer route.

CATHY: As an Israeli Arab, are you affected by the checkpoints?

AMIRA: Palestinians who are obliged to drive into East Jerusalem must plan on a two to three hour wait to get their cars inspected before being given permission to enter Jerusalem.

Everyday life for the Israeli Arab, even if they hold an Israeli passport and are citizens of the State of Israel, is almost as hard, and in some cases even harder, than their Palestinian counterparts in the occupied territories. Palestinians are looked at with suspicion, especially if they are a little dark skinned. They are afraid to take buses, to walk in parts of Jerusalem for fear of being attacked by Israelis. Many such incidents have already occurred since the second *Intifada* began.

CATHY: Can Arabs use the judicial system to protest Israeli confiscation of their lands?

AMIRA: Yes, there are a few brave souls who dare to contest their lost land. Do they get compensation? No. Does the Israeli Supreme Court ever accept to hear their case? If it does, it is not the Israeli Arab who wins.

CATHY: Why do so many Israelis occupy apartments in the Christian and Muslim Quarters of the Old City?

AMIRA: The Palestinians sell their apartments to them.

CATHY: Why would they do that?

AMIRA: They are given two choices: either the apartment is confiscated with no compensation, or they accept to sell at the price the Israeli wants to pay. These are very poor people who live in the Old City. They cannot afford to be thrown out of their apartments. Whatever compensation they get is better than nothing. In other words, they have no choice but to do as the Israelis say.

I will give you an example. In my parents' village, the Israelis continuously tried to give money to those people who had lost their homes, in order to be able to say that the Arabs sold them their homes, and that they, the Israelis, never took the houses by force. In some of these cases, people needed the money and could not afford to refuse. Others refused outright.

CATHY: Who are those people who still live in the Old City, in the Armenian, Christian and Muslim Quarters?

AMIRA: They are mostly very poor people who fled their villages in '48. They have no voice, practically no legal rights. They are residents of East Jerusalem, but not Israeli Arabs. They cannot vote for the *Knesset*, the Israeli Parliament. I can vote. I am an Israeli citizen. We have eight Palestinian representatives in the *Knesset*, and we represent twenty percent of the Israeli population. Of course, our elected officials are not in any coalition and, therefore, their powers are very limited. However, it is a beginning.

CATHY: Do you see any glimmer of hope in the foreseeable future?

AMIRA: I am extremely pessimistic about the future. Somehow, someday, we must have our Palestinian state. The Israelis for now resist this idea. They say they are ready to make peace, but only on their terms. Israelis rarely respect viewpoints other than their own.

YASMINE

SURVIVOR OF THE DEIR YASSIN MASSACRE

Yasmine heads the Center for Palestinian Women, an organization that monitors women's working conditions. In order to reach her office, I had to leave my taxi two city blocks away and walk through an Israeli checkpoint. As soon as I found her office in a building pockmarked with bullet holes and broken windows, I had to climb three flights of stairs. Yasmine graciously invited me into her spacious, sunny office as though I were her only appointment of the day when, in reality, at 9:30 AM her phones were already ringing nonstop. Before we began the interview, she instructed her secretary to hold all her calls. She then closed the door and returned to her desk. "Now we can talk," she said, smiling.

YASMINE: I'm from a village called Deir Yassin. Have you ever heard of it?

CATHY: No.

YASMINE: It was located in a largely Jewish area in what is now called West Jerusalem.

CATHY: Why is this so significant?

YASMINE: In 1942, the people in my village signed a nonaggression pact with their Jewish neighbors. When the fighting broke out in '48, they did not think it was necessary to ask for protection from the Arab High Committee. After all, they had sworn to live in peace with their Jewish neighbors.

However, on April 9, 1948, *Irgun* and Stern gang members, lead by Begin and Shamir, both of whom later became Israeli Prime Ministers, entered our village and slaughtered many people. They lined men, women and children up against walls, and shot them. Two hundred and fifty-four people were killed. I lost many family members: my father and grandfather, my brother, my oldest sister and her son. My mother lost a brother.

CATHY: What happened to you after that?

YASMINE: I was only five years old at the time, but I remember very vividly my mother grabbing me into her arms and running from the village.

CATHY: How did you survive?

YASMINE: Thanks to the generosity of other family members in other villages, until we finally settled in Ramallah in 1960. There, my mother got a job teaching school.

CATHY: After the massacre what happened?

YASMINE: When the news spread to other villages, people got very frightened and began fleeing. This led to the flight of Palestinians from places like Haifa, Jaffa, Tiberias, Safed, Acre, Lydda, Ramleh, Majdal and Beersheba.

On October 29, 1948, there was another terrible massacre near Hebron, in a place called Duweima. This crime was not even uncovered until 1984, and only then by an Israeli journalist.

It was easy enough at the time, particularly when so many people fled, to cover up a crime like Deir Yassin. Bulldozers moved into a village once all of the Palestinians had fled. Houses were razed to the ground. Even trees were uprooted and plowed under. This process eliminated all evidence of any prior existence very rapidly.

In Tantura, near Haifa, Jewish militia murdered 200 Arab fighters, who had already laid down their arms, after the village surrendered in May, 1948. The village was razed in June, 1948, to make way for a kibbutz and a swimming pool. This particular massacre received a lot of press recently because an Israeli by the name of Teddy Katz wrote his masters' thesis on the event. Even though his thesis was awarded an unusually high grade, an academic committee at Haifa University ordered the suspension of his thesis. They gave him six months to submit a revised one.

Of course, the objective of all the massacres was to destroy the urban Palestinian communities. Even before the mass exodus, Palestinians were already suffering from economic deprivation. Food convoys were not allowed into villages and, in some parts, mass starvation was common. Houses were demolished and people were harassed. We now know that this was all part of Ben-Gurion's plan to rid Palestine of the Palestinians. His campaign was very successful.

CATHY: Why are there such diverging views of Israeli history?

YASMINE: Modern Israel is guided by Zionist ideology and its romantic stories about war heroes. No one wanted to hear about Palestinians driven from their homes in acts of ethnic cleansing. In the last decade, several Israeli historians have attempted to set the record straight. They are called the "new historians."

CATHY: What remains of Deir Yassin today?

YASMINE: Nothing. It was completely razed and incorporated into Jerusalem. You will not find it on any map. It is as though it never existed.

CATHY: Tell me something about yourself.

YASMINE: I begin each day by getting out of bed and getting dressed for work. More often than not, I arrive at the Qalandya checkpoint to be told that it is closed, and that I cannot enter Jerusalem.

I backtrack and walk miles over dirt roads to get to al-Ram, which is near the next checkpoint. From there, I can usually get a taxi into Jerusalem. Sometimes I have to walk into Jerusalem before finding a taxi. I repeat the same routine every night after a long day of work.

CATHY: Where do you find the courage to face these daily hardships?

YASMINE: I have no choice. I do not have the luxury of staying in bed and doing nothing. Many people count on me for help. Until very recently, I was monitoring working conditions in a clothing factory.

CATHY: An Israeli-owned factory?

YASMINE: Yes.

CATHY: Describe the working conditions.

YASMINE: It is very long hours for very little pay, from five in the morning till five in the evening. The Israeli employer does not pay a Palestinian, particularly a woman, a decent wage. The only good thing about the *Intifada* now is that the Israelis suffer with us. There is no work, no production and, therefore, no profit for the factory owners. The worst part is that many of the husbands of these women are in jail, and there is no money coming in.

CATHY: What happened to the men who were taken from the refugee camp near Jenin two days ago?

YASMINE: I know there were about 500 men rounded up. In the Balata camp, near Nablus, the Israelis did the same, and in Tulkarim, too. All in all, there were about 800 men. No one knows where they are.

CATHY: You are very nicely dressed today. Is this how you walk from Ramallah?

YASMINE: Yes.

CATHY: In these same clothes?

YASMINE: Yes, I leave my house in the clothes I wear to work. I do not change clothes once I get here. And yes, even nicely dressed, we have to walk around the checkpoint at Qalandya, over dirt roads. It is a question of pride, you see. Why should I allow the Israeli soldiers to make me feel less than who I am? I do not have a lot of money, but I enjoy dressing nicely. I even wear my heels over dirt roads. No, I will not change this part of my life.

CATHY: Are there still a lot of Israeli Army tanks at the Qalandya checkpoint?

YASMINE: Yes, of course, and all throughout Ramallah. Soldiers are everywhere. They have several checkpoints inside Ramallah, too.

You know, many of us start out every morning to go to work. It is like a throw of the dice. Some of us succeed, but many are obliged to return home because the Israeli soldiers refuse to let them pass at a checkpoint. Look at the checkpoint outside my office. Did you see how many cars were lined up this morning waiting to get through the checkpoint?

CATHY: I counted over one hundred!

YASMINE: This goes on every morning. People trying to get to work in Jerusalem have to wait in long lines, sometimes two to three hours. It is an incredible hardship.

For trucks transporting produce, it is especially difficult, particularly with this awful heat wave, because the Israelis often hold up the trucks for days. Obviously, by the time the trucks are allowed to pass, their produce has spoiled. What can they sell, then, to feed their families?

Sometimes, after making Palestinians sit in their cars for hours, the Israeli in charge of the checkpoint will announce that the road has been closed, and that no more cars will pass that day.

We are totally at the mercy of these people. Sometimes, I think their only purpose is to frustrate us, to humiliate us. We are proud people, and we are patient people. At least, I hope we can continue to be patient. Some days it is very difficult.

Yesterday, the Israelis claimed they were looking for a man. The soldiers came into our building. They told us to leave. They planned to seal off the building, so we had to leave or risk being locked inside. It was closed from twelve noon to 6:30 in the evening.

CATHY: Describe your work, what do you do in an average day?

YASMINE: My organization monitors activities throughout the territories and Jerusalem, particularly those that affect women. We report this information to the Palestine Monitor, which is an NGO that keeps track of abuses, the round-up of men in camps, etc. Today, I will be doing a documentary on women's conditions in Israeli factories.

CATHY: How do you see things here evolving?

YASMINE: I do not know. It is almost too difficult and too painful to even think about. Every morning, when I leave my house and say good-bye to my mother, I never know if I will see her again. We do not know, from one minute to the next, what will happen to us. So how can I answer your question?

CATHY: Do you go through the motions of your daily routine and just not think?

YASMINE: Yes, this is the only way. If we think too much, it is very bad for our morale. Even me, I am a strong person, and I still find it extremely difficult at times. Yesterday, I walked from the Qalandya checkpoint all the way to Jerusalem. I did it because I had to.

CATHY: Do you have any contact with Israeli women?

YASMINE: No!

CATHY: Not even through your work?

YASMINE: No, I cannot. The Israelis massacred my family in my village. They took our land, our house, and now they want even the twenty-two percent of Palestine, the only thing we Palestinians have left. No, I cannot talk to these people.

Another major reason is that my house in Ramallah faces Psagot, the Israeli settlement. Every day, Israeli tanks peer out from behind the fortress walls at those of us living in Ramallah. At any minute of the day or night, they can fire on us whenever they wish.

We are helpless before them: my mother, my sister and me. We are alone face-to-face with these settlers and their army protection. What can I say? That I like these people who make me scared, who intimidate me when I leave my house, who make me fear for my life every time I walk to my car?

CATHY: If you had a message for the Americans, what would it be?

YASMINE: Palestinians have a lot of patience, but it is beginning to wear thin. Please ask your government to use its influence to force Israel to end its occupation of our land!

OMAR

TEACHER OF ARABIC

I met Omar at the American Colony Hotel on Nablus Road. We sat at a quiet corner table just off a busy lobby full of foreign correspondents and their camera crews preparing to venture out to some hot spot in either the West Bank or Gaza. While I waited for Omar to arrive, I watched, fascinated, as each crew painstakingly attached huge PRESS posters on top and along the sides of their vehicles. This was supposed to protect them from snipers, Israeli soldiers at checkpoints and Palestinian gunmen tired of biased media coverage.

For the past thirty years Omar has taught Arabic as a second language to thousands of students at the Hebrew University of Jerusalem.

OMAR: I majored in Education and Arabic at Hebrew University. Upon graduation, I applied for, and was accepted into their Masters Program. One day, my advisor said, "You understand, don't you, Omar, that no matter how good your dissertation is, your grade will never be higher than an eighty-two?" I did not respond.

For financial reasons, it took me longer than the planned two years to finish all my requirements. When I finally turned in my dissertation, my advisor read it and said, "I've never read anything finer. You have done a splendid job. But you remember what I told you, don't you?"

I shook my head, refusing to admit I had remembered. "No, I do not recall," I replied.

"I said that no matter how good your work was, your grade would never be any higher than an eighty-two."

I received a 79. Do you know why I could not get a higher grade?

First of all, I expressed an interest in going on to do my PhD in Arabic and Education. Can you guess the grade I would have needed from my Masters degree to get into their doctoral program? Eighty-two.

No Palestinian has ever been admitted into any doctoral program at Hebrew University. No Palestinian has ever been given tenure. I am named outstanding teacher by my students, every single year, and have been for the last thirty years. All I get in return is a yearly contract, with no job security.

And you know what? I learned, later, that my advisor took the work I did for my Masters thesis and presented it at an international conference as his own.

CATHY: Why do you put up with the humiliation?

OMAR: For a while, I actually took time off to write, but I could not stay away. I kept running into my former students, who were successful in whatever they ended up doing professionally. And I said to myself, "I played a small part in forming that young man or woman."

You might call it vanity, but I decided that I owed it to my students to go back to teaching. I owed it to the Palestinians to help in some small way, to make their educational experience a better one. It is what I do best. It is what I love to do and I must do it well if I see such successful former students all around me.

CATHY: Do you have any hope for the future?

OMAR: None whatsoever. I am totally pessimistic. Ariel Sharon does not want to make peace with the Palestinians. He will never dismantle the settlements, not a single one of them.

CATHY: What will happen then?

OMAR: Transfer. Sharon will try to push us out of Palestine.

CATHY: He couldn't possibly get away with such a thing.

OMAR: Maybe not, with the way things are now. But what if he manages to weaken the Palestinian Authority so much that it crumbles? What if Arafat's rivals try to step in to fill the power vacuum, but one of the radical groups takes hold instead? They increase the suicide bombers. They increase the violence against the Israelis and, in so doing, give Sharon the perfect excuse to expel all Palestinians, claiming they are a threat to Israel's survival.

CATHY: I hope you are wrong, Omar.

SHIRA T.

PROFESSOR AT HEBREW UNIVERSITY

I visited Shira in her lovely home located in a quiet neighborhood a short distance from the university. We sat in a cluttered living room full of over-stuffed chairs and books lying about on tables, in piles on the floor, strewn across the length of the long dining room table.

CATHY: I discovered during my week in Ramallah that Palestinians know practically nothing about Israelis. How are Israelis and Palestinians ever going to work together toward peace if they do not speak the same language, or understand each others' mentality?

SHIRA: I do not know the answer to that. I was brought up in a very Jewish household. We had Arab servants. That was as close as I came to knowing a Palestinian. I do not think that attitude has changed very much.

CATHY: Did you communicate with the Arab servants?

SHIRA: Yes, only because they were obliged to learn some Hebrew. Of course, I felt no obligation back then to learn Arabic. They needed us to employ them, and they needed to be able to communicate with us. Even now, if Israelis have relations with Arabs, which is very rare, it usually is not for anything personal. Israelis, for the most part, have no interest in forming friendships with Palestinians.

In fact, Israelis do not even like criticism. Look at your current American Ambassador to Israel. He dared to criticize Sharon's policy and got called a Jew-boy, and was invited to leave.

CATHY: Earlier, we spoke about Arafat refusing Barak's generous offer. But did you know that Barak did everything he could to scuttle the peace talks at Camp David?

SHIRA: No, all I remember was that President Clinton got on Israeli television and said it was all Arafat's fault.

CATHY: When the Palestinian negotiators called their counterparts on the Israeli side after Clinton's statement, they were told, "Oh, well, you understand. Clinton felt obliged to say this to make Barak look good in the Israeli polls back home."

SHIRA: You are telling me things I have never heard before.

CATHY: Why was the Israeli public so willing to believe that Arafat refused the generous offer?

SHIRA: Why? People believe what they can live with. As long as Arafat did not cooperate, and Barak was ready to give everything away, their conscience was clear. We tried to negotiate and look what those horrible Palestinians did. They refused.

CATHY: Could you, as an Israeli woman curious to know what was happening in Ramallah, walk up to the Qalandya checkpoint and get waved through by an Israeli soldier?

SHIRA: No, I would not be permitted to cross. They would say that it was for my own protection.

CATHY: Did you know that Daniel Barenboim wanted to cross into Ramallah last week to give a concert?

SHIRA: The papers here said that they were protecting him from every possible danger, and that it was their obligation to do so.

CATHY: Have you ever attended a pro-Palestinian demonstration?

SHIRA: Yes, about six weeks ago. It was held just behind Hebrew University. The Israelis had closed off a road leading to a Palestinian hospital. This measure effectively prevented any Palestinian from getting medical attention at that hospital.

Hundreds of Israelis decided to show up for a mass demonstration to lend support to the Palestinians who were protesting. We were met by the border patrol, who are known for their extreme brutality. They threw tear gas, and hit us with large batons. One of my friends, a seventy-year-old woman, sustained a severe blow to her head. She was rushed to the hospital. We were all beaten, and I will tell you quite honestly that I was never so scared in all my life.

CATHY: Why would they beat Israelis?

SHIRA: In their eyes, we were traitors for siding with the enemy and we needed to be taught a lesson.

CATHY: Do you know the saying "Ignorance is bliss"?

SHIRA: Yes, of course.

CATHY: I think this is how most Americans deal with the Israeli-Palestinian conflict. Israelis apparently do the very same thing.

SHIRA: For the most part, yes.

CATHY: I can almost excuse the American public. The Israeli-Palestinian conflict is a complicated one, and their lives are not directly affected by what happens here. How does one excuse the willful blindness of the Israeli society?

SHIRA: Oh, but it isn't willful blindness. Israelis have a clear conscience. They are convinced their leaders are doing everything possible to secure an agreement with the Palestinians. It is Arafat who will not cooperate.

In this society, Arafat is a very easy man to hate. He has been vilified for years, and most Israelis are convinced he wants to kill them.

CATHY: They would rather live in fear of a suicide bomber than open their eyes to the truth?

SHIRA: Yes, especially since things are not really that bad. "We can live with it," is something I hear all the time at the university.

CATHY: Is it true that Ben-Gurion's plan for a Jewish homeland never included any Palestinians?

SHIRA: Yes, that was his plan from the very beginning, and that attitude has not changed one bit. Just look how we treat Israeli Arabs. When they protested Sharon's visit to the Temple Mount [which ignited the current *Intifada*], the military rushed into their neighborhood, fired on their demonstration and killed thirteen innocent Palestinians.

CATHY: How did Israelis react to the actions of the Israeli Arabs?

SHIRA: There were calls to take away their Israeli citizenship.

CATHY: Were Barak and Sharon in agreement that Sharon should make that visit to the Temple Mount?

SHIRA: Absolutely, the whole thing was orchestrated to get a reaction from the Palestinians.

CATHY: Please explain.

SHIRA: Sharon needed a rebellion so he would have an excuse to go into the occupied territories and crush the Palestinians. That was his plan all along.

RABBI COHEN

CHAPLAIN, UNITED STATES AIR FORCE

Rabbi Avraham Cohen grew up in Mt. Lebanon, a suburb of Pittsburgh, Pennsylvania, in a liberal Jewish home. After graduating from Northwestern University in 1987 he felt the need to deepen his attachment to his Jewish heritage. He moved to Israel in 1989 with the goal of settling on a kibbutz, possibly becoming a Rabbi and helping to build a Jewish State.

CATHY: Tell me more about your motivations for moving to Israel.

RABBI: I have experienced a lot of anti-Semitism in my life, mostly in the form of name calling. I was very conscious of, and proud of, being Jewish and was deeply disturbed by Jewish persecution throughout Western History, including the Crusades, the pogroms and the Holocaust. Then there were the wars to annihilate the State of Israel and drive the Jews into the sea. Though I was only three years old during the Six Day War, I have vivid emotional memories of the jubilation exhibited by my entire family and the people at temple after Israel won such a crushing victory over the Arabs.

CATHY: Did you end up in a kibbutz in Israel?

RABBI: No, I enrolled instead in a *yeshiva* (seminary) called *Aish HaTorah*, which was a place which was geared to men from my background: well-educated, secular, with a keen interest in Judaism. I graduated from Tennenbaum College of Judaic Studies in Jerusalem in 1999 as an Orthodox Rabbi.

CATHY: How did an Orthodox Rabbi trained in Jerusalem come to serve as a chaplain in the U.S. Air Force?

RABBI: I met a chaplain in the U.S. Air Force who lives in Israel; he helped me. A *yeshiva* in Jerusalem has a Rabbinic training program called *Ohr Lagol*, which means "lamp to the Diaspora." This program trains rabbis to be Jewish religious leaders in the countries of their upbringing. They pay a stipend which is funded by private donations and by the Israeli Ministry of Education and Religion. It is conditional upon the graduate serving in the Jewish community outside of Israel for two years.

CATHY: After your two years of service will you return to Israel?

RABBI: I plan to serve in the Air Force for twenty years and then retire to Israel. I own a home in Beitar-Illit, a settlement with about 20,000 inhabitants which straddles the Green Line in Jerusalem.

CATHY: What does it mean to be an Orthodox Rabbi?

RABBI: Becoming Orthodox in Israel is a process. Orthodox Judaism believes that all aspects of Jewish life should be a reflection of Jewish tradition which are derived from Jewish sources. These include the *Torah* (Old Testament), oral *Torah* which includes the *Talmud* and the *Midrash*, or oral tradition, which goes into the nuts and bolts of the written *Torah*.

Orthodox Jews believe that the written *Torah* is the word of God dictated to Moses in the desert. Every word came directly from God. All principals of *Torah* law, all aspects of human experience are expressed in God's law. Every human interaction and behavior finds an expression in Jewish law.

According to Hirsh, a Jewish scholar in the 19th Century, Judaism is a religion created by God to describe man. All other religions are created by man to describe God.

An Orthodox Jew believes that the *Torah* is the living revelation of God's will and how he wants everyone to behave. There are Jewish laws for Jews that are encapsulated in the seven laws of the sons of Noah. These include things like "don't kill, don't steal, don't commit adultery, don't worship idols, create a fair and just legal system, etc." These are the guiding principles which God wants us to adhere to.

CATHY: These sound like the Ten Commandments I grew up learning as a Catholic.

RABBI: Similar, but one of the ten commandments is different for the Jewish People and that is "to lead me out of the house of bondage." I literally believe that my ancestors were in Egypt. My father said that his father said that they were Levites. When I go to Israel and I go to the ancient Levitical city I believe that my roots have come from there, that I descend from one of the three sons of Levi.

"Remembering the Sabbath" is one commandment specific to Jews and setting it apart from the regular weekdays is important. There are thirty-nine principles of labor, and we must dissent from those categories so as to respect the Sabbath. Obviously if you aren't Jewish you aren't obligated to that specific principle. If a Jew violates the Sabbath I would have an obligation as a Rabbi to reprimand him.

CATHY: Can we talk, please, about the issues facing Israel today?

RABBI: An Orthodox Jew in Israel has a split vision of the issues. The ideal solution will be the Messianic Redemption which means the re-establishment of the Jewish Dynasty, the *Sanhedrin* (the highest judicial and ecclesial council of the ancient Jewish nation), the rebuilt Temple upon the Temple Mount and an end to all war and hostilities which will lead to global peace.

CATHY: How does this differ from the Christian Fundamentalist vision?

RABBI: We disagree on what the Messiah's name will be. Jesus is not part of the equation. We would consider him a false Messiah.

Under the Messianic Redemption all people – Palestinians, foreign nationals, Muslims, Christians, atheists – would enjoy all fundamental God-given human and civil rights: equality under the law, the right to livelihood, freedom of worship and expression, right to face one's accuser, the right to a robust defense, a right to life, right to property, and so forth. Everyone has these basic rights.

The Orthodox position is that in the absence of the Messianic Redemption, or until it occurs, we need to come to some type of negotiated settlement with the hostile Palestinian population.

However, there are objective limits as to what we can agree to in terms of autonomy, military capacity, strategic land, and so forth. These are objective military questions which are determined by the military experts and beyond that line we cannot and will not compromise.

Any diplomatic movement or military posturing on the part of the Israeli government which would endanger lives, security and future generations would be irresponsible and negligent.

I believe that the majority of Israelis are of the opinion that we have offered everything we can to the Palestinians. We have demonstrated a willingness to reach a compromise but there is a certain price which is too high and we are not willing to make peace at any cost.

The peace movement in Israel is not of this vein. They reflect a small percentage of the population, less than one percent. The majority of Israelis are either Orthodox (thirty-five percent) or secular moderates (forty percent) who are middle-of-the-roaders.

Religion and politics have a lot to do with one's attitudes and persuasions. The traditional Orthodox position is that the historical biblical boundaries of Israel are the legitimate boundaries.

Under the Messianic Redemption these boundaries will be restored with the acquiescence of the neighboring states. Once the Messiah comes it will be a divinic [sic] monarchy based upon the rule of *Torah* law and morality. He will have universal acceptance as the leader we have been waiting for. He will redistrict those boundaries and make them permanent.

Obviously at the moment things are in a state of flux. What may be impossible today may be possible tomorrow. If Israel discovers oil and undercuts the leverage of OPEC (the Organization of Petroleum Exporting Countries), or if it discovers the vaccine for the Avian flu, or if America invades Iran, and the Middle East over the next twenty or thirty years becomes a democracy to the degree that Europe is today, then there will be room to change our negotiating position.

However, under the present conditions, with a resurgent Islamic fundamentalist front funded and stockpiled by Iran and like-minded states and the moderates in the Arab world who have at best a tenuous hold on power, this doesn't give Israel a lot of room to negotiate. Let's face it. We are probably the most hated of all peoples in the region. After us come the leaders of Arab nations.

CATHY: Can trust be built between the moderate Palestinians like Abbas and the Israeli leadership?

RABBI: I believe it can, but only after Palestinian moderates as well as the rest of the world, including the US, declare war on Islamofascism.

CATHY: I've not heard that term used before.

RABBI: It was coined by Benjamin Netanyahu. It is imperative that the Arab world denounce Islamo-fascism. It will require the weight of international institutions to crush the movement. We have done our part in footing the bill for this job but it will take greater powers to prevail because the dangers to Israel are so great. It is literally a matter of life and death for us.

CATHY: Was the Gaza withdrawal undertaken for demographic reasons?

RABBI: History will be the judge of that. Military intelligence says that this was a bold move on the part of Sharon. He essentially created military symmetry along that seam of friction by removing all Israeli targets within Gaza. In so doing, he rendered any cross-border volleys an act of war and made the Palestinian Authority responsible for any such acts.

As a military officer the withdrawal may have also made sense to him in terms of cost of defending the Israeli positions in Gaza. When this same money could have been spent on research and development, on budget considerations and other aspects of Israeli security, the cost of protecting settlers living there was too high.

CATHY: Couldn't the withdrawal have been carried out in coordination with the Palestinian Authority instead of unilaterally?

RABBI: No one, except perhaps Iran, could fault Israel for responding the way it did in Gaza. History will be the judge of Sharon's move.

CATHY: What about some form of negotiations?

RABBI: What can Israel negotiate on? What you are asking is peace at all costs and I say no.

There are two ways to have peace. The Palestinians could evacuate the entire country and move to Los Angeles or the Israeli Army could invade all Palestinian population centers and evacuate all people who left willingly, and kill the remaining who refuse. These are the two ways of gaining peace now.

And if Israel were then attacked by the Arab world it could use its vast arsenal of nuclear weapons to defend itself.

Obviously, neither of these solutions are [sic] practical. So we have to look at what is practical at the present time. The peace-now-at-all-costs approach approximates the former proposal. It may not be just a unilateral evacuation of the whole country. It would be protracted and bloody.

The other alternative, of transfer or destruction of Palestinians, might be the other extreme approach with no negotiations and constant warfare, but people don't want this. The other alternative would be to look at concerns for constant warfare.

CATHY: I believe that most Israelis, like most Palestinians, are tired of warfare and want some sort of solution even if it means concessions.

RABBI: I can tell you that the traditional Jewish and Orthodox camp more than likely do not feel this way. In the broad scope of Jewish history we could have given up many times. Many have done just that, perhaps because of pressures to assimilate and to disappear into the woodwork, but most have not.

Being a Jew means that you believe that God created the Jewish people to be his custodian of his *Torah*, to live in the Land of Israel, to bear light unto the nation, and to teach morality, good governance, and to live in brotherhood and harmony.

We may face an inquisition. We may face crusades. We may be caught up in pogroms. We may be persecuted in a Holocaust. Even now we see an assault on our integrity, but this too will pass. And in the end the Jewish people will survive as always.

CATHY: That is a very powerful statement.

RABBI: Think about this. In Roman times we lost the same amount of people as we did during the Holocaust. In a one-on-one fight with Germany, we could beat the shit out of them today. The Nazis killed us down to our children but we rallied back and look at how strong we are today.

If the Israeli army could be time-warped back to Nazi Germany, imagine what we could do to them.

We are an indestructible people because the *Torah* is indestructible.

World civilizations resemble the Jewish ideal. They accept the Jewish definition of human and civil rights. In the broad scope of history, therefore, the Jewish people have won.

My view is that some day cooler heads will prevail in the Arab world. They will acknowledge that they have this world power [Israel] in their neighborhood who is the leading manufacturer of medical technology. It is the center of the diamond industry. It has the most number of Nobel prize winners than any other country [sic]. It has the highest per capita rate of published articles in scientific journals in the entire Middle East. Recently Bill Gates referred to Israel as "the Middle East's Silicone Valley."

They will want to make peace with us. Yes, we will face the tip of the sword before that happens. Maybe even a gas chamber, but we have been there before. It is not new for us.

CATHY: In Lebanon people frequently talked of having a federation of nations one day where Arabs could travel freely to Tel Aviv for the latest medical treatments, or for cultural events and the like. This is not a new concept.

RABBI: Times have changed. For this to happen now we will need first a global effort to defeat fanaticism. We would like to see Israel extend a hand to its neighbors but we don't need to spill blood to get peace now. We are perfectly content to let the Messiah do this.

A Jew can violate a commandment only if it is to save a life. If you are starving you can eat pork. There are three commandments we must obey: do not kill, do not worship false idols and do not commit adultery. We must give up our lives if we are forced to do any of these things. That is the difference between Orthodox Jews and Islamic fundamentalists. Our religion does not allow us to kill other people.

CATHY: Is there any room for negotiations between Israel and the Palestinians?

RABBI: Under the present circumstances there is nothing more to talk about because the moderates are too weak and the rejectionists are too powerful. We need a global concerted effort to crush the Islamic fundamentalists. The more moderate Arab Muslims need to prevail. Algeria is dealing with its extremists and so is Egypt. The other Arab leaders need to do the same.

CATHY: Are the Americans dealing with extremism in Iraq the right way?

RABBI: That is what we are supposed to be doing: strengthening the moderates and their values. Ultimately, we hope the Iraqis do this. We can hope things will get done peacefully but I am not optimistic that will happen.

Orthodox Jews do not glorify the idea of war but they do not turn the other cheek either. There are certain things worth dying for and family is one of them. It is worth living hardships to protect your family and to give your children a better life.

If combating an enemy hell-bent on destroying your life and civilization is the only way to survive then you fight and defeat them. Abraham was put in a situation where he did not have a choice. He was asked to sacrifice his son. This will not happen to us. Rabbis in Nazi Germany were asked to give the names of all the Jews in their community or else all the children would be killed. Sometimes your choices are impossible to choose from. Your community or your children is not an easy choice.

The world is now faced with that same Holocaust choice: confronting Islamo-fascism or being crushed by it.

It is naïve to expect Israel will endanger itself when confronted by such an evil. The more Israel gives up, the greater the rejectionist camp grows. When you have a malignant threat, you deal with the threat first. You have to treat the cancer so the body will recover.

CATHY: In Jimmy Carter's newest book *Our Endangered Values*, he addresses the issue of fanaticism. Have your read the book?

RABBI: Jimmy Carter is an anti-Semite.

CATHY: Is it because in the late '70s he urged Israel and Egypt to make peace?

RABBI: Carter embodies the vision of blaming Israel while ignoring the cancer of Islamo-fascism.

TWO ISRAELI SOLDIERS

I faced a dilemma when I reached the Wailing Wall in the Jewish Quarter of the Old City. I was looking for someone to interview, preferably a woman, but the plaza was empty. I had gone through a bit of a hassle to get past the metal detector and the security guards. It was late afternoon, and my remaining daylight hours were limited. When I noticed a young Israeli soldier heading in my direction, I knew what I needed to do.

"Excuse me," I said, stepping into his path. "I am an American visiting Jerusalem for the first time. I'd like to learn more about the Israeli-Palestinian conflict. Would you have time to talk to me?"

At first, he seemed unsure of how to respond to this unusual request. Confounded by my smile and apparent friendliness, he finally acquiesced.

"Sure, I'll talk to you."

"Perhaps we could sit back there," I said, turning and pointing to the cement benches on the opposite side of the Wailing Wall.

I must admit, before I continue, that I went into this interview feigning complete ignorance and, therefore, could not direct the conversation as much as I would have wished, or asked the kinds of questions I would have liked to have had the soldiers answer.

"This is such an incredibly spacious area," I said, once we got seated.

The young soldier smiled proudly at what he assumed was a compliment. He was only twenty-four and probably did not know that this area had been part of an Arab neighborhood before the '67 war.

As we began to converse, an older soldier, obviously quite curious, walked over. I introduced myself.

"Won't you join us?" I asked. "I know very little about your conflict with the Palestinians. I would be grateful for any information the two of you could give me."

"Look, all we want to do is live in peace," said the first soldier. "*They* don't want peace."

"Who are they?" I asked, "the Palestinians?"

"Yes, we tried to live peacefully and establish a homeland for ourselves. But what happened? The Arabs declared war on us."

"I am a bit confused," I said. "When was this?"

"This was in 1947–48."

"Were there Palestinians living here then?" I asked.

"At that time, they were not called Palestinians," said the first soldier. "There were just small clusters of people scattered about the country. When we wanted to establish a country, Ben-Gurion tried to work out a compromise. He was even willing to sacrifice land just to get their cooperation. They refused. That was when all the Arab countries and their armies started a war, and we were forced to defend ourselves."

"Ever since Israel declared its independence in 1948, we have had to defend ourselves," explained the second soldier. "We must have a strong army, a strong defense, because we live surrounded by Arabs who want to destroy us."

"Do you perceive all Arabs as a threat?"

"No, not all of them," said the first soldier. "We had an Arab who worked in our garden. He was quiet and respectful. He knew his place."

"Our greatest enemy is Arafat. He is a terrorist," said the first soldier. "He wants to destroy Israel and throw us into the sea. He sends bombers to our cafes, our pizza parlors. He kills innocent people. How do you want us to talk peace with someone like that?"

"Isn't he the Palestinians' elected leader?" I asked. "If so, there is no one else to talk to."

"We cannot. It is impossible to talk to that terrorist, any terrorist."

"Look," interrupted the second soldier. "I was in Lebanon. We went there to protect our settlements in the north. We were nice to the local people, and what happened to us? We had to leave because we kept getting attacked by terrorists there."

"How long were you stationed in Lebanon?" I asked.

"Six months."

"How long did the Israeli Army stay in Lebanon?"

"I'm not sure … I think it was about twenty years."

"Why did you have to stay so long?"

"We had to fight the *Hezbollah* terrorists," he replied. "Do you know who the *Hezbollah* are?"

I shook my head.

"Well, they are crazy people with lots of arms. They attack our northern border. They do not want peace. They say they want to destroy Israel. It is totally crazy. We are surrounded by all these crazy people."

"What do you think Ariel Sharon should do in the face of all these threats?" I asked.

"He must remain strong, and never show weakness. Look, right now Sharon is doing a good thing. He is sending troops into the refugee camps. I know a lot of these soldiers, and they tell me that they ask the people very nicely to get out of their houses so they can search for weapons. We must collect all their guns so that they cannot attack us.

"And you know what? Just because we go into people's houses, certain countries are starting to call us bad people."

"I have even heard people refer to us as occupiers," said the second. "It is very hard for us to hear this kind of criticism. We are not bad people. All we want is to live in peace."

"There was a major war in 1967," I said. "What happened?"

"Egypt started a war," said the first. "We resisted their advances, then pressed on to take more land so we could protect ourselves against the Arabs."

"Is this why you took over the land in the West Bank, to protect yourselves?" I asked.

"That was never Arab land," said the first soldier. "That is Judea and Samaria. Just look in the Bible. That land belongs to us."

"Let us put politics aside for a minute. I would like to talk to you as a mother who has children a little older than yourselves. Surely you don't want to have to spend the rest of your lives carrying guns and fearing for your safety. Do you see a solution?"

"No," said the first soldier. "There is no solution."

"What about the two-state solution? What about Israelis and Palestinians living side by side in two separate states?"

"That will not work. The Palestinians do not want to live in peace," replied the second. "Besides, they will never be satisfied until they push all the Israelis into the sea."

"What about the option of transferring the Palestinians to other Arab countries?"

"That might be a good solution," said the first.

"No," retorted the second. "That will not solve any of our problems because then all the Arab countries will be at war with us."

"So what is the solution?" I asked.

"I do not know," replied the first.

"You two are in your mid-twenties. Do you still go out? Do you take your girlfriends to nightclubs? Are you scared?"

"I still go out," said the second. "I am afraid, but I still go out with my friends."

"To be honest," said the first, "I go out much less."

"We want to live in peace," insisted the second. "We are a peaceful people. We are not Hitlers."

"Our people are dying," said the first. "Innocent people are being killed by suicide bombers who think they will go to Heaven and have seventy-two virgins if they kill Israelis.

"Now they are arming themselves with weapons," he continued. "This proves they are not interested in peace."

"Look," said the second. "I served in Lebanon. I also served in the West Bank. I do not like to see people die. I do not like to see women die. But what can we do? We must defend ourselves."

[**Author's Note:** I concluded my interview here. The sun was setting and I still had to traverse the Old City alone. I shook hands with the two soldiers and wished them well.]

THREE TEENAGE GIRLS, AGES 14 TO 16

I interviewed three teenage girls at a Ramallah school. They are intelligent and inquisitive. They speak Arabic, French and English fluently. They are restless and scared. More than anything else, they want to lead normal lives.

GIRLS: The situation is very difficult for us. We cannot go anywhere. The Israelis continually bomb our neighborhoods. Every day people die. Yesterday, fifty people were killed. It was really horrible.

CATHY: Do any of you have to pass through Israeli checkpoints to get to school?

GIRLS: I live in Jerusalem. I have a blue card, which means I am a resident of Jerusalem. Technically, I have the authority to pass through the checkpoint at Qalandya. However, the soldiers do everything in their power to make it as hard as possible

CATHY: Give me an example.

GIRLS: Most days the checkpoint is closed, even for those of us who have blue cards. Like everyone else, I am obliged to walk the mountain road, which runs parallel to the checkpoint. This is a very difficult and dangerous road because, if the Israeli soldiers see us, they take aim at us.

CATHY: When the checkpoint is open, how long does it take you to pass?

GIRLS: With my blue card, usually a few minutes, sometimes half an hour. Of course, that is if I walk through the checkpoint. If my parents were to drive me to Ramallah, we would have to wait in line three to four hours.

CATHY: How many checkpoints do you have to cross to get to school?

GIRLS: Because I am coming from Jerusalem, I have two; one at al-Ram, the other at Qalandya.

CATHY: Why are there so many Israeli checkpoints?

GIRLS: They say it is because they are stopping terrorists and making Israelis more secure. We think it is just to humiliate us, to make our lives more difficult.

CATHY: What do you think about the suicide bombers?

GIRLS: No innocent civilians should have to die, but you have to understand that these people are just trying to be liberated.

When Palestine was still under English domination, the Israelis, like Begin, did terrible things. The English called them terrorists. If you had asked Begin back then, he would have said they were obliged to do whatever they could to end British rule. In the end, they got their own state.

Why is it any different now? The blacks in South Africa were called terrorists, too, but all they wanted was their freedom. Why are we so different?

CATHY: You are fourteen to sixteen years old. You have lived your whole lives under Israeli occupation. How do you feel about this?

GIRLS: We are always frightened. We live in fear of being bombed, of seeing tanks in our neighborhoods and soldiers roaming our streets, imposing curfews. It is awful.

Sometimes, my parents see important people they knew walking in the street here in Ramallah. Even though they are good friends, my parents are afraid to stop and talk to them. They are scared the Apache gunships hovering overhead will assassinate them, too. It is a horrible way to live.

CATHY: Do you relax when you are around your friends?

GIRLS: No, all we manage to do is talk about the war, about the occupation, about who lost a house or who was wounded. At our age, we are supposed to be enjoying ourselves. I have an eight-year-old sister. She should be growing up in a happy environment. All she knows is war and destruction.

All we want is an end to the occupation. We want to be able to travel freely around Palestine. Right now, we cannot even leave Ramallah. I cannot visit my grandmother in the next village. We missed my uncle's wedding two weeks ago because we could not get a permit to travel. Any time we want to leave, we have to apply for a permit. The Israelis take their sweet time and, in the end, they deny us permission to leave.

I know there are many good Jews who do not think badly of Palestinians. However, there are many who abuse their religion. They think it is all right to kill Palestinians and steal their land.

Judaism, like any other religion, is a religion of God, and God said, "Thou shalt not kill."

So, I have to wonder if those particular Israelis practice their religion. If they did, they would not act like this toward us. They claim that because they are Jewish, they are entitled to this land.

The Jews called themselves the "Chosen People," but God loves everyone; the Muslims, the Christians, the Jews, equally. So, no one people is special. We are all equal in the eyes of God. The Israelis should not be using the excuse that they are the Chosen People to steal our land.

Just yesterday, the Israelis killed fifty Palestinians, and nothing happened. It was as if they had killed some ants. Does the whole world believe that they are the Chosen People?

Why does no one side with us? When we kill, we are called terrorists. When the Israelis kill, they are retaliating, or acting in self-defense.

CATHY: What is your opinion of Ariel Sharon?

GIRLS: He has a long history of killing us. He says he wants peace, but what kind of peace is this? He hates Palestinians. He wants our land. A lot of Israelis do not like Sharon for what he does.

CATHY: But they elected him. How do you explain that?

GIRLS: My mother once told a French Jew that Sharon was crazy. The French woman replied, "Sharon is the only one who can bring peace. Yes, his methods are very harsh, but they are necessary." My mother said that this is probably why the Israelis voted for Sharon. He promised a lot of things to his people. Maybe now, the Israelis like him less because he has not succeeded in making Israelis feel secure. If anything, he has made them feel less secure.

Even for the Israeli Arabs in East Jerusalem, it is not safe anymore. They are attacked by Israelis and beaten up. They are very frightened.

CATHY: If Sharon falls, who will come in his place?

GIRLS: Maybe Netanyahu, maybe Peres. What does it matter? They are all the same, except Rabin. He was different. He was willing to make peace, but look what happened to him. An Israeli extremist killed him.

Look at your President Bush. What is he doing? Of course, Mr. Clinton was not any better. Contrary to what the press says, Clinton and Barak did not want any of the Camp David accords written down. They wanted Arafat to agree to their terms, all of which were oral. This just shows me that Israel and its leaders, and even the Americans, do not want peace. And if they do, they only want it on their terms.

I do not think our thoughts and aspirations are any different from most Israelis. I believe in peace. If we could all just forget the past and move forward, I think we could learn to live in peace together.

We should begin to think of each other as human beings, not as Israelis and Palestinians, and show each other respect.

CATHY: If you were in charge of the Palestinian Authority now, what would you do to implement peace?

GIRLS: I would forget about Jerusalem, boundaries, the right of return, and just be one nation. We are all brothers and sisters, all from one family.

Forget the leaders, the generals. All they want is war.

I am certain most Israeli children have the same feelings, the same imagination of life, as it can and should be. We will talk with them. They will understand that we can, that it is possible to live together.

Right now, young Israelis live healthy childhoods. They go to sports events, attend parties, play outdoors. All we do is wake up, go to school, return home, listen to machine gun fire, to Apache gunships firing missiles, and tanks rolling down our streets. We cannot sleep. We have to get up early to go to school. Our grades are dropping because we cannot concentrate on our studies.

This is our life, and it affects us in horrible ways. Most of us have yellow skin and black circles under our eyes. We feel sick all the time.

We have been deprived of our childhoods. And now we are teenagers. This is not a happy time for us.

CATHY: Do your teachers give you lots of homework?

GIRLS: Yes, every day. And on top of that, both our teachers and parents think we have it easy. They don't understand the pressure we are under. They push us all the time to work hard, to study. We cannot take it. We are only children.

CATHY: Maybe they are just trying to distract you from what is going on around you?

GIRLS: No, they just want to cram as much as possible into our heads, whether we can handle it or not, just in case the schools close for any length of time.

In the beginning, it was easy to keep up. We were strong then. Now, we are weary of being scared all the time.

We used to have a club, where we could go and hang out with our friends. The Israelis destroyed it. Now, our parents are afraid to let us leave the house, so they oblige us to stay home all the time.

CATHY: Are there Palestinians who collaborate with the Israelis?

GIRLS: Yes, of course.

CATHY: Do you know anyone who works for the Israelis?

GIRLS: No, not personally, but it could even be a ten-year-old boy. Anyone could be an Israeli agent.

CATHY: Why would someone want to do this against his own people?

GIRLS: Blackmail and torture are the most common ways of recruiting young men.

CATHY: Even ten-year-old boys?

GIRLS: Yes, of course. The Israelis say, "We will give you 100 shekels if you do such and such." If the boy does not accept, they beat him up. He gets frightened and agrees to cooperate.

I've heard that young girls are asked to work for the Israelis. When they refuse, they are kidnapped, drugged and raped. Photos are taken of them. The Israelis tell the girls that if they do not cooperate, they will show the photos to their families.

[**Authors Note:** I could not verify these stories.]

CATHY: What do the Israelis want in return?

GIRLS: They want these girls to work as informants, and to get other girls to do the same.

CATHY: Does this go on in Ramallah?

GIRLS: We are not sure, but we hear our parents talking about it. They do not think we are listening when they are chatting with their friends, but we hear them say these things. We do not know specifically where this is happening.

There was a Palestinian in Jenin who was working for the Israelis. He offered a young woman coffee, drugged her, raped her, and took many pictures of her naked body. She was told that if she did not cooperate with the Israelis, the photos would be shown to her family. She killed herself because she could not live with her guilt. And she did not want other girls to be hurt like her.

226

BRIEF HISTORY OF THE MIDDLE EAST – 1914 TO PRESENT

THE OTTOMAN EMPIRE EXTENDED OVER THE ENTIRE MIDDLE East, Greece, Asia Minor and the Balkans, lasting four centuries, from 1516–1918.

In the early 1900s, Eastern European Jews colonized Palestine. This was a very European pattern. The native population did not really count. This was clearly Chaim Weizman's thinking when he addressed the 1914 World Zionist Congress in Paris. Referring to Palestine, he called it "a land without people for a people without land," despite the fact 700,000 Arabs already lived there.

In the late 19th century, 20,000 Jews moved to Palestine to escape pogroms in Russia and Romania due to rampant anti-Semitism. In 1896, Theodor Herzl, President of the Zionist World Congress, asked the Ottoman Turks if they would give Palestine to the Jews so they could establish a homeland. The Turks refused. Following the abortive 1905 Russian revolution, a second wave of Jews immigrated to Palestine. Between 1900 and 1939, Zionist settlement villages in Palestine increased from twenty-two to two hundred.

1914–1918

In World War I the Ottoman Turks were allied with Germany against England and France. Sir Henry McMahon, British High

Commissioner of Egypt, aware of Arab frustrations with their Turkish rulers, wrote to Sharif Hussein, the leader of the Hashimite Arabs, asking him to revolt against the Ottoman Empire. In exchange for that assistance, Hussein asked that all Arab lands under Ottoman control be given their independence. In the Hussein-McMahon correspondence, 1915–16, England promised if Hussein did his part, the British would help create independent Arab governments in Ottoman-held territory.

On June 5, 1916, Hussein revolted against the Ottoman Turks. The British sent in T.E. Lawrence – Lawrence of Arabia – to help the Arabs assist the Allies against the Ottoman Empire. However, in February, 1916, in the Sykes-Picot Agreement, France and Britain had already secretly agreed to divide the Ottoman Empire between themselves, with Britain taking Iraq and Palestine, explicitly ignoring the promise made to Sharif Hussein. Chaim Weizman used his influence to persuade Lord Arthur Balfour, a member of the British Parliament, to write the 1917 Balfour Declaration, which officially endorsed the establishment in Palestine of a national home for the Jewish people. Two years later, Balfour wrote, "In Palestine, we do not propose even to go through the form of consulting the wishes of the present inhabitants of the country ... The four great powers are committed to Zionism, and Zionism, be it right or wrong, good or bad, is rooted in age-long tradition, in present needs, in future hopes of a far profounder import than the desires and prejudices of the Arabs who now inhabit that ancient land."[34]

In October, 1918, the Ottoman Empire signed the Mudros Armistice; Britain and France continued to promise the Arabs the right of self-government. The Covenant of the League of Nations recognized the independence of the former Ottoman provinces.

---

34   Chomsky, Noam. *The Fateful Triangle: The United States, Israel and the Palestinians.* South End Press, Boston, 1983, p. 90.

1919

In an effort to reconcile the claims of the Arabs, Woodrow Wilson dispatched the King-Crane Commission to the former Arab provinces of the Ottoman Empire to ascertain the wishes of the inhabitants regarding post-war settlement of their territories.[35] The commission reported that the Zionists looked forward to a practically complete dispossession of the present non-Jewish inhabitants of Palestine, and estimated that the latter ... "nearly nine-tenths of the whole, are emphatically against the entire Zionist program." The Commission warned that to subject them to this program would be a gross violation of the principle of self-determination, and of the peoples' rights, although it kept within the forms of law. The Commission, while expressing sympathy for the Jewish cause, recommended limitations on Jewish immigration and abandonment of the goal of a Jewish state.[36]

1920

The League of Nations made France the mandatary of Syria and Lebanon, and England of Palestine, Jordan and Iraq. The mandatary did not own the mandate. The mandatary was supposed to teach the mandate to govern itself like a democracy.[37] The Arabs of Palestine never accepted the legitimacy of this ruling.[38]

Instead they found themselves being run off land they had owned for generations because the Ottoman Turks had secretly sold Palestinian land to Zionist colonists. Without the knowledge of the Arabs, the Ottoman Land Code had been instituted in Syria and Palestine in 1858.[39] As a result, anti-Zionist riots broke out, resulting in the deaths of scores of Jews.

---

35 David, Ron. *Arabs and Israel for Beginners.* Writers and Readers, New York 1993, p. 92.

36 Chomsky, *op. cit.*, p. 91.

37 David, *op. cit.*, p. 90.

38 Chomsky, *op. cit.*, p. 90.

39 David, *op. cit.*, p. 98.

1922-1936

The Jewish population in Palestine continued to grow from about 86,000 – eleven percent of the total – to 400,000, thirty percent. Most of this increase occurred between 1933 and 1936, following the rise of Hitler in Nazi Germany.[40] Arab leaders asked Britain to halt Jewish immigration. In May, 1936, a general strike ushered in the three-year Arab Revolt. In response, the British government sent in the Peel Commission to investigate the causes of unrest. It recommended a three-way partition of Palestine into a Jewish state, an Arab state united with Transjordan, and certain districts under British Mandate.[41] In August, 1937, the Twentieth Zionist Congress rejected the Peel Commission. David Ben-Gurion said, "Just as I do not see the proposed Jewish State as a final solution to the problems of the Jewish people, so I do not see partition as the final solution of the Palestinian question … After the formation of a large army in the wake of the establishment of the State of Israel, we will abolish partition and expand to the whole of Palestine."[42]

APRIL, 1939

In an attempt to end the Arab Revolt, which killed 329 Jews and 3,112 Arabs,[43] the British government stated that they had already fulfilled their pledge to establish a Jewish national homeland in Palestine; that indefinite Jewish immigration and transfer of Arab land to Jews was contrary to Article 22 of the Covenant of the League of Nations; that within the next five years only 75,000 Jews would be allowed in Palestine; and an independent Palestinian state would be considered within the next ten years.[44]

---

40 Flapan, Simha. *The Birth of Israel: Myths and Realities*. Pantheon Books, New York, 1987, p. 18.

41 *Ibid.*

42 Tzur, Zeev. *From the Partition Dispute to the Allon Plan*. Tel Aviv, 1982, p. 12. See Flapan, Simha, p. 22.

43 David, *op. cit.*, p. 103.

44 *Op. cit.*, p. 104.

This declaration so enraged the Zionists that they not only stepped up their terrorism against the Arab population, they began aiming more of it at the British. In 1944, the Stern Gang, headed by Yitzhak Shamir, murdered a British minister. The *Irgun*, headed by Menachem Begin, was responsible for many terrorists attacks against British subjects.[45]

MAY, 1939

The US Congress held hearings on whether or not to admit 20,000 Jewish children into the US to escape Hitler. Congress voted "no." A ship named the *St. Louis* left Germany with some 900 Jews aboard. Even though they had US immigration permits, they were not allowed to dock, and Belgium finally accepted the ship.

1941

When the massacre of Rumanian Jews began, a Turkish minister came up with a plan to save 300,000 people. The US refused to help. Instead of making it easier for Jewish refugees to get into the US, America passed new immigration laws in 1941, making it almost impossible for Jews to enter the US.[46]

SPRING, 1942

The Nazis began using gas chambers to kill large numbers of Jews. Despite this atrocity, influential Zionist leaders never tried to persuade the US to open its doors to save the Jews from the concentration camps. In his book, *America and the Survivors of the Holocaust*, Leonard Dinnerstein wrote, "Unspoken publicly, but in the air privately, was the Zionist concern that few European Jews would resettle in Israel if the possibility existed of getting to the US."[47]

---

45   *Ibid.*

46   *Op. cit.*, p. 109.

47   Dinnerstein, Leonard. *America and the Survivors of the Holocaust.* Columbia University Press, New York, 1982. Quoted in David, *op. cit.*, p. 111.

Morris Ernst, an advisor to President Roosevelt, wrote of his shock at the refusal of American Jews to give those beaten people of Europe a choice, rather than insisting they emigrate to Palestine or suffer the consequences. He suggested a program that would free the US of the hypocrisy of closing its doors while making sanctimonious demands on the Arabs.[48]

After World War II the Jewish Agency was responsible for resettling Jewish displaced persons. At a certain point, the *Irgun* and Stern gangs moved into the displaced person camps. Using threats and brutality, they encouraged the poor Jews who had just survived the Holocaust to go to Israel.

1947

President Truman, who was behind in the upcoming elections, demanded the immediate admission of 100,000 displaced Jews into Palestine. The Arabs refused. Truman asked the British to force the Arabs into accepting. The British replied, "As soon as the Zionists disband their 65,000 man underground." The Zionists responded by blowing up the King David Hotel in Jerusalem, and killing ninety-one Britons.[49] Great Britain turned the matter over to the newly formed United Nations.

In November, the UN General Assembly, under enormous pressure from the US, recommended that Palestine be provisionally partitioned into a part-Arab, part-Jewish state.[50] The UN-imposed partition gave the Jews fifty-six percent of the total land area, and it created conditions for unlimited immigration under Jewish sovereignty.[51] Addressing his people on December 3, Ben-Gurion declared that "the borders are bad from a military and political point of view. In the area allotted to the Jewish state, there

---

48   *Op. cit.*, p. 111.

49   *Op. cit.*, p. 113.

50   *Ibid.*

51   Flapan, *op. cit.*, p. 31.

are not more than 520,000 Jews and about 350,000 non-Jews, mostly Arabs ... This composition does not provide a stable basis for a Jewish state ... Arrangements are not final, not with regard to the regime, not with regard to borders, not with regard to international agreements."[52]

MARCH, 1948

After Truman won the election, the US government went on record opposing the forcible partition of Palestine. On March 19, it called on the UN to stop all such efforts. On March 30, the US called for an immediate truce. The Zionists refused.[53] The Jewish Agency announced that a provisional government was being formed in the Jewish portion of Palestine.[54]

Nahum Goldmann, who was President of the World Zionist Organization from 1956 to 1968, charged that the Arabs were not consulted about the partition of Palestine in 1947, and their willingness to negotiate a political compromise that might have prevented the 1948 war was vetoed and undermined by Ben-Gurion before May, 1948.[55]

MAY 15, 1948

Israel declared its independence and Arab armies crossed the border. Attempts to arrange a truce had been successfully thwarted, not just by Ben-Gurion but by King Abdullah of Jordan, who had made a secret deal with the Jewish Agency to control the newly partitioned Arab part of Palestine.[56] Most of the fighting took place on

---

52 *Op. cit.*, pp. 32–3.

53 David, *op. cit.*, p. 114.

54 Green, Stephen. *Taking Sides: America's Secret Relations with a Militant Israel*. William Morrow, New York, 1984, p. 25.

55 Goldmann, Nahum. *Le Monde Diplomatic*, August, 1979; cited in Flapan, *op. cit.*, pp. 156–7.

56 *Loc. cit.*, p. 186.

territory the UN had assigned to the future Palestinian state, and not the portion assigned to the State of Israel. The newly declared State of Israel was not fighting for its survival, as it proclaimed, but to expand its borders at the expense of the Palestinians. The Zionist army of over 90,000 not only outnumbered the Arabs three-to-one, but had modern weapons, including up-to-date fighter and bomber airplanes with well-trained pilots.[57] Simha Flapan wrote, "Like most Israelis, I had always been under the influence of certain myths that had become accepted as historical truth. One such myth was that all the Arab states, unified in their determination to destroy the newborn Jewish State, joined together to invade Palestine and expel its Jewish inhabitants. Another myth was that the Arabs started the war. Arabs had agreed to a last-minute American proposal for a three-month truce, on the condition that Israel temporarily postpone its Declaration of Independence. Israel's provisional government rejected the American proposal by a slim majority of 6–4."[58]

JANUARY, 1949

David Ben-Gurion was elected Israel's first prime minister; Chaim Weizman became President. Israel was admitted to the UN in May.

By the time an armistice was signed in the Summer of 1949, between 600,000 and 700,000 Palestinian Arabs had been evicted from, or fled from, areas that were allocated to the Jewish State, or occupied by Jewish forces during the fighting, and were *de facto* integrated into Israel. During and after the exodus of the Palestinians, every effort was made to prevent their return, from razing villages to the promulgation of laws.[59]

---

57 David, *op. cit.*, p. 120.

58 Flapan, *loc. cit.*

59 *Op. cit.*, p. 83.

In his memoir,[60] Nahum Goldmann said that he urged Ben-Gurion not to declare a Jewish State, but rather to hold out for finding some way of accommodation with the Palestinians that could lead to a unified bi-national state, a state that would recognize the national and political rights of both the Palestinian people and the Jewish people.

Ben-Gurion, in a conversation some years later with Mr. Goldmann, responded to this notion of accommodation. "Why should the Arabs make peace? If I were an Arab leader, I would never make terms with Israel. This is natural: we have taken their country. Sure, God promised it to us, but what does that matter to them? We have come here and stolen their country. Why should they accept that?"

Mr. Goldmann remained critical of Israel's diplomacy. He felt that America's support of Israel was causing considerable harm. When he died in August, 1982, after a lifetime of service to the Zionist cause, Prime Minister Begin did not attend his funeral, and no official statement of grief was issued by the Israeli government.[61]

Upon learning of Mr. Goldmann's death, Yassir Arafat sent the following condolence: "The Palestinians mourn the death of Nahum Goldmann. He was a Jewish statesman of a unique personality. He fought for justice and legitimate rights of all people."[62]

1950

Following King Abdullah's plan, Jordan annexed the West Bank. Meanwhile, Egypt kept control of the Gaza Strip to prevent the emergence of any autonomous Palestinian aspirations.

---

60 Goldmann, Nahum. *The Jewish Paradox: A Personal Memoir.* Grosset and Dunlap, New York, 1978, pp. 99–100.

61 Chomsky, *op. cit.*, p. 98.

62 *Ibid.*

1951

In July, King Abdullah – who had made a secret deal with the Jewish Agency to control the newly partitioned Arab part of Palestine – was assassinated at point-blank range on the steps of the Al-Aqsa Mosque by a Palestinian.

1954

Ben-Gurion had stepped down as Prime Minister, handing over power for one year to Moshe Sharett. At that time Prime Minister Sharett entered into peace talks with Gamal Abdul Nasser of Egypt.[63] Even after Egypt gained its independence in 1936, Britain maintained a presence in the Suez Canal. Nasser had become Egypt's leader in a military coup in 1952. He nationalized the Suez Canal and forced Britain out of Egypt. For his forceful actions, Nasser is remembered as the first great Arab leader.

FEBRUARY 28, 1955

Israeli terrorists attack American installations in Gaza. The Israelis had it planned so that the attack is blamed on Egypt. The Israelis are apprehended and sent to an Egyptian prison. Ben-Gurion blames the blundering terrorists on his Defense Minister, Pinchas Levon. Evidence later surfaces which proves Ben-Gurion was behind the terrorist attacks. His motive? He and Chief of Staff, Moshe Dayan, wanted a war with Egypt, and Sharett's peace talks would have deprived them of that.[64] Nasser, in the meantime, has broken off the peace talks. Knowing that his army is ill-equipped, he asks the Americans for supplies and technical assistance, which they refuse. Nasser turns to the Russians, who supply him with Czech arms. Israel then claims Nasser and Egypt are a threat to the security of Israel.

---

63   Rokach, Livia. *Israel's Sacred Terrorism: A Study based on Moshe Sharett's Personal Diary and Other Documents.* Third edition, Chapter 10, p. 3. Association of Arab-American University Graduates, Belmont, MA, 1986.

64   *Ibid.*

OCTOBER, 1955

Ben-Gurion ordered Dayan to prepare invasion plans. According to Moshe Dayan,[65] Ben-Gurion was determined not to miss any politically favorable opportunity to strike at Egypt. The opportunity came in July, 1956, when Nasser nationalized the Suez Canal, an act which was within Egypt's legal rights. France and Britain were so outraged at Nasser's actions that they joined with Israel to invade the Sinai and destroy Nasser.

OCTOBER 29, 1956

Israel attacks Egypt, occupying the entire Sinai. French military equipment pours into Israel, while French and British warships bombard the Egyptian coast. President Eisenhower demands that Israeli forces withdraw from Egyptian territory.

According to Moshe Sharett's *Personal Diary*, Israel began planning the re-conquest of the Sinai soon after its forced withdrawal in 1956. Sharett also wrote that as early as 1954, American Zionist leaders knew of Israel's intention to occupy the West Bank, which was ultimately done in June, 1967.[66]

1964–1966

At a summit in Cairo, Arab leaders called for the creation of the Palestinian Liberation Organization (PLO). As Palestinian leaders suggested at the time, the charter did not stipulate that the Palestinian people had the right to self-determination and, if necessary, the right to fight to regain the UN-promised portion of the original Palestine. Instead, the Arab summit's purpose in creating the PLO was to restrain the resistance movements so as not to be drawn into a conflict with the State of Israel.

Yassir Arafat formed *Fatah* in 1965. He believed that the Pales-

---

65   *Loc. cit.*, p. 6.

66   Rokach, *op. cit.*, p. 3.

tinians could count only on themselves and that the only realistic way of regaining the portion of Palestine they had lost was through armed struggle.

JUNE 5, 1967

Israel announces to the world that the Egyptian Air Force has initiated hostile actions. However, it is the Israelis who attack the Egyptians, and destroy virtually the entire Egyptian Air Force on the ground. General Peled, one of the architects of the Israeli attack, admitted, "To pretend that the Egyptian forces massed on our frontiers, and were in a position to threaten the existence of Israel, constitutes an insult, not only to the intelligence of anyone capable of analyzing this sort of situation, but it is an insult to the Israeli army."[67]

Prime Minister Begin, in a speech to the Israeli National Defense College, said, "The Egyptian army concentrations in the Sinai do not prove that Nasser was really about to attack us. We must be honest with ourselves. We decided to attack him."[68] Israel claimed that Nasser's threat to close the Straits of Tiran constituted an act of war, but Nasser had already agreed to a compromise, worked out by Russian and American negotiators, whereby he would not close the Straits.

Israel accused Syria of shelling the Syria-Israel border when, in fact, Israeli provocations were incessant and well documented. Israel's need for water also played a role in the 1967 attack. The invasion completed Israel's encirclement of the headwaters of the Upper Jordan River and the West Bank's two aquifers, which currently supply all the groundwater for northern and central Israel.

As a result of the June, 1967, war, 500,000 Palestinians fled, or were expelled from, Israeli-occupied territory in the West Bank and Gaza. On July 15, 1967, only five weeks after the end of the war,

---

67   Interview with General Peled, *Ha'aretz*, March 19, 1972.

68   *Jerusalem Post*, August 20, 1982.

Israel quietly established its first settlements in the occupied territories, despite promises to Washington that it had no intention of doing so. Thirty-five years later, in 2002, there are approximately 427,000 Israeli settlers living in Arab East Jerusalem and the West Bank.

NOVEMBER 22, 1967

UN Resolution 242 is unanimously passed by the Security Council, requiring the establishment of a just and lasting peace in the Middle East, which should include the withdrawal of Israeli armed forces from territories occupied in the recent conflict.

1969

Yassir Arafat became President of the Executive Committee of the PLO.

1970-1971

While Syria actively supported the Palestinian resistance movements, Jordan resisted. In the end it was unable to prevent the PLO from establishing itself on Jordanian soil.

Because of the PLO's attacks on Israel from its bases in Jordan, Israel began attacking Jordan. King Hussein reasoned that if he did not restrain the PLO, Israel would destroy his country. This resulted in "Black September," a confrontation between the PLO and the Jordanian army which led to the PLO's expulsion from Jordan.

Arafat moved his PLO headquarters to the Sabra-Chatilla refugee camps in Beirut.

In the same period a PLO splinter group came into being, the Popular Front for the Liberation of Palestine (PFLP). Its leader, George Habash, ordered the hijacking of four Western airlines planes, forcing them to land in Jordan. The brutal treatment of the Jewish passengers so enraged King Hussein that he sent his army to crush the group.[69]

---

69   David, *op. cit.*, p. 135.

SEPTEMBER, 1972

A Palestinian group called Black September murdered nine Israeli Olympic athletes and one trainer in Munich. In retaliation, Israel bombed Lebanon, killing one hundred civilians.[70]

OCTOBER, 1973: THE YOM KIPPUR WAR

The Arab defeat in June, 1967, left Israel in control of the West Bank, Gaza, Syria's Golan Heights and the Egyptian Sinai.

Egypt and Syria launched a surprise attack against Israeli forces occupying the Sinai and the Golan Heights. The attacks came in part because Israel rebuffed several Arab attempts at peaceful settlement, including Egyptian President Sadat's 1971 offer of full peace; and as the Secretary-General of the Arab League said, "Arab action is justifiable under Article 51 of the Charter of the United Nations. There is no attempt to acquire new territory, but to restore and liberate the occupied territories."[71]

The Egyptians beat the Israeli Defense Forces back across the Suez Canal, and Ariel Sharon – who had just quit the army over a dispute – was called back. In a brilliant military maneuver, he confused the Egyptians, breaking through their advancing lines. He sent half his men to attack the Egyptians in the rear, the other half marched on Cairo. By the time the UN ordered a cease-fire on October 22, Sharon was within 63 miles of Cairo.[72]

Skirmishes continued until the intervention of the US and Russia on October 25. The Yom Kippur war ended with an agreement negotiated by US Secretary of State Henry Kissinger in which Israel agreed to withdraw to the eastern edge of the Suez Canal.

---

70 *Op. cit.*, p. 139.

71 *Sunday Times*, London, October 14, 1973.

72 David, *op. cit.*, p. 130.

APRIL 14, 1975

Civil war begins in Lebanon. The conflict lasts 15 years.

1977

Egyptian President Anwar Sadat became the first Arab leader to visit Israel and address the *Knesset*. Yassir Arafat offered Israel a full peace treaty; Israel refused.

MARCH, 1978

Israel invades Lebanon. Forced to withdraw, Israel leaves a proxy army in its place, the South Lebanese Army (SLA). According to Moshe Sharett's *Diary*, Ben-Gurion had developed a plan as early as 1954 to Christianize Lebanon, i.e., invent and create from scratch the intra-Lebanese conflict, and to partition and subordinate the entire country to Israel. This was more than fifteen years before the Palestinian presence became a political factor in Lebanon.

NOVEMBER, 1978

Arafat declared, "The PLO will accept an independent Palestinian state consisting of the West Bank and Gaza ... We will give *de facto* recognition to Israel."[73]

MARCH 26, 1979

Israel and Egypt sign a peace treaty, brokered by President Jimmy Carter, ending a thirty year state of war.

OCTOBER 6, 1981

Anwar Sadat is assassinated by four members of the Muslim Brotherhood, who are also members of the Egyptian Army. At a ceremony commemorating the October, 1973, war, they open fire directly on the president as their unit passes the reviewing stand.

---

73   Kennedy, Jon. "Letters to the Editor." *Daily Princetonian*, October 9, 2002.
     www.dailyprincetonian.com/archives/2002/10/09/opinion/5649.shtml

JUNE 6, 1982

The Israeli Army, led by Ariel Sharon, invades Lebanon to destroy the PLO. The invasion begins in Southern Lebanon, moving rapidly up the coast to Beirut. During seventy-two days of bombing, some 20,000 Lebanese and Palestinians are killed. The Israelis claim they invaded Lebanon in self-defense. However, between August, 1981, and May, 1982, the PLO maintained a truce on Lebanon's southern border, sponsored by the US and Saudi Arabia. Israel, according to UN records, violated the truce 2,777 times.

SEPTEMBER 18, 1982

1,200 Palestinians are massacred in the Sabra-Chatilla refugee camp in Beirut. The killings are carried out by Lebanese Christian militiamen.

FALL, 1982

Saudi Arabia, Iraq, Syria and Jordan all offered peace with Israel; Israel refused.

DECEMBER, 1987

The first *Intifada* (Palestinian uprising) began in reaction to the killing of six Palestinian children by Israeli soldiers. When it ended in 1993, eighty-five Israelis and 900 Palestinians had lost their lives.

AUGUST 29, 1993

Israel and the PLO agree in the Oslo Accords to a time-table on Palestinian self-rule.

SEPTEMBER 13, 1993

Prime Minister Rabin and Arafat sign the Oslo Accords at a White House ceremony. The document calls for limited autonomy in parts of Gaza, and Jericho in the West Bank, with some vague promises of self-government after five years.

Israel intended this agreement to function as a civilian arm of the Israeli military occupation forces, i.e., to make the PLO Israel's enforcer in the territories. According to Dr. Israel Shahak, Chairman of the Israeli League of Human and Civil Rights, "The deeper intention of the agreement was to create an apartheid system. Why did Yassir Arafat sign a document that resulted in the permanent imposition of a Bantustan upon his people?"[74]

By the early 1990s, Palestinians were disillusioned with Arafat's one-man, one-rule policies. His leadership was corrupt and ineffective, and the people demanded a change. Unwilling to give up control, Arafat signed the Oslo Accords, essentially duping his people into believing that they would realize their dream of a Palestinian state.[75]

NOVEMBER, 1995

Israeli Prime Minister Rabin was assassinated by Israeli fundamentalist Yigal Amir.

SEPTEMBER, 2000

Accompanied by 1,000 Israeli soldiers, Ariel Sharon visited the Haram al-Sharif Mosque in East Jerusalem, Islam's third holiest site. As non-Muslims are forbidden entry, Palestinians viewed this as a deliberate desecration of their sacred shrine. The following day, Israeli troops returned to the Mosque. In the ensuing riot, several Palestinians were killed, setting off the Second *Intifada*.

OCTOBER 7, 2000

The United Nations Security Council unanimously adopts Resolution 1322, stating that it was Sharon's desecration of the Harem el-Sharif Mosque which was responsible for the start of the Second *Intifada*.

---

74 Shahak, Israel. "Oslo Agreement Makes PLO Israel's Enforcer." *Washington Report on Middle Eastern Affairs*. Nov/Dec., 1993, pp. 7–16.

75 Reinhart, Tanya. *Israel/Palestine: How to End the War of 1948*. Seven Stories Press, New York 2002, p. 17–18.

During the Second *Intifada* Palestinian extremists – *Hamas*, Islamic Jihad and al-Aqsa Martyr's Brigade – resorted to escalating numbers of suicide bombers. Up through August, 2005, there have been sixty-eight suicide bombings, killing 587 Israelis. In addition, 500 Israeli soldiers and settlers have been killed. Twelve of the suicide attacks were prior to the current *Intifada*.

Some 4,000 Palestinians have lost their lives during the current *Intifada*.

NOVEMBER 11, 2004

Yasser Arafat dies in a Paris hospital under mysterious circumstances after falling ill in his headquarters in Ramallah. Although viewed as a terrorist by many, he fought tirelessly for a homeland for his people. The 70-year-old Mahmoud Abbas (Abu Mazen) was elected President to succeed Arafat.

SEPTEMBER, 2005

Ariel Sharon unilaterally withdraws from Gaza.

NOVEMBER 10, 2005

Amir Peretz, former *Histadrut* (labor union) chairman, defeats Shimon Peres, the long-time leader of Israel's Labor Party. Peretz's election could lead to new elections in Israel as early as March, 2006. Peretz favors negotiations with the Palestinians and a two-state solution.

JANUARY 4, 2006

Prime Minister Ariel Sharon suffers a massive stroke and falls into a coma. His illness comes as he prepares for the March 28 Israeli election as head of Kadima, a new centrist party.

JANUARY 25, 2006

Hamas stuns the world by winning the long anticipated Palestinian election. US President George W. Bush fails to understand that

Hamas won because of allegations that the Palestinian Authority was corrupt and plagued with nepotism.

Hamas, which has maintained a year-long truce with Israel, has not, as of this writing, ended its call for the destruction of Israel. However, seventy-seven percent of Palestinians who voted for Hamas are not only opposed to calls for the destruction of Israel but want a negotiated settlement.

Israel insists it will not negotiate with a terrorist organization which calls for the destruction of the State of Israel.

FEBRUARY 4, 2006

Acting Israeli Prime Minister and head of Kadima, Ehud Olmert, faces two strong opponents in Israel's upcoming election: Benjamin Netanyahu, current leader of Likud and champion of the settler movement, and Amir Peretz, the new head of Labor.

As this book goes to print the future for ordinary Israeli and Palestinian citizens is once again looking increasingly bleak.

CONCLUSION

SEPTEMBER 2000 TO PRESENT

FOR THE MOST PART THE ISRAELI GOVERNMENT HAS SUCCEEDED in making the occupation of the West Bank and Gaza invisible. This has been done through imposing thousands of regulations and a civil administration that is run by the military. Dr. Jeff Halper, Coordinator of the Israeli Committee against House Demolitions in Jerusalem, calls the system "the Matrix of Control." According to him, it is composed of three layers:

1. Military actions, both in response to the *Intifada* and in normal times, which include using undercover units and collaborators who undermine the fabric of Palestinian society;

2. Creating "facts" on the ground: expropriation of land; construction of more than 200 settlements; carving the occupied territories into areas which confine Palestinians to some 190 islands; a massive system of highways for Israeli-use only; control over aquifers and exploitation of holy places;

3. The most subtle, bureaucratic or legal restrictions: these entangle Palestinians in a web including closures; work discrimination; entrance and travel permits restricting movement; displacement through exile, deportation and induced emigration; land expropriation; house demolition; transfer schemes; a freeze on the natural development of Palestinian

towns and villages; restrictions on the planting of crops and their sale. All these come under bureaucratic controls.[76]

These conditions remain largely invisible to the outside world, and therefore are rarely – if ever – covered by the media. What is visible – and is routinely reported – is the series of mindless suicide bombing attacks by young Palestinians, which in the end labels the Palestinians as terrorists.

The UN Committee on the Exercise of the Inalienable Rights of the Palestinian People issued a report on October 31, 2001, in which they voiced their grave concern at the severity of the Israeli military response to the current *Intifada*.[77]

Repression: The Committee noted that, in addition to the use of plastic, rubber-coated metal and live ammunition, the Israeli military continued to use heavy and sophisticated weapons in an excessive and indiscriminate manner, such as Apache gunships, air-to-surface and heavy anti-tank missiles, tanks, missile boats and F16 fighter planes. Article 32 of the Fourth Geneva Convention prohibits assassinations and any brutalization of the civilian population.[78]

Assassinations: The Israeli security apparatus has resorted to selective assassinations of Palestinian activists and political leaders using special undercover units, snipers and helicopter gunships. Article 146 holds accountable individuals who have committed grave breaches of the Convention. This includes willful killing, torture, etc.[79]

Incursions: Israeli incursions into areas under full Palestinian control, which violate the spirit and letter of the Oslo Agreement.

---

76 Report of the International Meeting on the Question of Palestine, Madrid, 17–18 July, 2001. Division of Palestinian Rights, United Nations, Document No. 01-63718, dated 27 November 2001, paragraphs 44 and 45.

77 Paragraph 19, UN General Assembly Official Records No. A/56/35, 31 October, 2001.

78 *Ibid*, Paragraph 20.

79 *Ibid.*, Paragraph 27.

The incursions result in the destruction of public and private property. Article 43 reads: "Any destruction of the Occupying Power of real or personal property, including house demolitions ... is prohibited."[80]

Destruction: An alarming increase in the demolitions of Palestinian houses and other property in the West Bank and Gaza.[81]

Settler Violence: During 2001, the number of Israeli settlers in the West Bank and Gaza – excluding East Jerusalem – increased by 17,000, and has now reached nearly 227,000. Under the protection of Israeli soldiers, settler groups resort to the use of firearms, hit-and-run incidents, torture, beatings and murder. The Fourth Geneva Convention forbids an occupying power from making its presence a permanent one. Article 3 prohibits outrages upon personal dignity, in particular, humiliating and degrading treatment, a routine element in Palestinian life under Israeli occupation.[82]

Collective Punishment: The Palestinian economy has experienced extreme difficulties and continues to show signs of rapid disintegration as a result of the Israeli military occupation. Protracted closures and restrictions on movement of goods and labor force have decimated practically all sectors of the economy. Collective punishment is prohibited under the Fourth Geneva Convention. Article 39 stipulates: "Those residents of occupied lands who have lost their gainful employment shall be granted the opportunity to find paid employment."[83]

Control of Water Supply: Israel has full control over Palestinian water resources, with thousands of Palestinian families deprived of connections to water networks. Some 200,000 Palestinians are forced to rely on alternative water sources. Settlers

---

80 *Ibid.*, Paragraph 24.

81 *Ibid.*, Paragraph 25.

82 *Ibid.*, Paragraph 27.

83 *Ibid.*, Paragraph 28.

routinely use bulldozers to rupture Palestinian water pipelines, while Israeli army snipers target Palestinian water storage tanks. Article 33 of the Fourth Geneva Convention prohibiting pillage would pertain to Israel's extensive use of West Bank and Gaza water resources, especially as they are denied to the local Palestinian population.

The UN Committee on the Exercise of the Inalienable Rights of the Palestinian People has been submitting its report to the UN General Assembly every year for the last twenty-four years. It is the UN Security Council, controlled by the United States and its allies, which has ensured that the recommendations of the UN Committee remain unimplemented.[84]

RECENT DEVELOPMENTS

THE SEPARATION (SECURITY) WALL

In 2002, Israel began construction of a Separation Wall, explaining that it was necessary to protect its citizens from Palestinian terrorists. There is evidence to support the claim. According to Benjamin Netanyahu, former Prime Minister of Israel, since its construction the wall has contributed to a drop in attacks on Israelis. Former Israeli Defense Minister Benjamin Ben Eliezer reaffirmed this: "In the first eleven months from August, 2003, to the end of June, 2004, we have seen only three suicide bombings with an overall decline of more than ninety percent."[85]

According to Peace Index, a survey published on March 1, 2004, eighty-four percent of the Israeli public – which includes large numbers of Israeli Arabs who live in Israel-proper and are also victims of suicide bombers – unanimously supports Israel's

---

84   Jayaprakash, N.D. "The Palestinian Saga: Seething with Rage: Part Three."
      CounterPunch, June 28/30, 2002, p. 7.

85   "Israel's Security Fence." www.jewishvirtuallibrary.org/jsource/Peace/fence.html

security fence. This widespread approval reflects the realization that the fence will significantly reduce terrorist attacks.

According to figures supplied by the Israeli government, the fence has saved lives. Between August, 2001, and August, 2002, fifty-eight people were killed or wounded in Israeli towns near the West Bank Arab towns of Jenin and Tulkarim. Since the wall was erected, only three Israelis have been killed. From the northern West Bank into Israel from April to December, 2002, there were seventy-one attacks. In all of 2003 there were only five. According to an article in *The Times of London* on January 26, 2005, five thousand people have been killed in Israel and Palestine since 2000, a thousand of them Israelis.[86]

To determine the efficacy of the fence we have only to look at Gaza, where a fence was erected in 1996, resulting in fewer Gaza residents participating in terrorist attacks within Israel.

Palestinians believe that if Israeli security was the primary concern of the Israeli government, the fence would have been built along the 1967 Green Line, and not at some points up to fifteen miles inside the West Bank, to include eighty percent of all Israeli settlements. The planned route of the wall does not expropriate any Israeli land. Palestinians believe that if the wall were built along the Green Line, it would not disrupt the lives of hundreds of thousands of Palestinians, and could eventually lead to much better relations with the Israeli government. Former Israeli Defense Forces Deputy Chief of Staff, Matan Vilnai, appears to agree with this line of thinking. "We need to have a fence in order to have good friends on the other side. We need the fence to safeguard a Jewish democratic state. The fence is one precaution we must take to have peace. But it needs to be built on the Green Line."[87] The UN Commission on Human Rights concluded that "There is no compelling

---

86   "Abbas-Sharon Summit on Cards after Contacts Resume." *The Times of London*, January 26, 2005.

87   Szymanski, Tekla. "Israel's Security Fence: Back to the Wall?" www.tekla-szymanski.com/engl8fence.html

evidence that suicide bombers could not have been as effectively prevented from entering Israel if the wall had been built along the Green Line."[88]

While still under construction, the Separation Wall is expected to be at least 650 kilometers in length and twenty-five feet tall.[89] The Wall will include watchtowers and a buffer zone thirty to one hundred meters wide with electric fences, trenches, cameras, footprint detection fields, sensors and security patrols. The total cost will be approximately five billion American tax dollars.

The Wall will divide the West Bank into three non-contiguous enclaves, meant to be the future Palestinian State. While President George W. Bush called the fence a problem for the viability of a future Palestinian state, this did not stop Israeli Foreign Minister Silvan Shalom from insisting that Israel would continue building its security fence in the West Bank along its planned route, despite the President's suggestion that it was an obstacle to peace.[90]

The Israeli government also has plans for a separation barrier in the Jordan Valley, on the eastern edge of the West Bank, which will extend 143 kilometers up to a line approximately ten kilometers west of the Jordan River. Israeli settlements already exist in the Jordan Valley. The fact that the Israeli government is currently offering houses to new Israeli buyers in established settlements along this line in the Jordan Valley is further evidence of Prime Minister Sharon's intention to preserve this area as part of Israel.

According to *B'Tselem*, the Israeli Information Center for Human Rights, nearly 490,500 Palestinians will be affected by the barrier's route, preventing access to primary urban centers where essential services such as hospitals, schools, markets and places of worship are available. From Jenin to Qalqiliya in the northwestern

---

88 "UN Report Blames Israel for Building Wall to Confiscate Land." Reuters, Sept. 25, 2004. www.globalexchange.org/countries/mideast/palestine/2499.html

89 The Berlin Wall was 155 kilometers long and 11.9 feet tall.

90 Dunn, Ross. "Israel to Continue Building Security Fence Despite US Opposition." *Voice of America News*, August 10, 2003.

part of the West Bank, sixteen villages west of the Wall have been annexed to Israel, and some fifty villages have been separated from their farmland and means of financial support. A number of villages will lose their only source of water. This is particularly true in Qalqiliya in the northern part of the West Bank, the most important agricultural area in the West Bank, where two thirds of its land – including all underground wells – has already been confiscated for Israeli use.

In the Wall's first construction phase, more than thirty-one groundwater wells will be in the annexed land. Israeli bulldozers have already destroyed 35,000 meters of water pipes used by Palestinians for both agricultural and domestic use. A number of villages will lose their only source of water. The area planned for the first phase of the Wall's construction is among the most fertile in the entire West Bank, and the bulldozed land includes acres of cultivated fields, orchards and greenhouses.

By the time the Jerusalem part of the wall is completed, ninety percent of Arab East Jerusalem will have been absorbed by Israel. Palestinians wonder whether Israel has another motive for building the Separation Wall on its present course. Recent statements by Israeli government officials – if they are official and not reflective of their own personal views – do nothing to quell these suspicions. According to Ehud Olmert, Israel's Deputy Prime Minister, "The Wall has nothing to do with security. It's purpose is to maximize the number of Jews [in East Jerusalem] while minimizing the number of Palestinians."[91] Haim Ramon, a Jerusalem cabinet minister, in an interview on Israeli radio on July 31, 2005, said, "The barrier makes Jerusalem more Jewish. The safer and more Jewish Jerusalem becomes it can serve as a true capital of the State of Israel."[92]

---

91   Butta, Diana. "Israel's Unilateral Disengagement." *Arabic Media Network*, July 31, 2005.

92   "Israel Admits Wall is not just about Security, not Temporary." PNGO Information Clearinghouse: *The Palestine Monitor*. July 31, 2005.

Thomas L. Friedman correctly summed up what people on both sides of the debate are feeling when he wrote, "Israel is building a fence and walls around the West Bank to deter suicide bombers ... For Palestinians the fence is part of a web of Israeli checkpoints and fences inside the West Bank, and the sealing of all exits but one from many Palestinian villages. This has transformed the West Bank into a series of cages ... If Israelis were building a fence around the West Bank, and then removing all the checkpoints inside, it would make great sense. But they can't, because the West Bank Jewish settlements also have to be protected ... I have enormous sympathy for Israelis trying to deter suicide bombers. But, to build a fence without a border, and without facing up to the contradictions of having Jews on both sides of it, will only bring more trouble."[93]

On July 9, 2004, the International Court of Justice ruled against Israel's Separation Wall by a vote of 14–1 with US Justice Thomas Buergenthal dissenting.[94]

THE E-1 CORRIDOR ("THE JERUSALEM ENVELOPE")

E-1 is short for "East 1," the name given to the land northeast of Jerusalem and west of the Ma'aleh Adumim settlement in the West Bank. Ma'aleh Adumim, the largest settlement in the West bank, and home to 25,000 Israeli settlers, is located fourteen kilometers due east of Jerusalem. Former Israeli Prime Minister Yitzhak Rabin established Ma'aleh Adumim in 1975. Thereafter each successive government offered housing subsidies, income tax reductions and low-interest loans to prospective residents. Since housing in Jeru-

---

93　Friedman, Thomas. "One Wall, One Man, One Vote." *New York Times*, September 14, 2003.

94　The Advisory Opinion of the ICJ on 9 July, 2004, issued an official document titled "Legal Consequences of the Construction of a Wall in the Occupied Palestinian Territory" in which the court almost unanimously found Israel's West Bank Barrier (termed "Israel's Apartheid Wall" by Palestinians and the "Terror Prevention Fence" by Israel) to be illegal under international law.

salem is expensive, these incentives had great appeal to average secular Israelis who were looking for a nice place to raise their families.

Included in the E-I project is a plan to build the easternmost part of its fence around Ma'aleh Adumim, twenty-five kilometers from the Green Line or about half the width of the West Bank. As a comparison, this is two-thirds of the way to Jericho, which is thirty-five kilometers east of Jerusalem and a short distance from the Jordan Valley.

Israel plans to fill in this E-I corridor with 3,500 houses, an industrial area, tourist attractions, sport and recreation areas, a police station, cemetery, a site for refuse disposal and recycling and an area for mining and quarrying. The E-I link to the Ma'aleh Adumim settlement will extend over fifty-three square kilometers, an area bigger than Tel Aviv and half the size of Paris. If implemented, this comprehensive plan will also link the area around Ma'aleh Adumim to the municipal boundaries of Jerusalem, and include the neighborhoods and villages to the east of the city. According to Israeli officials, the area does not currently have any inhabitants so no Palestinians would be displaced. For the convenience of the Palestinians, Israel plans to build tunnels and overpasses to obviate the need for Palestinians to detour to the east around Ma'aleh Adumim.

According to the Palestinians, the settlement of Ma'aleh Adumim was established on lands confiscated from individual Palestinians in the villages of Abu Dis, Al Izriyyeh, Al Issawiyyeh, Al Tur, Anita, and from the Jahalin and Sawahareh Bedouin tribes.

The E-I corridor with its proposed link to Ma'aleh Adumim would impede territorial contiguity between the southern and northern West Bank, essentially breaking the West Bank into two parts. Israeli officials disagree with this assessment, insisting the real issue is convenience not contiguity, because Palestinians will still have a passage which will connect north and south to the east of Ma'aleh Adumim.

Palestinians also believe the E-I corridor would sever access to

East Jerusalem for Palestinians in the West Bank, and sever access to the West Bank for Palestinians residing in East Jerusalem. In their opinion this would impede any durable peace agreement and preclude the establishment of a viable, contiguous Palestinian state.

If the E-1 corridor is built, could the Palestinians have contiguity via by-pass roads or tunnels? Palestinians could travel between the northern and southern West Bank via a road – which does not yet exist – through the Judean desert, looping around the Ma'aleh Adumim bloc and the expanded area of Jerusalem, whose outskirts would stretch nearly to Jericho which is thirty-five kilometers from Jerusalem. That would be some detour! And if the Palestinians agreed to the thirty-five kilometer detour they wonder if the as yet to be constructed road will be checkpoint-free.

Will the Ma'aleh Adumim–E-1 corridor be constructed? If Israel is serious about wanting to make peace with the Palestinians, the future of these areas must be left to negotiations and not determined by unilateral acts. This is particularly true at a time when President Abbas needs to demonstrate to the Palestinian people that diplomacy and negotiations are the only route to achieving Palestinian aspirations. Unilateral acts by Israel will only undermine President Abbas; such acts also publicly defy and embarrass the United States, waste goodwill towards Israel around the world and pointlessly consume valuable Israeli political capital. Some observers expect that under a future peace agreement Ma'aleh Adumim will remain part of Israel provided there is a land swap to compensate the Palestinians for the territory taken. There is no similar consensus on the E-1 corridor.[95]

The Bush Administration opposes the E-1 project. On September 2, 2005, the Israeli government gave assurances that the project would be put on hold for the present. In fact, construction began

---

95   Etkes, Dror. "What is E-1?" Text by Peace Now Settlement Watch Director, May, 2005.

on the E-I infrastructure in mid-2004, including the clearing of roads for major highways leading to the planned residential areas, and site preparation for the planned police station.[96]

In an interview, Vice Prime Minister Ehud Olmert said, "It is absolutely clear that at a certain point in the future Israel will create continuity between Jerusalem and Ma'aleh Adumim. There is not even an argument that in the end we will have to build the project. When conditions are ripe, we will raise the issue with the Americans again. In the meantime, we will not do anything behind the back of the Americans."[97]

SHARON'S UNILATERAL DISENGAGEMENT FROM GAZA

In August, 2005, Prime Minister Ariel Sharon carried out what he called a "unilateral disengagement" from the Gaza Strip.[98] The operation was brilliantly carried out by Israeli soldiers who exercised great care so as not to harm fellow Jews.

Unfortunately, *Hamas* and some of the other extremist Palestinian groups did not act as gallantly as the Israeli soldiers. As soon as the settlers and soldiers cleared out, many of the extremists rushed to desecrate graves and burn down the abandoned synagogues. This was disgraceful, senseless behavior. They should have known not to show such blatant disregard for another religion. *Hamas* did a great disservice not only to themselves, but to their fellow Palestinians. The Palestinian Authority should have sent in security forces ahead of the pullout to prevent such abominable acts of desecration. The PA – knowing the whole world was watching – could and should have done everything in its power to demonstrate to the world that the Palestinians were up to the task

---

96 *Ibid.*

97 Lefkovits, Etgar. "Israel won't build near Ma-aleh Adumin." *The Jerusalem Post*, September 2, 2005.

98 "Unilateral" meant that he acted without prior consultation with the Palestinian Authority.

of ensuring security and acting with dignity in the aftermath of the decolonization of the Gaza Strip.

Gaza, an area one-eighth the size of Rhode Island, represents one percent of historic Palestine. The Strip is approximately twenty-five miles long and seven miles wide, and is home to 1.4 million Palestinians.

The 7,800 Israeli settlers who occupied the Strip for thirty-eight years comprised one half of one percent of the population in Gaza, yet they occupied twenty percent of the land. An additional ten percent was under Israeli military control.

The Palestinian economy was for the most part agricultural. After their lands were confiscated and their orchards uprooted to make way for Israeli settlements, Palestinians were obliged to become day laborers inside Israel. When former Prime Minister Barak and then Ariel Sharon closed off Gaza and the West Bank from Israel for long periods of time, denying Palestinians the right to enter, Palestinians suddenly found themselves without work and without money, unable to feed their families. According to the World Bank, eighty-six percent of Gazan households depend on food relief from the UN or other humanitarian agencies.

During Israel's thirty-eight year occupation of Gaza, Palestinians were not allowed to build a seaport along the Mediterranean to export their goods. Similarly, they were forbidden to reconstruct an old, abandoned airport. Unless the Israeli government reverses these decisions – which they have yet to do – Palestinians will remain without a seaport or airport. Since the only way in and out of Gaza is through the Eretz checkpoint manned by Israeli soldiers, Israel will still be able to cut off the supply of food and medicine, raw materials, water, fuel, gas and electricity at will.

The Palestinian Authority plans to revitalize the Palestinian economy of the Gaza Strip, where unemployment reached almost ninety percent in some areas, encouraging investment and creating jobs. In order to accomplish this, Israel's cooperation is necessary. Israel still strictly controls all access in and out of the strip for both people and goods. If the current levels of absolute control continue, the Gaza Strip will be cut off from the West Bank and the rest of the world. For the Gazan economy to improve, and for the evacuation of the settlers to be a model of success for hopefully future settlement withdrawal in the West Bank, Israel will have to ensure that Palestinians and their goods are provided free movement, and that Palestinians are allowed to live free from Israeli control over their every movement.

Currently Palestinians need Israeli permits to travel within the occupied West Bank, between the West Bank and Gaza, and into Israel. Palestinians living in Gaza need Israeli permission to cross international borders to visit other countries. Less than thirty percent of West Bank residents receive permission; in Gaza only ten percent obtain travel permits.

Israel can improve the Palestinian economy by removing its barriers and checkpoints, and allowing Palestinian goods to move more freely. The economy of the Gaza Strip can be revitalized and improved by creating certainty among investors. The World Bank is in agreement with this conclusion. "Palestinian economic recovery depends on a radical easing of internal closures throughout the West Bank and Gaza, the opening of Palestinian external borders to commodity trade and sustaining a reasonable flow of Palestinian labor into Israel."[99]

In an odd but candid interview in October, 2004, Dov Weisglass, Prime Minister Sharon's political and legal advisor, told the Israeli press, "The primary goals of the proposal to withdraw the Jewish settlers from Gaza were to strengthen Israel's hold on its more numerous settlements in the West Bank and to freeze the political process as a way to indefinitely block the creation of a Palestinian state. What I effectively agreed to with the Ameri-

---

99 "Disengagement: The Palestinian Economy and Settlements." World Bank, June 15, 2004, cited in the UN *Office of the Coordination of Human Affairs (OCHA) Report*, June 22, 2005.

cans was that part of the settlements would not be dealt with at all, and the rest will not be dealt with until the Palestinians turn into Finns."[100] Mr. Weisglass, who speaks with Secretary of State Condoleezza Rice almost every day, said that he estimates that "out of the 240,000 settlers in the West Bank, 190,000 will not be moved from their place."[101]

Asked by journalists why the Gaza withdrawal plan had been unveiled, he responded: "In the fall of 2003, we faced both international and internal erosion; the economy was stagnant. Thousands of Israelis were refusing to serve in the military. The blame fell squarely on us and we knew we had to do something to get the Americans and the international community off our backs. The disengagement plan supplied the amount of formaldehyde that was necessary so there would not be a political process with the Palestinians. As a result you prevent the establishment of a Palestinian state and you prevent a discussion on the refugees, the borders and Jerusalem."[102]

Dov Weisglass's remarks were made in a public interview with Israeli journalists. Since these were not remarks made by the Prime Minister himself there is no way to know whether or not they are official, or merely the personal comments of Mr. Weisglass. Whether the Gaza pullout was a calculated maneuver on the part of the Sharon government, or merely a way to alleviate a demographic time bomb – the 1.4 million Palestinians in Gaza under Israeli military occupation – or merely to draw attention away from his expansionist policies in the West Bank – as argued by Rabbi Lerner[103] – remains to be seen.

---

100   Anderson, John Ward. "Sharon Aide Says Goal of Gaza Plan is to Halt Road Map." Washingtonpost.com, October 7, 2004, p. A14.

101   *Ibid.*

102   *Ibid.*

103   Lerner, Rabbi Michael. "Stop the Murders of Israelis and Palestinians: How many more will have to die?" *Tikkun*, July/September, 2003. www.networkingtheinternet. com/zxm198.htm

If that is the Prime Minister's real goal, and if he succeeds, he will incorporate fifty-five percent of the West Bank into Israel. This will leave forty-five percent of the West Bank for 2.4 million Palestinians. Palestinians in Gaza and the West Bank would be left with only ten percent of historic Palestine and live in a kind of archipelago of Israeli settlements, each "island" cut off from the other and surrounded by Israeli areas. The islands would be artificially connected by Israeli-controlled roads, bridges and tunnels, to create the illusion of a viable, contiguous state.

The actual effect would be to create distinct communities with no physical connection to a neighboring community. This is quite different from territorial contiguity, which implies a continuous area in which Palestinian life – consisting of commerce, economy, education, health services and political activity – functions and flows normally, and hopefully flourishes as an integral part of Israel's long-term security and regional stability.[104]

To an outside observer this may seem a reasonable solution. Perhaps some of these challenges could be overcome in a negotiated settlement by way of mutually agreed-upon ideas involving innovative transportation schemes, land-sharing and land-swap agreements.[105] What about the Separation Wall? Would that not have to be dismantled as well?

A flourishing Palestinian state should counteract the forces of extremism. An independent Palestine that invites the extremists to participate, giving them an incentive to reform – as it did the *Hizbullah* in Lebanon – would be better able to guarantee security for Israel.

A recent study attempted to cut through the issues of "islands" and contiguity. In early 2005, the Rand Corporation made recommendations for a future Palestinian State. Rand envisioned a

---

104 Etkes, Dror. *Op. cit.*

105 *Ibid.*

140-mile corridor between the northern West Bank and Gaza – where one does not currently exist – to include rail line, highway, aqueduct, energy network and fiber optic cable, linking Palestine's major towns and cities. Under the Rand proposal, The Arc would generate 100,000 to 160,000 new jobs over five years and add thousands more in new businesses built along the corridor. Overall cost estimates run around thirty-three billion dollars in the first ten years of a new state.[106]

The study does not consider how the Israelis and Palestinians will be able to reach a settlement and create a Palestinian state. Instead it focuses on what would happen if such a state were created. The study also neglects to take into account the existing Israeli settlements in the West Bank, and Israel's continuing refusal to discuss any plans to relinquish control of the crossing between Gaza and the West Bank.

UNITED STATES LOAN GUARANTEES TO ISRAEL

The Israeli government is the largest recipient of US financial aid in the world, over one-third of all US aid to foreign countries. "It is in the United States' national interest to promote the existence of a stable, democratic and militarily strong Israel at peace with its neighbors."[107] According to the US State Department in November, 2002, "... the US is committed to maintaining and enhancing Israel's security and qualitative edge over any combination of adversaries."[108]

The Palestinian Authority also receives US aid. In 2003, it was twenty million dollars; in 2004 they received the same amount; in 2005 the figure jumped to $200 million. The 2006 Foreign Opera-

---

106 Hanley, Delinda C. "Rand's Blueprint for Palestine: Fairy Tale or Nightmare?" *The Washington Report on Middle East Affairs*, July, 2005.

107 US Department of Defense Joint Report to Congress, March, 2001.

108 "United States Aid to Israel: Funding the Occupation." *The Palestine Monitor*. www.palestinemonitor.org/factsheet/US_Aid_to_Israel.htm

tions Appropriations Bill currently being passed through Congress allocates an additional $150 million in aid to the Palestinians.

US law prohibits the President from providing military aid to any country that engages in a consistent pattern of gross violations of internationally recognized human rights. Under the 1967 US Arms Export Control Act, it is illegal to use US weapons to carry out extra-judicial killings. This act stipulates that weapons sold to friendly countries be used solely for internal security and legitimate defense.[109]

The US law authorizing loan guarantees to foreign countries gives President Bush the power to withhold portions of those loans based on both Israeli and Palestinian performance in Middle East peace efforts. The international community should support, and even applaud, the withholding of funds to both the Israelis and Palestinians until they seriously agree to enter into negotiations with the end goal of permanent status.

ISRAEL'S DEMOGRAPHIC PROBLEM

There are approximately 4.8 million Palestinians living in Israel, the West Bank and Gaza; the Jewish population stands at 5.1 million.

It is difficult to verify these numbers, since each side guards its statistics closely. It is obvious that each passing year weakens Israel's claim to be a democracy. Once the demographic balance shifts, Israel will no longer be able to dominate the greater number of Palestinians and still claim to be a democracy.[110] Should the demographics change in favor of the Palestinians, Israel will become a colonial-settler state like South Africa under apartheid. According

---

109 *Ibid.*

110 Shahak, Israel and Norton Mezvinsky. *Jewish Fundamentalism in Israel*. Pluto Press, London, 1999. Quoted in Brownfeld, Allan C. "Jewish Fundamentalism in Israel," book review in *Washington Report on Middle East Affairs*, March, 2000, pp. 105–106. www.washington-report.org/backissues/0300/0003105.html

to Jeff Warner of Americans for Peace Now, "Israel's security ultimately relies on Israel remaining a democratic state."[111] Demographics favoring the Palestinians challenge that status. Put more succinctly, Israel's survival as a democracy is dependent on the concessions it makes to ensure peace with the Palestinians.

RADICAL FUNDAMENTALISM: A THREAT TO ISRAEL'S SURVIVAL

What we see operating in Israel today are vocal, influential and politically powerful minorities of Israelis and Palestinians, who use religious extremism and skewed Zionist ideology for political gain to override the wishes of the majority.

Hamas was founded in late 1987 out of the Muslim Brotherhood, a religious and political movement in Egypt in the 1970s. *Hamas*' founding charter commits the group to the destruction of Israel and the replacement of the Palestinian Authority with an Islamic State on the West Bank and Gaza.

The Palestinians' largest and most influential movement, *Hamas* combines Palestinian nationalism with Islamic fundamentalism. The terrorist wing has carried out suicide bombings and attacks using mortars and short-range rockets in the Palestinian West Bank and Gaza, and inside the pre-1967 boundaries of Israel. *Hamas*' first suicide bombing inside Israel took place in April, 1993.

Hamas' annual operating budget is estimated at about fifty million dollars. This money comes from expatriates, Saudi Arabia, Iran and other moderate Arab countries. Much of this money is given to support *Hamas*' extensive social services network which funds schools, orphanages, mosques, healthcare clinics, soup kitchens and sports leagues. Only a small percentage of its budget is used to fund terrorist activities. According to Israeli scholar Reuven Paz, "Approximately ninety percent of its work is in social,

---

111 Warner, Jeff, Americans for Peace Now MAT. "Letters." *Jewish Journal*, June 24, 2005. www.jewishjournal.com/home/preview.php?id=14280

welfare, cultural and educational activities." While nothing can justify its terrorist activities, *Hamas* can at least claim to be free of corruption.

On the other hand, the Palestinian Authority is corrupt and does not provide these services. *Hamas* is a well-organized Palestinian challenge to the Palestinian Authority, and intends to participate in elections in early 2006. This is encouraging news. In order to garner votes from a Palestinian public tired of suicide bombings and Israeli aggression, *Hamas* will have to disavow any further use of suicide bombers.

Islamic Jihad is a loosely organized but highly selective group of Islamic extremists that spans the Middle East. It is another offshoot of the Muslim Brotherhood. These extremists broke away from the Muslim Brotherhood movement because they felt it had become too moderate. Islamic Jihad is less well-organized than *Hamas*, but shares the same goal of an Islamic State and the destruction of Israel. It does not have a social network; it is solely a terrorist organization with leadership and membership distinct from *Hamas*.

Al-Aqsa Martyrs Brigades is an armed Palestinian group loosely associated with Yasser Arafat's *Fatah* Organization. The Brigade has never been officially recognized nor openly backed by Mr. Arafat and *Fatah*, although Brigade members also tend to belong to *Fatah*, the late Palestinian leader's political faction. With the aim of making life difficult for the Israeli Army, Mr. Arafat allowed the Brigade to operate, which was both a military and a political miscalculation; Israel could claim that Yasser Arafat backed terrorism, and therefore was unfit as a partner for peace.

Gush Emunim (the Bloc of the Faithful) is a right-wing Jewish settler movement with over 300,000 members, founded in March, 1974, in the aftermath of the October, 1973, War. The major goal of *Gush Emunim* has been to establish Jewish settlements in the West Bank and the Gaza Strip, aided by the Israeli government. From 1977 to 1984, Israel's Likud government permitted the expansion of Israeli settlements beyond the Green Line. Successive Israeli governments have recognized *Gush Emunim* as an official settlement movement, allocating considerable funds for its activities.

Until 1967, religious Zionists in Israel were marginalized. After the June, 1967, war and the capture of East Jerusalem and the West Bank – which comprised the 'Land of Israel' – the future of these territories became a major controversy among Israeli policy makers. Many religious Israelis believe that the conquered territories belong to the Jewish people by Divine decree. As such, they should not be returned to the Palestinians. According to Israel Shahak, "*Gush Emunim* argues that what appears to be confiscation of Arab-owned land for subsequent settlement by Jews is in reality not an act of stealing but one of sanctification. From their perspective the land is redeemed when it is transferred from the satanic to the divine sphere: *Halacha* (Jewish law) permits Jews to rob non-Jews in those locales wherein Jews are stronger than non-Jews."[112]

The fundamental policies of *Gush Emunim* have gradually filtered down to mainstream Israeli politics, making land-centered nationalism the highest form of religious virtue. *Gush Emunim* presents a tough, muscular image of religious Judaism that has not been seen since the destruction of the Second Temple by the Romans nearly two thousand years ago – a disaster brought on by similar militant hysteria.[113]

The Israeli Settler Movement has as its aim to drive every Palestinian into exile. "Transfer" is the word they use.

G'vaot Olam (Hills of the World) was the first Hilltop Settlement. It was founded in 1998 by Avri Ran in Samaria, the biblical name for an area near Nablus, north of Jerusalem. Settlers choose hilltops because they dominate the valleys below and because they are easier to defend. According to Jewish tradition, the patriarch

---

112 Friedman, Robert. *Zealots for Zion*. Random House, New York, 1992, p. xxxiv.

113 Sparks, Allistair. "Israel's Two-State Solution is Dead." *The Star*, Johannesburg, South Africa, September 21, 2005.

Joseph is buried in Nablus and that has attracted some of the most ultranationalist Jewish settlers over the last three decades.

One of the settlers was Yigal Amir, the young extremist who assassinated Israeli Prime Minister Yitzhak Rabin on November 4, 1995. Messianic fundamentalists like Yigal Amir take their radical value system from extremist rabbis. Before he killed Rabin, he heard his rabbi say, "Anyone who hands over parts of the Land of Israel to gentiles will be punished according to the Jewish Law of the pursuer [a religious categorization that justifies preemptive murder to defend Jews whose lives are in danger]."[114]

Avri Ran believes the Jewish people must connect the mountain communities of Samaria to the Jordan Valley because this is an indispensable corridor of settlements for Israel's security. Over the last ten years or so, "the hilltop youth," as they are called, have become more radicalized. They tend to be second- and third-generation settlers, often children of members of *Gush Emunim*. *Gush Emunim* has maintained a close relationship with state institutions while the hilltop youth have not. Many of the hilltop settlers have had run-ins with Israeli security forces, and the government is very concerned about threats by the hilltop settlers to blow up the Temple Mount, Islam's third holiest site.

The Hebron Settlers. Hebron is home to some of the most extreme members of the Israeli settler movement. In 1968, sixty Orthodox Jews, disciples of Messianic Rabbi Tzvi Yehudah Kook, booked rooms in a Hebron hotel for Passover holiday and refused to leave. Today, the 450 settlers call their settlement Kiryat Arba, protected by 1,200 Israeli soldiers. The settlement of Kiryat Arba is located in the heart of Hebron, home to some 123,000 Palestinians. To protect the settlers, the Israeli army imposes curfew on the Palestinian residents of Hebron. Three times a week – between

---

114 Amir was a third-year law student at Bar-Ilan University and a member of *Eyal*, an extremist offshoot of the radical anti-Arab movement *Kach*, founded by the late Rabbi Meir Kahane.

the hours of 8:00 AM and 1:00 PM – the Palestinian residents of Hebron are allowed to leave their homes to run errands and stock up on food. At all other times they are confined to their homes.

According to a member of the Christian Peacemaker Team with whom I spoke, "They stone Palestinian houses, shoot holes in their water tanks, dump sewage in their water system, uproot fruit and olive groves and fire on any Palestinian who tries to get into his field to pick his crops."[115] According to the Christian Peacemaker Team, most of the Orthodox Jewish settlers are from Brooklyn, New York.

CHANGE IN PALESTINIAN LEADERSHIP

When Yasser Arafat died at the age of 75 on November 11, 2004, he was eulogized as the founder of Palestinian nationalism; the unifier of the various liberation and resistance movements; trouble-maker in Jordan and Lebanon; a compromiser with Israel for peace when he signed the Oslo Peace Accords; and an obstacle to peace during the last five years of his life. One cannot deny the legacy of a man who successfully re-invented himself from terrorist to politician, even statesman. He transformed Palestine from a community of refugees and stateless people to a nation-state-in-waiting, supported by global consensus; and he mapped the PLO's peace strategy toward a two-state solution.

On January 9, 2005, 70-year-old Mahmoud Abbas, who was Prime Minister for a brief period, became the new President of the Palestinian Authority. Since his election, Abbas' most difficult challenge has been trying to obtain some modest concessions from either Israel or the United States. While President Bush was full of praise for Mahmoud Abbas when the two met at the White House in June, 2005, the meeting resulted in no concrete action.

Nothing has changed for the Palestinian people. The occupation, the settlement and the Separation Wall construction con-

---

115 This was Brian, mentioned in Huwaida's interview.

tinue, as do the daily humiliations at Israeli checkpoints. For the Israelis, there has been a dramatic decrease in the number of suicide bombings due to the Wall. Increased security has helped the Israeli economy recover.

Abbas's greatest challenge comes from *Hamas*, Islamic Jihad and al-Aqsa Martyr's Brigade, who are committed to the overthrow of the Israeli state. In the spring of 2005, Abbas did succeed in obtaining a major concession from *Hamas*, whose leaders agreed to a ceasefire through the end of 2005, to give President Abbas some credibility as he tries to re-engage the Israelis in peace negotiations. Nonetheless, in late September, 2005, *Hamas* fired a series of rockets into Israel causing several injuries. This wanton escalation of violence is incomprehensible, since *Hamas* is trying to acquire political power in the West Bank for the upcoming Palestinian elections.

Unfortunately for President Abbas, Islamic Jihad did not agree to halt its attacks on Israel, and carried out two suicide bombings inside Israel, one on July 12, 2005, which tragically killed six Israelis, several of them teenagers; and the other in October, 2005, which killed six more.

POSSIBLE SOLUTIONS

THE BEILIN–ABU MAZEN DOCUMENT

A little-known document signed in October, 1995, between Yossi Beilin – Israel's Minister of Justice – and Abu Mazen – Arafat's advisor who would become President as Mahmoud Abbas in 2004, following Arafat's death – is still cited as a potential solution to some of the outstanding unresolved issues between the Israelis and Palestinians. This could be resurrected and applied today, since there is currently talk about legal status in the territories.

Since 1967, when settlement construction began in the West Bank, Israel has enacted laws and regulations to ensure that every aspect of their settlers' lives was like those of Israelis in Israel proper. By granting the same rights to the Israeli residents in the West Bank settlements, a system of segregation and discrimination has been established in which two populations in the same area are subject to different legal systems. While Palestinians are subject to military law and usually tried in military courts, Israelis who commit similar offences are subject to Israeli law and tried in civil courts inside Israel. Jewish settlers also enjoy all the rights of Jews in Israel, including complete freedom of movement, speech and organization. They participate in local and national elections, social security and health benefits, while Palestinians are limited in their freedom of movement by checkpoints and travel permits, and do not benefit from Israel's social security or health benefits.

Since Israeli Arabs living in Israel with citizenship rights abide by Israeli law, it makes sense for Israeli settlers who choose to stay in the West Bank – when it becomes a Palestinian state – to live there as citizens of that Palestinian state and abide by Palestinian law. Yasser Arafat signed away all but twenty-two percent of the original Palestine when he signed the Oslo Accords. Since only twenty-two percent of the land is up for negotiation, intelligent people – if the extremists are neutralized – should be able to come up with a solution which would enable both sides to agree on a settlement for peace. If there must be a wall, let both sides work together and come to some mutual decision on what status the Israeli settlers in the West Bank will have.

A just solution to the Palestinian crisis would nullify the radicals. Although they will have achieved neither an Islamic State nor the destruction of Israel, a flourishing Palestinian state with full employment and better social structures in place will provide less incentive for young men to turn to extremism.

The Beilin–Abu Mazen Document is part of a framework for concluding final agreements on status between Israel and the Palestine Authority. The following points have already been worked out by Beilin and Abu-Mazen:

1. It will end exclusive civilian residential areas for Israelis in the State of Palestine, a reference to the settlements;
2. Individual Israelis who choose to remain within the borders of a Palestinian state will be subject to Palestinian authority and law;
3. Individual Israelis who have their permanent domicile within the Palestinian State will be offered Palestinian citizenship, or given the choice to remain as alien residents without prejudice to their Israeli citizenship.

Perhaps the idea of citizenship in a future Palestinian state does not in and of itself constitute a framework for peace, but the concept should be given serious consideration. Since the Israeli government refuses to consider dismantling the major settlement blocks – which are some fourteen to twenty-five miles inside the West Bank – and the Palestinians have only their twenty-two percent option to bring to any negotiations, the choices are few unless both parties agree to work together. The establishment of a Palestinian state along the lines of the Beilin–Abu Mazen formula would guarantee the continued existence of the Jewish state, since by the very nature of their side-by-side existence each would guarantee the security of the other.

The Beilin–Abu Mazen Document, so clear and apparently so simple to implement – given the right leaders – also says, "Jerusalem shall remain an open and undivided city with free and unimpeded access for people of all faiths and nationalities."

THE GENEVA ACCORD

On December 1, 2003, a group of prominent members of the Israeli opposition and leading Palestinians signed a document called the Geneva Accord, which sets forth the principle that both the current Palestinian leadership and the Palestinian people are partners for peace. The Accord offers an opportunity for an alliance between moderate, pragmatic Israelis and Palestinians which would weaken the religious fundamentalists and extremists on both sides. Avoiding a victory by Palestinian extremists is just as important as Israel's necessity to separate itself from the fundamentalist Settler Movement.

Broadly speaking, this accord envisions a Palestinian state established on the pre-1967 borders; the dismantling of most Israeli settlements in the West Bank and Gaza; and shared sovereignty of Jerusalem. Unlike Bush's Road Map and the Oslo Accord, the Geneva Accord from the start spells out the boundaries of the final settlement.

The Geneva Accord proposes to annex only two percent of the West Bank; Prime Minister Ariel Sharon proposes to annex fifty-five percent. His strategy is to absorb the maximum land area of biblical Israel, with the largest number of settlements. The Geneva Accord favors Israel withdrawing from far more land and settlements, in order to end the occupation of the Palestinian people. Sharon justifies his unilateral approach by claiming there is no partner with whom to negotiate.

The Geneva Accord is not a perfect document; but given the deteriorating relations between the present Israeli and Palestinian leadership, even this flawed document should be given serious attention, and improved upon as necessary. The Accord envisions an Israeli withdrawal from most Palestinian areas and demonstrates a strong resolve to end all violence against civilians. If nothing else, the Geneva Accord provides an impetus for renewed talks; for this reason it has broad support from the international community.

Given the current disparity of power between the two sides, it remains to be seen whether the Geneva Accord is the best Israelis and Palestinians can hope to achieve. What is certain is that the US government has an opportunity here to make a sincere commitment to be part of an international team, and to deal in an even-handed manner with both parties, demanding they participate in honest and fair peace negotiations.

A ONE STATE SOLUTION

On September 12, 2005, during Prime Minister Ariel Sharon's visit to the US, reporters asked whether, after the Gaza withdrawal, he would also remove the 250,000 settlers living in the West Bank. "There are about a quarter-million Jews living in these areas," he replied. "There are religious families with many children. What am I supposed to say, 'You cannot live there any more?'" Asked if he would allow the West Bank settlements to continue expanding he replied: "What am I supposed to do, legislate that they are not allowed to have babies?"[116]

The expansion of West Bank settlements is not just a matter of natural population increase. Since 1967 successive Israeli governments have subsidized and encouraged more and more Israelis to establish new settlements and enlarge the existing ones.[117]

If the Israeli government is not going to dismantle settlements in the West Bank, and the US government is not going to pressure Israel to do so – even in the interest of regional peace and stability – then Professor Virginia Tilley of the University of Michigan has another solution. Mindful of the difficult and painful decisions her solution would require, she nonetheless advocates a one-state solution because, according to her, the number and size of settlements render the two-state solution unworkable. In addition to the settlements there is an extensive network of interlinking highways defined by high security fences that crisscross the countryside, cutting the proposed Palestinian state into twisted fragments of land.[118]

To cram the expanding Palestinian population into tiny, claustrophobic ghettos under a government unable to meet the most basic needs of its people, would lead to a catastrophe for both Israe-

---

116 Sparks, *loc. cit.*

117 *Ibid.*

118 *Ibid.*

lis and Palestinians.[119] To expect their misery to trigger a mass Palestinian exodus across the Jordan River into other Arab countries would lead to a destabilization of the region. In Lebanon the influx of hundreds of thousands of Palestinians led not only to civil war, but also acted as a rallying call for extremists to fight the Zionist enemy. Such enforced "ethnic cleansing" would also be morally destructive for Israel.[120]

The Israeli-Palestinian conflict is fueling anti-Western passions among Islamic radicals who see the Palestinian plight as a crime. This threat is not regional, it is global; therefore it is everyone's problem.[121]

These issues pose serious problems for Israel since the Zionist vision has always been a Jewish State with a Jewish majority; in a single secular state this would no longer be the case. Professor Tilley refers to South Africa's experience in abandoning apartheid for non-racial democracy and asks an interesting question. "Would a negotiated settlement for one state not defuse the destructive antagonisms between Israelis and Palestinians as it has done in South Africa and in so doing make Israel a much safer homeland for Jews than it is now?"[122]

JEWISH VOICE FOR PEACE AND OTHER GROUPS

Groups like Jewish Voice for Peace, Americans for Peace Now, Jewish Alliance for Justice and Peace, and *Brit Tzedek* – the Chicago-based movement led by Rabbi Arnold Jacob Wolf, one of America's most respected rabbis – are making enormous strides to change attitudes within the American Jewish community. According to Rabbi Wolf, "… the only possible solution lies in recognizing each other and defining each other with not just the right to exist but the

---

119 *Ibid.*

120 *Ibid.*

121 *Ibid.*

122 *Ibid.*

necessity to exist."[123] Collectively, these groups offer an alternative to AIPAC (American-Israel Political Action Committee), the powerful Jewish lobby responsible for coercing American government leaders into supporting Israel, right or wrong. In July, 2005, Rabbi Michael Lerner, head of the Tikkun Community, commented on National Public Radio that members of Congress, behind closed doors, agree that Israel should end the occupation, and that the US should take a more balanced approach to solving the crisis. He says the problem is that these same members of Congress flatly refuse to make these kinds of statements in public because they fear reprisals from AIPAC come election time.

Through grassroots organizing, education, advocacy and media outreach, Jewish Voice for Peace hopes to achieve a lasting peace that recognizes the aspirations of both Israelis and Palestinians for security and self-determination. Toward that goal, JVP has called upon the United States to suspend military aid to Israel until it participates in a peaceful settlement in good faith, and on US corporations to ban sales of the machinery they supply to the Israeli Army to demolish Palestinian homes.

With a membership of 2.5 million and an investment portfolio estimated at close to seven billion dollars, the US Presbyterian Church has decided selectively to divest their interests in certain companies doing business with Israel. In August, 2005, the church's Committee on Social Responsibility through Investment published the names of four international companies that aid the Israeli occupation. The list includes Caterpillar, which manufactures bulldozers used to build the Separation Wall; ITT Industries, which supplies communications, electrical and night-vision equipment to the Israeli Defense Forces (IDF); and United Technologies which supplies the IDF with helicopters and other military equipment. The decision to publicly identify these international cor-

---

123 Wolf, Rabbi Arnold Jacob. *L'Shana Tovah 5766*, October 1, 2005.

porations was made by the Presbyterian Church in July, 2004. Since that time the campaign has gained momentum in the mainline Protestant establishment in the US. In November, 2004, the Episcopal Church, the United Methodist Church and the United Church of Christ made similar decisions. These major Christian churches are the same ones who organized the boycott in the 1980s against South African apartheid. The American Catholic Church has not yet joined the campaign.

The Protestant churches, like many Christian churches worldwide, understand that holy places – like the Church of the Nativity in Bethlehem and the Church of the Holy Sepulcher in the Old City in Jerusalem – are at risk. Since the time of Christ, there has been a continuous Christian presence in Palestine. Of the 4.8 million Palestinians living in Israel and Palestine today, only two percent are Christian. The vast majority of Palestinian Christians have emigrated because of the daily struggles and challenges created by the Israeli occupation.

There is a great need for Christian communities world-wide who are not already actively engaged, to act now. The battle for control of the Holy Land is currently dominated by Jewish and Muslim Fundamentalists. In America, foreign policy – particularly decisions regarding Israel – are dictated by Christian Fundamentalists. A liberal Christian presence is urgently needed in order to counterbalance extremist views. The international community will lose access to the holy places sacred to the Christian heritage if it does not loosen the stranglehold of extremist groups in their respective communities.

Bethlehem, the birthplace of Christ, is now a closed military zone. The Israeli Army has set up checkpoints and roadblocks permitting only limited access to the city. This means pilgrims can no longer easily visit the Church of the Nativity. If Christians give up control over the Church of the Holy Sepulcher in the Old City of Jerusalem – Christianity's holiest site – it will be too late to act.

The only solution is a shared presence in the Holy Land.

IDEAS FOR CITIZEN INVOLVEMENT

According to Bill Moyers, former host of the PBS program NOW, the central task of all social movements is "... to win the hearts, minds and support of the majority of the populace. Because it is people who ultimately hold the power, they will either preserve the status quo or create change."[124]

Knowledge empowers people to demand change. In the months leading up to the second Gulf War there was an upsurge of popular protests worldwide. It was a remarkable grassroots movement which played a role in transforming the debate around the war. The American right-wing also did a remarkable job of mobilizing counter-demonstrations, ultimately convincing Americans that war with Iraq was a necessary evil, and they also did a remarkable job of getting George W. Bush re-elected.

Peace between Israelis and Palestinians is a cornerstone of world stability, a goal toward which every member of the international community should work. This festering crisis is not just a partisan issue; it affects the stability of the entire Middle East, where American servicemen and women are currently stationed. The war in Iraq and the Israeli-Palestinian conflict are used as a recruiting tool for Muslim extremists, who regard both Israel and America – which supplies Israel with financial support and military hardware – as complicit in Israeli occupation of Palestinian land. The occupation is a thorn in the side of 1.3 billion Muslims world-wide, most of whom are moderates. As such it poses a threat to American security.

We have the power to influence and shape the policies of our governments. Now is the time to exercise that right.

---

124 Moyers, Bill. "This is Your Story: The Progressive Story of America. Pass it on."
    Speech to the Take Back America Conference, June 4, 2003.

A WAY TO HELP

For fifteen years, the National Peace Foundation (NPF) has achieved positive results by bringing conflict resolution skills first to people living with war in the former Soviet Union, and now to the Middle East. NPF believes in creating alternatives to war and violence through citizen action. NPF decided that a national initiative was needed to respond to the frustration of Americans concerned about the government's involvement in the Middle East.

A year ago, Sarah Harder, President of NPF, asked me to sit on her Board of Directors and direct NPF's Middle East Projects. This past spring, NPF and Partners for Peace co-sponsored the biannual Midwest tour of "Jerusalem Women Speak: Three Women, Three Faiths, One Shared Vision." These tours bring one Muslim, one Jew and one Christian to the US to share their experiences and hopes for a just peace. Their frank discussions break taboos, dispel misconceptions and shatter illusions – all elements essential to fostering change. NPF will continue to collaborate with Partners for Peace.

NPF is also working with the Bereaved Family Circle – some 500 Israeli and Palestinian families who have lost loved ones because of the Israeli-Palestinian conflict – to bring speakers to the United States, seeking to resolve the ongoing crisis through dialogue and mutual understanding. NPF is committed to bringing this same message to communities across America.

Based on a model used with great success by Lilly and Len Traubman of San Mateo, California, NPF is working to initiate Israeli-Palestinian "Living Room Dialogue Groups" through its nation-wide member base. NPF believes that participation in conversations which cross information boundaries while building identification and respect for the 'other' is the best way to initiate change and bring about stability in the Middle East.

At the end of this book there are Discussion Questions. A more detailed packet of information is available upon request. If you would like to start a Dialogue Group in your community, or help by becoming a NPF member, please visit the Cathy Sultan home page at www.scarlettapress.com/authors/CathySultan.cfm, or write to:

National Peace Foundation
666 11th St. N.W.
Washington, D.C. 20001

ONLINE RESOURCES

news.independent.co.uk/world/fisk – *The Independent*, excellent source for Robert Fisk's articles

www.adl.org – Anti-Defamation League, pro-Israel site

www.afsc.org – American Friends Service Committee, Quakers dedicated to peace

www.aipac.org – American-Israeli Public Affairs Committee

www.ajc.org – American Jewish Committee, safeguarding welfare and security of Jews in US and Israel

www.ameu.org – Americans for Middle East Understanding

www.amnesty.org – Amnesty International

www.azm.org – American Zionist Movement

www.bbc.co.uk – BBC News

www.bitterlemons-international.org – good source for Middle East news

www.bnaibrith.org – B'nai B'rith International, promotes and protects interests of Jewish communities wherever they exist

www.btselem.org – B'Tselem, Israeli human rights organization

www.batshalom.org – Israeli women's group with ties to Palestinian's Jerusalem Link

www.camera.org – Committee for Accuracy in Middle East Reporting in America

www.campus-watch.org – Monitors Middle East Studies on campus www.coalitionofwomen.org – Coalition of Women for Peace

www.counterpunch.org – *CounterPunch*, political newsletter edited by Alexander Cockburn and Jeffrey St. Clair

www.cpt.org – Christian Peacemaker Teams, based in Chicago with a peacemaking program in Hebron, West Bank

www.dailystar.com.lb – *The Daily Star*, newspaper from Beirut, Lebanon

www.electronicintifada.org – The Electronic Intifada, excellent news site

www.endtheoccupation.org – US Campaign to End the Israeli Occupation

www.forusa.org – Fellowship of Reconciliation, an interfaith movement for peace

www.gush-shalom.org – excellent Israeli site run by Uri Avnery, former Knesset member

www.haaretz.com – *Haaretz*, Israeli newspaper

www.hadassah.org – Women's Zionist Organization of America

www.hillel.org – The Foundation for Jewish Campus Life

www.holylandtrust.org – Holy Land Trust, a Palestinian NGO working with children

www.hrw.org – Human Rights Watch

www.icahd.org – The Israeli Committee Against House Demolitions

www.imagine-life.org – Media-based human rights awareness campaign

www.indymedia.org – Independent Media Center, good news site

www.jewishvoiceforpeace.org – Jewish Voice for Peace

www.jpost.com – *The Jerusalem Post*, Israel's right-of-center English daily

www.kibush.co.il – information about Israeli occupation published by Israelis

www.lemonde.fr – *Le Monde*, French daily newspaper

www.machsomwatch.org – Women for Human Rights, Israeli women monitoring Israeli checkpoints for abuse www.mfa.gov.il – Israeli Ministry of Foreign Affairs

www.miftah.org – The Palestinian Initiative for the Promotion of Global Dialogue and Democracy

www.mwio.org – Media Watch International, advancing Israel's image by promoting accurate media coverage

www.palestinemonitor.org – good news site

www.pchrgaza.org – Palestinian Centre for Human Rights, based in Gaza City

www.refusersolidarity.net – Refuser Solidarity Network, supports Israelis who refuse to serve the Israeli occupation

www.rhr.israel.net – Rabbis for Human Rights, based in Israel

www.standwithuscampus.com – Pro-Israel site for students

www.stopthewall.org – excellent news site

www.thenation.com – *The Nation*

www.tikkun.org – *Tikkun Magazine: A Bimonthly Jewish Critique of Politics, Culture and Society*, edited by Rabbi Michael Lerner

www.washington-report.org – *Washington Report on Middle East Affairs*

www.weekly.ahram.org.eg – *Al Ahram*, newspaper from Cairo, Egypt

www.womeninblack.org – Women in Black

www.womeningreen.org – Women for Israel's Tomorrow, Israeli grassroots women's movement

www.ynet.co.il – *Yediot Aharonot*, an Israeli newspaper

www.zoa.org – Zionist Organization of America, speaking out for Israeli interests

zmagsite.zmag.org – *Z Magazine*, dedicated to resisting injustice, defending against repression, and creating liberty

SUGGESTED READING

Ateek, Naim Stifan. *Justice and only Justice.* Orbis Press, New York, 2001.

Aruri, Naseer. *Dishonest Broker.* South End Press, Massachusetts, 2003.

Carey, Ron. *The New Intifada.* Verso, London, 2001.
  – *The Other Israel.* The New Press, New York, 2002.

Carter, Jimmy. *Our Endangered Values.* Simon and Schuster, New York, 2005.

Chacour, Elias. *Blood Brothers.* Chosen Books, New York, 1984.
  – *We Belong to the Land.* Harper Collins Paperback, New York, 1992.

Chomsky, Noam. *The Fateful Triangle.* South End Press, Boston, 1983.

David, Ron. *Arabs and Israel for Beginners.* Writers and Readers Publishing, New York, 1993, 1996.

Ellis, Mark. *Toward a Jewish Theology of Liberation.* Orbis Books, New York, 1987.

Feiler, Bruce. *Walking the Bible.* William Morrow & Co., New York, 2001.
  – *Abraham.* William Morrow & Co., New York, 2002.
  – *Where God was Born.* William Morrow & Co., New York, 2005.

Finkelstein, Norman. *Image and Reality of the Israeli-Palestinian Conflict.* Verso, New York, 1995.

Flappan, Simha. *The Birth of Israel: Myths and Realities*. Pantheon Books, New York, 1987.

Friedman, Robert. *Zealots for Zion*. Random House, New York, 1992.

Hass, Amira. *Drinking the Sea at Gaza*. Metropolitan Books, New York, 1999.

Hirst, David. *The Gun and the Olive Branch*. Harcourt Brace & Jovanovich, New York, 1977.

Morris, Benny. *The Birth of the Palestinian Refugee Problem 1947–1949*. Cambridge University Press, Cambridge, 1989.

Pappe, Illan. *The Making of Israel: Myths and Realities*. I.B. Tauris, London, 1994.

Reinhart, Tanya. *Israel/Palestine: How to End the War of 1948*. Seven Stories Press, New York, 2002.

BIBLIOGRAPHY

Are, Thomas L. *Israeli Peace Palestinian Justice*. Clarity Press, Atlanta, 1994.

Armstrong, Karen. *The Battle for God*. Ballantine Books, New York, 2000.

Ateek, Naim Stifan. *Justice and only Justice*, Ballantine Books, New York, 2000.

Chomsky, Noam. T*he Fateful Triangle. The United States, Israel and the Palestinians*, South End Press, Boston, 1983.

David, Ron. *Arabs and Israel for Beginners*, Writers and Readers, New York, 1993.

Ellis, Marc H. *Toward a Jewish Theology of Liberation*, Orbis Books, New York, 1987.

Finkelstein, Norman G. *Image and Reality of the Israel-Palestine Conflict*. Verso, London, 2001.

Flapan, Simha, *the Birth of Israel: Myths and Realities*. Pantheon Books, New York, 1987.

Fox, Edward. *Sacred Geography*. Metropolitan Books, New York, 2001.

Friedman, Robert. *Zealots for Zion: Inside Israel's West Bank Movement*. Random House, New York, 1992.

Fromkin, David. A *Peace to End all Peace*. Avon Books, New York, 1989.

Green Stephen. *Taking Sides: America's Secret Relations with a Militant Israel*. William Morrow, New York, 1984.

Neff, Donald. *Fifty Years of Israel.* American Educational Trust, Washington, D.C., 1998.

Reinhart, Tanya. *Israel/Palestine.* Seven Stories Press, New York, 2002.

Reuther, Rosemary Radford and Marc Ellis. *Beyond Occupation: Jewish, Christian and Palestinian Voices for Peace.* Orbis Books, New York, 1989.

Shahak, Israel and Norton Mezvinsky. *Jewish Fundamentalism in Israel.* Pluto Press, London, 1999.

Shahak, Israel. *Jewish History, Jewish Religion.* Pluto Press, London, 1994.

– *Open Secrets. Israeli Nuclear and Foreign Policies.* Pluto Press, London, 1997.

– *Jewish Fundamentalism in Israel.* Pluto Press, London, 1997.

Shlaim, Avi. *The Iron Wall: Israel and the Arab World.* W.W. Norton and Co., New York, 2000.

Smith, Charles. *Palestine and the Arab-Israeli Conflict: A History with Documents.* Bedford/St. Martins, Boston, 2004.

Sykes, Christopher. *Crossroads to Israel 1917–1948.* Indiana University Press, Bloomington, 1994.

Tessler, Mark. *A History of the Israeli-Palestinian Conflict.* Indiana University Press, Bloomington, 1994.

Tilley, Virginia. *The One-State Solution.* University of Michigan Press, Ann Arbor, 2005.

Zunes, Stephen. *Tinderbox.* Common Courage, Monroe, Maine, 2004.

DISCUSSION QUESTIONS FOR READING GROUPS

1. Did you feel that the author presented a balanced account of her visit to Israel/Palestine? Use your answer to examine your own preconceived ideas and biases.

2. The Israeli government is building a separation wall around Jerusalem. In the long run what effect will this have on Israeli security?

3. Why does the author think there is little difference between the Israeli and American publics? What do you think might be possible differences?

4. Many Palestinians believe a two-state solution is no longer possible. What is your opinion?

5. Was there any information in the "Brief History of the Middle East" which surprised you?

6. Which interview did you find the most interesting? What did you learn from it?

7. Sam, the businessman from Ramallah, spoke of Arafat and Rabin. Why did he compare the two men? What did he mean when he said, "Being elected is not being a leader. It is simply being a politician?"

8. Why do you think the author insisted on carrying the Palestinian textbooks out of Ramallah? Use the information found in the Author's Note in Huwaida Arraf's interview to initiate a discussion.

9. The three Palestinian teenagers suggest that they and their Israeli counterparts can solve the crisis. Given a chance, are the people more likely than their leaders to solve the major differences?

10. According to Maha, America is a plutocracy of powerful people who run both the government and corporate America. What is your opinion?

ACKNOWLEDGMENTS

I am deeply indebted to my editor, Ian Graham Leask, who insisted, for this project, that I examine the Israeli-Palestinian crisis objectively since both sides have an historical narrative that needs to be better understood.

To Sarah Harder, for inviting me to sit on her Executive Board at the National Peace Foundation and for the opportunity to expand my work promoting peace between Israelis and Palestinians.

To my friend, Eileen Immerman, for always being there with her superior technical know-how when I need her.

To Ed Foreman who, once again, has transformed an otherwise ordinary text into something extraordinary.

And finally to Michel, my husband of 40 years, for allowing me to travel to Israel/Palestine in spite of the dangers in pursuit of this story. All my love.